Air War D-Day

Volume 1

The Build-Up

Other volumes in this series

Air War D-Day - The Build-Up

Volume 2   Assaults From The Sky
Volume 3   Winged Pegasus and The Rangers
Volume 4   Bloody Beaches
Volume 5   'Gold' - 'Juno' - 'Sword'

Air War D-Day

Volume 1

The Build-Up

Martin W. Bowman

First published in Great Britain in 2012 by
PEN & SWORD AVIATION
An imprint of
Pen & Sword Books Ltd
47 Church Street
Barnsley
South Yorkshire
S70 2AS

ISBN 978 1 78159 119 2

A CIP catalogue record for this book is
available from the British Library

Printed and bound in England
By CPI Group (UK) Ltd, Croydon, CR0 4YY

Pen & Sword Books Ltd incorporates the Imprints of Pen & Sword Aviation,
Pen & Sword Family History, Pen & Sword Maritime, Pen & Sword Military,
Pen & Sword Discovery, Pen & Sword Politics, Pen & Sword Atlas,
Pen & Sword Archaeology, Wharncliffe Local History, Wharncliffe True Crime,
Wharncliffe Transport, Pen & Sword Select, Pen & Sword Military Classics,
Leo Cooper, The Praetorian Press, Claymore Press, Remember When,
Seaforth Publishing and Frontline Publishing

For a complete list of Pen & Sword titles please contact
PEN & SWORD BOOKS LIMITED
47 Church Street, Barnsley, South Yorkshire, S70 2AS, England
E-mail: enquiries@pen-and-sword.co.uk
Website: www.pen-and-sword.co.uk

Contents

Acknowledgements 6

Glossary 7

Comparative Table of Ranks 14

Chapter 1   The Boys' Crusade 17

Chapter 2   'The Days are Really Long Now' 77

Chapter 3   'This Is It!' 129

Chapter 4   'Off We Go Into the Wild Blue Yonder' 153

Index 183

Acknowledgements

I am enormously grateful to the following people for their time and effort and kind loan of photos etc, not least to my fellow author, friend and colleague, Graham Simons, for getting the book to press-ready standard and for his detailed work on maps and photographs: My thanks to Ray Alm; Ed 'Cotton' Appleman; James Roland Argo; Peter Arnold; John Avis; Les Barber; Harry Barker; Mike Bailey; Carter Barber; Neil Barber, author of *The Day The Devils Dropped In;* E. W. D. Beeton; Franklin L. Betz; Bill Bidmead; Rusty Bloxom, Historian, Battleship Texas; Lucille Hoback Boggess; Prudent Boiux; August C. Bolino; Dennis Bowen; Tom Bradley; Eric Broadhead; Stan Bruce; K. D. Budgen; Kazik Budzik KW VM; Les Bulmer; Reginald 'Punch' Burge; Donald Burgett; Chaplain Burkhalter; Lol Buxton; Jan Caesar; R. H. 'Chad' Chadwick; Noel Chaffey; Mrs J. Charlesworth; Chris Clancy; Roy Clark RNVR; Ian 'Nobby' Clark; P. Clough; Johnny Cook DFM; Malcolm Cook; Flight Lieutenant Tony Cooper; Lieutenant-Colonel Eric A. Cooper-Key MC; Cyril Crain; Mike Crooks; Jack Culshaw, Editor, *The Kedge Hook;* Bill Davey; S. Davies; Brenda French, Dawlish Museum Society; John de S. Winser; Abel L. Dolim; Geoffrey Duncan; Sam Earl; *Eighth Air Force News; Eastern Daily Press;* Chris Ellis; Les 'Tubby' Edwards; W. Evans; Frank R. Feduik; Ron Field; Wolfgang Fischer; Robert Fitzgerald; Eugene Fletcher; Captain Dan Flunder; John Foreman; Wilf Fortune; H. Foster; Lieutenant-Commander R. D. Franks DSO; Jim Gadd; Leo Gariepy; Patricia Gent; Lieutenant Commander Joseph H. Gibbons USNR; Larry Goldstein; Bill Goodwin; Franz Goekel; Lieutenant Denis J. M. Glover DSC RNZNVR; John Gough; Peter H. Gould; George 'Jimmy' Green RNVR; Albert Gregory; Nevil Griffin; Edgar Gurney BEM; R. S. Haig-Brown; Leo Hall, Parachute Regt Assoc.; Günter Halm; Roland 'Ginger' A. Hammersley DFM; Madelaine Hardy; Allan Healy; Andre Heintz; Basil Heaton; Mike Henry DFC, author of *Air Gunner;* Vic Hester; Reverend R. M. Hickey MC; Lenny Hickman; Elizabeth Hillmann; Bill Holden; Mary Hoskins; Ena Howes; Pierre Huet; J. A. C. Hugill; Antonia Hunt; Ben C. Isgrig; Jean Irvine; Orv Iverson; George Jackson; Major R. J. L. Jackson; Robert A. Jacobs; G. E. Jacques; Marjorie Jefferson; Bernard M. Job RAFVR; Wing Commander 'Johnnie' Johnson DSO* DFC*; Percy 'Shock' Kendrick MM; the late Jack Krause; Cyril Larkin; Reg Lilley; John Lincoln, author of *Thank God and the Infantry;* Lieutenant Brian Lingwood RNVR; Wing Commander A. H. D. Livock; Leonard Lomell; P. McElhinney; Ken McFarlane; Don McKeage; Hugh R. McLaren; John McLaughlin; Nigel McTeer; Ron Mailey; Sara Marcum; Ronald Major; Walt Marshall; Rudolph May; Ken Mayo; Alban Meccia; Claude V. Meconis; Leon E. Mendel; Harold Merritt; Bill Millin for kindly allowing me to quote from his book, *Invasion;* Bill Mills; John Milton; Alan Mower; Captain Douglas Munroe; *A Corpsman Remembers D-Day Navy Medicine 85,* No.3 (May-June 1994); Major Tom Normanton; General Gordon E. Ockenden; Raymond Paris; Bill Parker, National Newsletter Editor, Normandy Veterans; Simon Parry; Albert Pattison; Helen Pavlovsky; Charles Pearson; Eric 'Phil' Phillips DFC MiD; T. Platt; Franz Rachmann; Robert J. Rankin; Lee Ratel; Percy Reeve; Jean Lancaster-Rennie; Wilbur Richardson; Helmut Romer; George Rosie; The Royal Norfolk Regiment; Ken Russell; A. W. Sadler; Charles Santarsiero; Erwin Sauer; Frank Scott; Ronald Scott; Jerry Scutts; Major Peter Selerie; Alfred Sewell; Bob Shaffer; Reg Shickle; John R. Slaughter; Ben Smith Jr.; *SOLDIER Magazine; Southampton Southern Evening Echo;* Southwick House, HMS *Dryad,* Southwick, Portsmouth; Bill Stafford; Allen W. Stephens; Roy Stevens; Mrs E. Stewart; Henry Tarcza; Henry 'Buck' Taylor; June Telford; E. J. Thompson; Charles Thornton; Robert P. Tibor; Dennis Till; Edward J. Toth; Walt Truax; Jim Tuffell; Russ Tyson; US Combat Art Collection, Navy Yard, Washington DC; Thomas Valence; John Walker; Herbert Walther; Ed Wanner; R. H. G. Weighill; Andrew Whitmarsh, Portsmouth Museum Service; 'Slim' Wileman; Jim Wilkins; E. G. G. Williams; Deryk Wills, author of *Put On Your Boots and Parachutes! The US 82nd Airborne Division;* Jack Woods; Len Woods; Waverly Woodson.

Glossary

21st Army Group	British and Canadian ground force assigned to the invasion of Europe.
36 Grenade	standard British Army hand-grenade (also known as a Mills bomb).
88 (German)	Originally designed as an anti-aircraft gun, used as an anti-tank gun and flak guns against aircraft. Its high velocity, flat trajectory and armour piercing capability made it a much feared weapon. The Germans first fitted it in the Tiger Mark I tank in 1942.
ABC ('Airborne Cigar')	A massive piece of equipment consisting of four VHF wireless sets. One scanned up and down the airwaves, seeking transmissions from enemy fighters. When a blip showed on the operator's CRT scope German-speaking special operator positioned half way down the fuselage between the main spar and the mid-upper turret, tuned one of the other sets to that frequency and listened in. If the speaker was a Jägerleitoffizier (JLO, or GCI-controller) the special operator would flood the enemy controller's instructions with interference.
ADS	Advanced Dressing Station, the next link in the evacuation chain behind the RAP.
All American	US 82nd Airborne Division.
AP	Armour Piercing shot.
APC	Armoured Personnel Carrier, an armoured tracked or wheeled vehicle designed to carry infantry into battle. Less heavily armoured than a tank.
ARK	Armoured Ramp Carriers (sometimes known as ARCs) equipped with folding bridges, could span demolished bridges or cross anti-tank ditches.
Armoured Bulldozer	a specially equipped version of the heavy-duty bulldozer produced by the Caterpillar Company.
ARV	Armoured Recovery Vehicle. Turretless Sherman or Churchill tank fitted with rescue and repair equipment to rescue damaged and broken down tanks.
ASR	Air/Sea Rescue.
ATS	Auxiliary Territorial Service (women's branch of the British Army).
AVRE	Armoured Vehicle Royal Engineers, a modified Churchill tank developed primarily for breaking enemy defence fortifications, armed with a 7.92mm BESA machine gun but its principal weapon was a huge 290mm (11.4 inch) spigot mortar firing a 44lb demolition round up to 260 feet. The AVRE could also carry fascines (huge bundles of brushwood) to fill in anti-tank ditches. On D-Day 180 AVREs were used by the 79th Armoured Division.
AVRE with SBG Bridge	a Churchill chassis adapted to carry a bridge which could be dropped in 30 seconds over a 30 foot gap, or surmount a 15-foot wall while supporting 40 tons.
Avro Lancaster	RAF four-engined heavy bomber.
Bangalore Torpedo	Named after the munitions factory in India where it was developed in World War I, consisted of an 8 feet long cast iron tube, containing between 10lb and 12 lb of Amatol HE with a primer and safety fuse. Tubes could be linked together. When the torpedo exploded, shrapnel fragments from the iron casing shredded the barbed wire and created a gap 2 to 10ft through the obstacle, especially barbed wire.
BAR	Browning Automatic Rifle, the standard squad weapon for the US Army.
BARV	Beach Armoured Recovery Vehicle, a turret-less tank with winches or small bulldozer blades for towing or pushing stranded vehicles off the beach.
Battalion	Infantry unit totalling between 600 and 1,000 men commanded by a lieutenant-colonel.
Battery	The smallest, self-contained sub-unit of artillery, in field and medium regiments, normally of eight guns in two equal troops.

Berlin Bitch	The voice of the Germany's English-language radio broadcasts, known more politely as 'Axis Sally'
Boase carpet	A carpet laid from a roller carried on the front of an AVRE.
Bobbin	A tank chassis which carried a 110 yard long roll of reinforced canvas matting 9 feet 11 inches wide, on a huge drum on the front of the hull that could be unrolled on soft wet sand or loose shingle to give other vehicles a surface that would provide traction.
Bocage	dense Norman countryside of small fields surrounded by large hedgerows on thick banks, often with sunken lanes in between.
Bofors	A 40mm quick-firing anti-aircraft gun of Swedish design.
Bren gun	British, magazine fed, .303 inch light machine-gun.
Brigade	British Army unit usually consisting of three infantry battalions or armoured regiments, commanded by a brigadier.
Brigade Major	Senior operations staff officer in a brigade, de facto chief of staff.
Buffalo	American Landing Vehicle Tracked, an amphibian with a water speed of 5 knots and land speed of 25 mph. Propulsion in the water was provided by grousers on the tracks. The later version had a stern ramp and could lift a jeep, Bren-gun carrier or 25-pounder field gun. The earlier models had no ramp and could carry 25 men.
C-47 'Skytrain'	American aircraft used for parachute drops and as a glider tug. Also known as a 'Dakota' (British).
Centaur	Variant of the Cromwell tank with a 97mm gun.
CIGS	Chief of the Imperial General Staff, the senior soldier in the British Army.
CO	Commanding Officer.
Concrete tetrahedral	Four-sided, dwarf, pyramids of concrete designed to impede tracked vehicles by ripping off their tracks, or hole landing-craft. Also known as dragon's teeth.
Corps	A formation of at least two divisions, commanded by a lieutenant-general.
COSSAC	Chief of Staff to the Supreme Allied Commander.
CP	Command Post.
Crab	a modified Sherman tank conceived by a South African officer, equipped with a revolving drum at the front which was fitted with weighted chains for clearing a lane 10 feet wide through minefields. These flailed through minefields at 1 mph, safely exploding the mines down to a depth of about 6 inches in their path. The 'Crab' retained the turret of a conventional tank and could be used in this role when required. The Crab had already proved successful at El Alamein in 1942.
Crocodile	a modified Churchill VII tank equipped with a flame-thrower that could engage enemy targets at 260-390 feet with 80 one-second bursts of flame. New flame-thrower fuel had been developed that was thicker and more viscous and consequently stuck to its target. 400 gallons of fuel were carried in a six ton trailer linked by a flexible hose to a flame gun in the hull machine gun position. Pressure from compressed nitrogen was used to force the fuel from the trailer to gun. When the fuel had been expended the trailer could be jettisoned and the Churchill became a conventional gun tank. It was often enough for a Crocodile to project unignited fuel into a wrecked bunker to induce the enemy to surrender. They hated this fearsome weapon and captured Crocodile crews were often executed.
CSM	Company Sergeant-Major.
Czech hedgehog	German beach obstacle consisting of sections of railway track welded together.
Dakota	Douglas C-47 transport aircraft.
Dannert Wire	a type of coiled barbed wire.
DCM	Distinguished Conduct Medal, British gallantry award for warrant officers, NCOs and soldiers.
DD tank	amphibious Duplex-Drive Sherman tank invented by the Austrian émigré and armoured vehicle designer, Nicolas Straussler. Fitted with a flotation screen

and rubber skirts and two boat screws, it could 'swim' ashore at a steady four knots (4.5mph). Also known as a 'Donald Duck'. On the beach, the crew would drop the skirts that had given the tank its buoyancy and would be able to engage enemy bunkers and defences with its 75mm gun.

D-Day	the term forever associated with 6 June 1944 but was a standard military expression for the day any operation was to begin. The D derived simply from the word day in the same way as H-Hour stood for the time when operations were to start.
DF	direction-finding, a radio receiver system for searching for and locating the source of enemy radio signals.
DFC	Distinguished Flying Cross (RAF) for officers.
DFM	Distinguished Flying Medal (RAF) for NCO air-crew.
Dingo	Small lightly armoured, turretless, four-wheeled scout car, used by armoured commanders for command, reconnaissance and liaison, when a command tank was not suitable for the occasion.
Division	Army unit consisting of two or more brigades (12,000-18,000 men), commanded by a major-general.
D-minus-one	the day before D-Day.
D-plus-one	the day after.
DSC	Royal Naval decoration usually for junior officers.
DSM	Royal Naval decoration for sailors and Petty Officers.
DSO	Distinguished Service Order (British award for officers for acts of gallantry and distinguished leadership).
DUKW	American six-wheeled amphibious vehicle, known as a 'Duck' built by General Motors.
DZ	Drop zone (for paratroopers and/or parachuted supplies).
E-boat	Allied term for small, fast, German motor torpedo boat.
Eighty-eight	Allied term for a German 88mm anti-aircraft gun. It was used to great effect against tanks as well as aircraft and against advancing infantry on the beaches.
Element C	Beach obstacles, also known as 'Belgian gates'
ENSA	Entertainments National Service Association, the organization that arranged morale-boosting concerts for British servicemen
FAA	Fleet Air Arm
FFI	Forces Francaises de l'Interieur: organization of the Resistance into the semblance of an army under the command of General Koenig in London.
Flail	see Crab.
Flak	fliegerabwehrkanone.
FTP	Francs-tireurs et Partisans: Communist-led part of the Resistance
Gammon grenade	a powerful hand grenade that could be primed to explode on impact (British)
GI	a US Army soldier.
GOC	General Officer Commanding.
H₂S	an advanced RAF radar system used for navigation and night bombing.
Hamilcar	Large glider built by General Aircraft. It had a crew of two and was 68 feet long with a wing span of 110 feet. Capable of carrying a Tetrach small tank; its other possible pay-loads were two Bren Gun Carriers or two Scout Cars. Used exclusively by the British, 412 Hamilcars were built during the war.
Handley Page Halifax	RAF four-engined heavy bomber.
Hawker Typhoon	RAF rocket-firing fighter-bomber, known as the 'tank-buster'.
Hawkins Grenade	anti-tank grenade (British).
HE	High Explosive.
H-Hour	The time that the first wave of craft touch down in an amphibious operation; or the leading troops cross the Start Line in a land battle.
Higgins boat	The standard American beach landing craft. Officially known as an LCVP.
Hobart's 'funnies'	Specialized armoured vehicles, the brainchild of Major General Sir Percy Hobart, an officer who had already made a name for himself as an armoured

innovator in the 1930s, who was made responsible for developing the specialised tanks when the Chief of the General Staff, General Sir Alan Brooke gave him command of the 79th Armoured Division.

Honey tank	Light, reconnaissance tank of American design.
Horsa	British troop-carrying glider.
IO	Intelligence Officer.
Jäger	German Army equivalent of light infantry or chasseurs
K-ration	US compact meal (and cigarettes) issued for battlefield conditions
'Jedburgh'	American, British and French three-man teams, consisting of two officers and a radio operator, parachuted into France before and during the battle for Normandy, their task being to train and advise Resistance groups
Kangaroo	British APC, based on Canadian-produced Sherman tank with turret removed. It could carry eight infantrymen.
KOSLI	King's Own Scottish Light Infantry.
KP	US military slang: 'kitchen police/patrol'. The U.S. military uses 'police' as a verb to mean 'to clean' or 'to restore to order.'
Kubelwagen	the Wehrmacht's slightly larger and heavier counterpart to the Jeep and made by Volkswagen.
Landser	German equivalent of a GI or ordinary soldier, but usually indicating an experienced front-line infantryman
LBV	Landing Barge Vehicle, a converted barge or lighter used mostly for carrying stores.
LCA	Landing Craft Assault, a small landing craft capable of carrying an infantry platoon (30-40 troops).
LCA (HR)	Landing Craft Assault (Hedgerow), a converted LCA equipped with 24 spigot mortars to blast a path through minefields.
LCF	Landing-Craft Flak, a converted LCT to give close anti-aircraft protection to craft approaching the beach. Equipped with eight 2-pounder Bofors and four 20mm Oerlikons, or four Bofors and eight Oerlikons.
LCG	Landing Craft Gun, a number of versions of which were produced, based on the LCT hull. Their purpose was to provide close support for troops landing on a defended beach.
LCGL	Landing Craft Gun Large armed with two 119mm (4.7 inch) naval guns and between two and seven 20mm Oerlikon guns or two 17-pounder and 2 pounders (40mm/1.57 inch).
LCI (L)	Landing Craft Infantry (Large), 300 feet long and which could carry around 200 assault troops and land them down gang-ways lowered on each side of the bow.
LCI (S)	Landing-Craft Infantry (Small) adapted from coastal forces craft. Landed infantry down gangplanks launched over rollers. Originally designed for raids, these craft proved far too vulnerable for assault against defended beaches. They had unarmoured high octane petrol tanks.
LCM	Landing Craft Mechanised, a small landing craft which could carry 100 troops, one small tank or two smaller vehicles.
LCP	Landing Craft Personnel, a small landing craft which could carry up to 40 troops.
LCS (M)	Landing, Craft Support (Medium), a small assault ship equipped to provide close fire support and which carried Forward Observation Officers (FOOs) equipped with radios and powerful binoculars who would direct fire and correct fire onto enemy positions.
LCT	Landing Craft Tank, a flat-bottomed craft capable of taking six Churchills or nine Shermans, or a mix of trucks, armoured vehicles and stores and landing them over a bow ramp on shallow beaches. The main type of LCT used on D-Day was the LST(2) designed by John C. Niedermair and mass produced in the US for the RN and USN. It could carry 20 Sherman tanks.
LCT (A)	Landing Craft Tank (Armoured) Armour was added so these could go into

the beach at H Hour with firepower from two tanks. A wooden ramp of heavy timbers was built so the two tanks side by side up forward could fire going into the beach. The ramp raised them high enough so they could fire over the bow ramp.

LCT (R)	Landing Craft Tank (Rocket), a converted LCT British landing craft armed with up to 1,064 5-inch barrage rockets fired electrically dead ahead in a ripple salvo immediately before an assault.
LCVP	Landing Craft Vehicle and Personnel. The American model for the LCA, also known as a 'Higgins boat'. It carried about 30 troops.
Lee-Enfield	Standard British rifle.
Lieutenant (JG)	Lieutenant Junior Grade (US Navy).
LSI	Landing Ship Infantry, a sea-going troop ship (usually a converted passenger ship) that came in various sizes. The largest carried about 1,400 troops and 24 LCAs, the smallest about 200 troops and 8 LCAs.
LST	Landing Ship Tank, larger than an LCT, with a displacement of 2,000 tons with opening bow doors and a ramp. It could hold 20 tanks. It could beach if required.
Luger	German service pistol.
'Mandrel'	British airborne radar-jamming device which effectively shielded an incoming force by jamming the long range Freya radars.
MC	Military Cross (British gallantry award).
MG-42	German machine gun known to the Allies as a 'Spandau'.
ML	Motor Launch.
M-l 'Garand'	American .30 calibre semi-automatic gas operated service rifle designed by John Garand of the Springfield Arsenal in the late 1920s. It had a an 8-round box magazine.
MM	Military Medal (British), a decoration for gallantry for warrant officers, NCOs and private soldiers.
MO	Medical Officer.
MP	Military Policeman.
MTB	Motor Torpedo Boat.
'Mulberry' harbour	code name for the prefabricated artificial harbours towed across the Channel after D-Day.
NF	Night Fighter
NAAFI	Navy, Army and Air Force Institute.
NCO	Non-commissioned officer.
Nebelwerfer	German mortar with six barrels. Known to the Allies as a 'Screaming Mimi'.
Oboe	British targeting system for blind bombing.
OC	Officer Commanding.
ODs	Olive drab(s) US uniform.
Oerlikon	Swiss-designed 20-millimetre automatic anti-aircraft gun.
OKW	Oberkommando der Wehrmacht: the Supreme Command of the Wehrmacht, which directed all other theatres, especially OB West, during the battle for Normandy.
OP	Observation Post.
OSS	Office of Strategic Services: American counterpart to SOE.
Ost-Battalion	a battalion formed from Osttruppen.
Osttruppen	The German term for 'Eastern troops': captured Soviet and East European troops (mostly from the Rosskaya Osvoboditel'naya Armiya: Russian Liberation Army of former Red Army soldiers, led by General Andrei Vlasov) who served in German uniform under German officers and NCOs in France.
P-38 Lightning	US fighter-bomber built by Lockheed.
Panzerfaust	simple and effective shoulder-launched anti-tank rocket-propelled grenade mass-produced for German infantry.
PE and PHE	plastic (high) explosive.
Petty Officer	Naval equivalent to sergeant.
Phoenix caisson	a prefabricated section of a 'Mulberry' harbour.

PIAT	Projector Infantry Anti-Tank (a platoon-level British hand-held anti-tank weapon similar to the American Bazooka.
Pfc	Private First Class.
PIR	US Parachute Infantry Regiment.
PLUTO	code name (and acronym derived from Pipeline Under The Ocean) - an oil supply line from Britain to Port-en-Bessin in Normandy, which was installed after D-Day.
PR	Photographic Reconnaissance
Priest	A self-propelled (SP) 105mm artillery piece mounted on a tracked chassis.
RAAF	Royal Australian Air Force
RAMC	Royal Army Medical Corps.
RAP	Regimental Aid Post, i.e. a field hospital.
RCAF	Royal Canadian Air Force.
RE	Royal Engineers.
Regiment	(British Army) the armoured corps equivalent of the battalion, consisting of three tank or 'sabre' squadrons and a headquarters squadron. Artillery batteries were also grouped into regiments.
REME	Royal Electrical and Mechanical Engineers.
Rhino ferry	A flat barge used for carrying vehicles and artillery into the invasion beaches
Rhinoceros	hedge-cutting Sherman tank an invention credited to US Army Sergeant Culin, designed to punch breaches into the high-banked hedges of the Normandy bocage by driving straight into the hedge at 10-15 mph, cutting the bank and removing a complete section of the hedge without being forced to stop.
RHQ	Regimental Headquarters.
RNZAF	Royal New Zealand Air Force
Rommelspargeln	'Rommel's asparagus' - an obstacle consisting of two pieces of steel or timber in the shape of a diagonal cross with an upright pole to stabilise them with a Tellermine (Plate mine) on top and designed to destroy ships at low tide and gliders inland.
RSM	Regimental Sergeant-Major.
RT	Radio Telegraphy.
RV	rendezvous.
SAS	Special Air Service: British special forces, organized into two brigades for the invasion of Europe, but including French and other national units and sub-units.
'Serrate'	British equipment fitted to aircraft designed to home in on the radar impulses emitted by the German Lichtenstein ('Emil-Emil') airborne interception radar. Serrate got its name from the picture on the cathode ray tube (CRT). When within range of a German night-fighter, the CRT displayed a herringbone pattern either side of the time trace, which had a serrated edge.
Scorpion	modified Matilda tank equipped with a rotating flail of chains for clearing minefields.
Screaming Eagles	US 101st Airborne Division.
SHAEF	Supreme Headquarters Allied Expeditionary Force.
Shaped Charge	explosive charge shaped in order to focus the blast in a particular direction.
Short Stirling	RAF four-engined heavy bomber.
Snake	a long pipe of explosive pushed ahead of an AVRE into a minefield and detonated to clear a path
SOE	Special Operations Executive, the secret British organisation set up in 1940 to encourage resistance and carry out sabotage in enemy-occupied territory.
SP gun	Self-propelled gun, i.e. a mobile artillery piece or heavy machine-gun mounted on a tank base or a truck chassis.
Spandau	Allied term for the German MG-42 machine gun.
SS	German acronym for Schutzstaffel - 'protection squad'. The SS was a paramilitary organization within the Nazi party which provided Hitler's

	bodyguard and constituted the German security forces.
Sten gun	British 9mm calibre sub-machine gun, a poor weapon with little stopping power and prone to firing accidentally.
Stick	An aircraft load of parachute troops due to drop on one DZ in one run over it.
Stonk	Slang for mortar or artillery barrage.
Stützpunkt	strongpoint.
TCS	Troop Carrier Squadron (US).
Teller mine	German anti-tank mine.
Terrapin	Inferior British equivalent to the DUKW.
Tetrach	British Light tank privately developed by Vickers from 1937 and known originally by the company project name 'Purdah'. It was accepted for service by the British Army in 1938 as the Light Tank Mk VII. Production began in 1940 but was soon halted when it was realized that light tanks were increasingly vulnerable on the modern battlefield. The Tetrach was powered by Meadows flat-12 petrol engine and had a top speed of 40mph and range of 140 miles. It had a crew of three and was armed with a 2-pounder gun and one 7.92mm Besa machine gun.
Thompson	Tommy gun - sub-machine gun (American).
tobruk	German look-out or machine-gun post, sunk into the ground.
USAAF	United States Army Air Force.
VC	Victoria Cross (highest British award for gallantry in the face of the enemy).
Very light	a coloured flare fired from a pistol.
W/T	wireless telegraphy.
WAAF	Women's Auxiliary Air Force (British).
Waffen	Combat divisions (a military elite) of the SS.
Weasel	A small amphibious truck with caterpillar tracks.
Wehrmacht	Regular German army.
Wiederstandnesten (WN)	'Resistance nests'
Wren	Member of the Women's Royal Naval Service.

Comparative Table Of Ranks

Wehrmacht	US Army equivalent	British Army Equivalent	SS
Reischmarschall	no equivalent	no equivalent	
Generalfeldmarschall	General of the Army	Field Marshal	
Generaloberst			SS-Oberstgruppenführer
General der Infantrie/Artillerie/Flieger/Fallschirmjäger			
	General	General	SS-Obergruppenführer
Generalleutnant	Lieutenant General	Lieutenant General	SS-Gruppenführer
Generalmajor	Major General	Major General	SS-Brigadeführer
	Brigadier General	Brigadier	SS-Oberführer
Oberst	Colonel	Colonel	SS-Standartenführer
Oberstleutnant	Lieutenant Colonel	Lieutenant Colonel	SS-Obersturmbannführer
Major	Major	Major	SS-Sturmbannführer
Hauptmann	Captain	Captain	SS- Hauptsturmführer
Oberleutnant			SS-Obersturmführer
Leutnant	1st Lieutenant	Lieutenant	SS-Untersturmführer
Fahnenjunker	2nd Lieutenant	2nd Lieutenant	SS-Junker
Stabsfeldwebel	Flight Officer		
Oberfähnrich	no equivalent		
Oberfeldwebel	Master Sergeant		
Fähnrich	Officer candidate		
Feldwebel	Sergeant	Sergeant	
Unteroffizier	Staff Sergeant		
Obergefreiter	Corporal	Corporal	
Gefreiter	Private First Class		
Flieger	Private Second Class		

'We have gained a foothold on the continent of Europe.'
General Sir Bernard Law Montgomery, C-in-C 21st Army Group, referring to Operation Overlord, 6th June 1944.

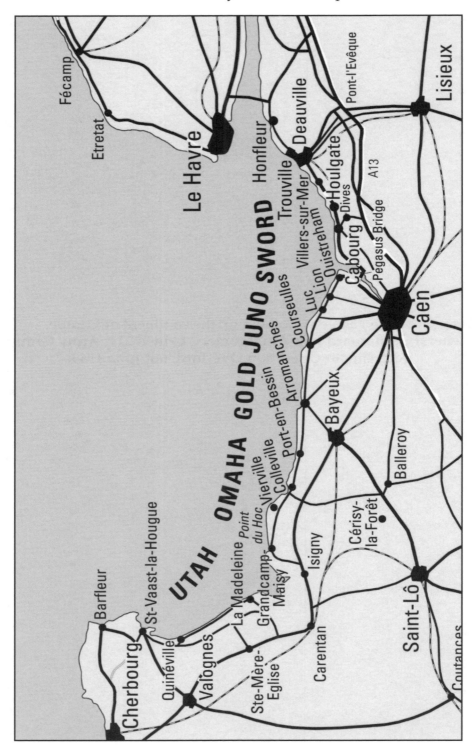

Chapter 1

The Boys' Crusade

Soldiers, Sailors and Airmen of the Allied Expeditionary Force! You are about to embark upon the Great Crusade... The eyes of the world are upon you. The hopes and prayers of liberty-loving people everywhere march with you. In company with our brave Allies and brothers-in-arms on other Fronts, you will bring about the destruction of the German war machine, the elimination of Nazi tyranny over the oppressed peoples of Europe and security for ourselves in a free world... Much has happened since the Nazi triumphs of 1940-41... The tide has turned! The free men of the world are marching together to Victory!

Pre-D-Day address by General Dwight D. Eisenhower, Supreme Allied Commander-in-Chief, Allied Forces of Liberation.

'Unless we can land overwhelming forces and beat the Nazis in battle in France, Hitler will never be defeated. So this must be your prime task.'

Winston Churchill's orders to Lord Louis Mountbatten commanding Combined operations in 1942. In spring 1943 at the Anglo-American 'Trident' conference the British Chiefs of Staff committed themselves to Overlord and the Combined Chiefs issued their Directive to General Frederick E. Morgan, who had been appointed Chief of Staff to the Supreme Allied Commander (Designate) 'COSSAC' at the Casablanca Conference:

'To mount and carry out an operation, with forces and equipment established in the United Kingdom and with target date 1 May 1944, to secure a lodgement on the Continent from which further offensive operations could be developed. The lodgement area must contain sufficient port facilities to maintain a force of some 26 to 30 divisions and enable that force to be augmented by follow-up shipments from the United States or elsewhere of additional divisions and supporting units at the rate of three to five divisions per month.'

The target date of 1 May 1944 for invasion was later postponed a month to enable extra landing craft to be built and the initial assault was expanded from three to five Army divisions. Overlord proceeded in London under the direction of General Morgan and Brigadier-General R. W. Barker, who set up an Anglo-American HQ for the eventual Supreme Commander and to prepare an outline plan for the invasion of North-West Europe from Britain. But where would the attack take place?

'The Pas de Calais has many obvious advantages such as that good air support and quick turn-around for our shipping can be achieved. On the other hand, it is a focal point of the enemy fighters disposed for defence and the maximum air activity can be brought to bear over this area with the minimum movement of his Air Forces. Moreover, the Pas de Calais is the most strongly defended area of the whole French coast... Further this area does not offer good opportunities for expansion... the Caen sector is weakly held; the defences are relatively light and the beaches are of high capacity and sheltered from the prevailing winds. Inland the terrain is suitable for airfield development and for the consolidation of the initial bridgehead; and much of it is unfavourable for counter-attacks by panzer divisions. Maximum enemy air opposition can only be brought to bear at the expense of the air defence screen covering the approaches to Germany and the limited number of enemy airfields within range of the Caen area facilitates the local neutralisation of the German fighter force... In the light of these factors it is considered that our initial landing on the Continent should be effected in the Caen area with a view to the eventual seizure of the lodgement area comprising the Cherbourg-Brittany group of ports.'

Seine Bay, the area of Normandy chosen for the assault, is 50 miles across. It stretches from Barfleur, where, in 1066 William of Normandy set sail for the invasion of England, eastwards to the mouth of the Seine. Because it was ultimately intended that American forces should be supplied directly from the United States, their troops were assigned to the western sector, while the British and Canadian beaches were in the eastern sector. The invasion would necessitate 24 different embarkation points spread over 1,000 miles of British coastline, made necessary by the total loading capacity in 24 hours, since the assault and follow-up had to load simultaneously. The British would load from Yarmouth to Portsmouth and the Americans from Southampton to Milford Haven. Each of the 24 points required its own embarkation camp, marshalling and concentration area and special road layout - many of which had to be either built or greatly improved.

'Broadly, the requirements for the coastline and hinterland where the huge embarkation operation was to take place, were: no tide, so that loading at the hards or ramps could take place 24 hours out of 24 and hinterland which was hard and flat, with good road access or surface with no need for road building or improvement, with loading points where one wanted them and not dictated by inland access. The hinterland also needed to be suitable for construction of embarkation camps, with marshalling camps behind them where men and vehicles were to get into their craft loads and - further back - concentration areas to which units were to proceed from their home stations. Good road access from one to another was imperative. Added to that, good depth of water at loading points was essential, so that craft could load without danger.

'North Africa for the Sicily landings was perfect: no tide, no road problems on the hard sand and camps and areas could be established precisely where required. England, on the other hand, could not have been worse. The change of tide around our shores is so great (24 feet each 24 hours), our coastline is intricate and deep water rarely lies close in. Also, the coastal roads and lanes are so winding and the country inland from the coast so enclosed for creating camps or areas, which could feed from one to the other...The operation, which could have been mounted on 15-20 miles of the African coast, was spread from Yarmouth to Milford Haven... spreading well over 1,000 miles with its estuaries and inlets. Even with the large number of embarkation points the loading of vehicles for the assault and follow-up had to begin six days before D-Day... D-Day was not only the greatest combined operation ever undertaken: It was the greatest that ever will be.'

Brigadier Tom Collins, Director of Movements for Continental Operations October 1943-June 1944.

'In 1942, when the planners were planning the invasion, they came to the conclusion that it wouldn't be feasible to have an invasion in which the stores came over the beaches. That was for two reasons: one, there's a 25-feet rise and fall of tide on the Normandy beaches and you can only discharge at certain times either side of high tide, so that the amount of time you had for discharge was limited and the amount of stores you could get over would be limited. The other was that if there was a storm or bad weather on the beaches, nothing could come ashore and the prospect of capturing a fortified port was negligible. It was only then that the bright boys - British boys - thought up the idea of an artificial harbour which would be built in pieces in England, towed a hundred miles to the beaches and there put down, piece by piece by piece. And so came about the building of the 'Mulberry' harbours. The combined Chiefs of Staff, British and American, said that this project was so vital that it might be described as the crux of the whole operation and it must not fail because it was the only way we could safeguard the getting of stores to support the operation.

'I'd been to a meeting in the morning and I was taken to lunch at the 'In and Out Club' in Piccadilly. I had my usual black civil service case in which I had locked the papers for the meeting and I placed it under the table during lunch. Afterwards I went back to Norfolk House in St. James Square but when I arrived, I realised I hadn't got the case. I'll never forget that moment. I'd left it in the 'In and Out Club' and it contained not merely the plans of 'Mulberry' but also information as to where we were going to invade. At that moment, I wanted to die. I wanted to be instantly shot - not that that would have helped much, but I really have never forgotten to this day my feelings of utter horror. I rang up the club and the hall porter answered and said, 'Yes sir, a case was left here and I've got it in my cubby hole' and I galloped the whole way from Norfolk House to the club and he handed it over to me. It was still locked.'

Brigadier Arthur Walter, Director of Ports and Inland Water Transport.

'We were told that we should be proud to have been selected from the corps of Royal Engineers to take part in this operation; that we would be responsible for the construction of the piers and pier heads in the field; that the success of the invasion of Europe depended on us. In fact they told us that this project was so vital that it might be described as the crux of the whole operation. I was not at all thrilled by this information; quite apart from a natural reluctance to get involved in anything that looked so dangerous, I was appalled to think that the British Army was so desperate, so near the bottom of the barrel that they had to choose me. And, if it were really true that the success of the assault on Europe depended in any way on me, then I could not see much hope for the Allied Armies.

'Something of these unhappy thoughts must have shown in our faces (my forebodings were shared by the others); we were assured that orders had already been passed to every RE Unit in the United Kingdom to send, immediately, their finest, bravest and most highly skilled soldiers to join this crack invasion force, because 'Mulberry' Must Not Fail. Alas, what really happened was that every unit in the UK seized this golden opportunity to unload on to us their most formidable and desperate criminals.'

An officer in the 969th and 970th Port Floating Equipment Companies.

'We arrived at what seemed like a huge office block without windows, sixty foot high. We were told to clamber up on top, not knowing at the time that this lump of concrete was actually floating - and when we got to the top we found that it was just a huge hollow concrete box. Next to it was a tug. We thought the tug was tied to it but, in fact, it was tied to the tug and the tug towed us away. There we were on top of this thing. There was nothing we could do. We just had to sit there while we were towed along at four knots, which isn't very fast and as the dawn began to break we found ourselves in a bay by Dungeness where we promptly went down inside this concrete box, opened the sluices and sunk it on the sand and wondered what the hell we were doing - 'cos nobody tells you anything. We soon realised why they asked for volunteers, because these things had never been taken across an ocean. I mean, it was like trying to drag a brick across the Thames.'

Ordinary Seaman Kenneth Bungard aboard craft towing 'Mulberry' Harbour caisson.

'We've got a fairly big job on. Something comparable to the city of Birmingham hasn't merely got to be shifted; it's got to be kept moving when it's on the other side…We must take everything with us - and take it in the teeth of the fiercest opposition. We are in fact, undertaking the greatest amphibious operation in history, so vast in scale and so complex in detail that the supreme consideration must be the orderly carrying out of a Plan.'

A US Supply Officer who was interviewed by *Picture Post* on 6 May 1944. Truck, Jeeps, transports and staff cars cause a vast traffic snarl-up in the days before D-Day. In Andover, Hampshire, office workers are given 15 minutes extra at lunchtime to cross the street.

'Everywhere along that road and all the others in England, there were endless convoys of army vehicles - miles and miles of them… moving along bumper to bumper - division after division. [The 820th Engineers] had pulled out of their aerodrome in Suffolk and were headed south, to take part in the invasion. As bulldozers rumbled past and the motorgraders and the shovels and the trucks, I stood up in the front of the Jeep and shouted and waved: 'So long, Pete! Good luck, Tommy! … Take it easy now John… Good luck, good luck!'

Robert S. Arbib Jr. *'Here We Are Together: The Notebook of an American Soldier in Britain.*

'The final conference for determining the feasibility of attacking on the tentatively selected day, June 5, was scheduled for 4 am on June 4. However, some of the attacking contingents had already been ordered to sea, because if the entire force was to land on June 5, then some of the important elements stationed in northern parts of the United Kingdom could not wait for the final decision on the morning of June 4.

'When the commanders assembled on the morning of June 4 the report we received was discouraging. Low clouds, high winds and formidable wave action were predicted to make landing a most hazardous affair. The meteorologists said that air support would be impossible; naval gunfire would be inefficient and even the handling of small boats would be rendered difficult. Admiral Ramsay thought that the mechanics of landing could be handled, but agreed with the estimate of the difficulty in adjusting gunfire. His position was mainly neutral. General Montgomery, properly concerned with the great disadvantages of delay, believed that we should go. [Sir Arthur] Tedder disagreed. Weighing all factors, I decided that the attack would have to be postponed. This decision necessitated the immediate dispatch of orders to the vessels and troops already at sea and created some doubt as to whether they could be ready 2¼ hours later in case the next day should prove favourable for the assault. Actually the manoeuvre of the ships in the Irish Sea proved most difficult by reason of the storm. That they succeeded in gaining ports, refuelling and readying themselves to resume the movement a day later represented the utmost in seamanship and in brilliant command and staff work.

'The conference on the evening of June 4 presented little, if any, added brightness to the picture of the morning and tension mounted even higher because the inescapable consequences of postponement were almost too bitter to contemplate.

'At 3.30 the next morning our little camp was shaking and shuddering under a wind of almost hurricane proportions and the accompanying rain seemed to be travelling in horizontal streaks. The mile-long trip through muddy roads to the naval headquarters was anything but a cheerful one, since it seemed impossible that in such conditions there was any reason for even discussing the situation.

'When the conference started the first report given us by Group Captain Stagg and the meteorological staff was that the bad conditions predicted the day before for the coast of France were actually prevailing there and that if we had persisted in the attempt to land on June 5 a major disaster would almost surely have resulted. This they probably told us to inspire more confidence in their next astonishing declaration, which was that by the following morning a period of relatively good weather, heretofore completely unexpected, would ensue, lasting probably thirty-six hours. The long-term prediction was not good but they did give us assurance that this short period of good weather would intervene between the exhaustion of the storm we were then experiencing and the beginning of the next spell of really bad weather.

'The prospect was not bright because of the possibility that we might land the first several waves successfully and then find later build-up impracticable and so have to leave the isolated original attacking forces easy prey to German counteraction. However, the consequences of the delay justified great risk and I quickly announced the decision to go ahead with the attack on June 6. The time was then 4.15 am, June 5. No one present disagreed and there was a definite brightening of faces as, without a further word, each went off to his respective post of duty to flash out his command the messages that would set the whole host in motion.

'A number of people appealed to me for permission to go aboard the supporting naval ships in order to witness the attack. Every member of a staff can always develop a dozen arguments why he, in particular, should accompany an expedition rather than remain at the only post, the centre of communications, where he can be useful. Permission was denied to all except those with specific military responsibility and, of course, the allotted quotas of press and radio representatives.

'Among those who were refused permission was the Prime Minster. His request was undoubtedly inspired as much by his natural instincts as a warrior as by his impatience at the prospect of sitting quietly back in London to await reports. I argued, however, that the chance of his becoming an accidental casualty was too important from the standpoint of the whole war effort and I refused his request. He replied, with complete accuracy, that while I was in sole command of the operation by virtue of authority delegated to me by both governments, such authority did not include administrative control over the British organisation. He said: 'Since this is true it is not part of your responsibility, my dear General, to determine the exact composition of any ship's company in His Majesty's Fleet. This being true,' he rather slyly continued, 'by shipping myself as a bona fide member of a ship's complement it would be beyond your authority to prevent my going.'

All of this I had ruefully to concede, but (forcefully pointed out that he was adding to my personal burdens in this thwarting of my instructions. Even, however, while I was acknowledging defeat in the matter, aid came from an unexpected source. I later heard that the King had learned of the Prime Minister's intention and, while not presuming to interfere with the decision reached by Mr Churchill, he sent word that if the Prime Minister felt it necessary to go on the expedition he, the King, felt it to be equally his duty and privilege to participate at the head of his troops. This instantly placed a different light upon the matter and I heard no more of it.

'Nevertheless my sympathies were entirely with the Prime Minister. Again I had to endure the interminable wait that always intervenes between the final decision of the high command and the earliest possible determination of success or failure in such ventures. I spent the time visiting troops that would participate in the assault. A late evening visit on the 5th took me to the camp of the US 101st Airborne Division, one of the units whose participation had been so severely questioned by the air commander. I found the men in fine fettle, many of them joshingly admonishing me that I had no cause for worry, since the 101st was on the job and everything would be taken care of in fine shape. I stayed with them until the last of them were in the air, somewhere about midnight. After a two-hour trip back to my own camp, I had only a short time to wait until the first news should come in.'

Dwight D. Eisenhower.

'My dear Winston,

'I want to make one more appeal to you not to go to sea on D-Day. Please consider my own position. I am a younger man than you, I am a sailor and as King I am the head of all the services. There is nothing I would like better than to go to sea but I have agreed to stay at home; is it fair that you should then do exactly what I should have liked to do myself?'

HM King George VI's letter to Winston Churchill on 2 June which helped dissuade the Prime Minister, who tried to justify his demand on the grounds that he was also Minister of Defence, from his determined desire to sail with the invasion fleet. He had arranged to go aboard HMS *Belfast*.

'It is true that the hour of the invasion draws nearer, but the scale of enemy air attacks does not indicate that it is immediately imminent.'

Feldmarschall Gerd von Rundstedt, Commander-in-Chief West, reporting to Adolf Hitler on 30 May 1944.

'If every one of the requirements I had been given was to be insisted on, it was easy to deduce that Overlord might not get underway for another hundred years or more.'

Group Captain John Stagg, Chief Meteorological Officer, a tall lean Scot, who one Royal Navy admiral described as 'six feet two inches of Stagg and six feet one of gloom'. The transport aircraft needed a cloud ceiling of not less than 2,500 feet over their targets and 3-mile visibility. The medium bombers ceiling had to be 4,500 feet and they also needed 3-mile visibility. The heavy bombers wanted no more than 5/10ths cloud cover below 5,000 feet and a ceiling of 11,000 feet over their targets. For the navy, the winds were not to exceed 12 mph onshore or 18 mph offshore. The paratroopers could not operate in winds exceeding 20 mph and in gusts. The army wanted dry conditions to operate heavy vehicles off the main roads.

'I was born on 21 August 1920 in Gonsenheim near Mainz in Hesse, Germany. Mainz is about thirty miles away from Frankfurt and was a city of a hundred thousand before the war. Gonsenheim, about ten thousand, was a very small village. I grew up as a typical German teenager and although I was Jewish, I was not really any different from any of the other kids. Our whole thing was World War I. My father and my uncles fought in the war; two of my uncles got killed and I grew up that way. Very patriotic and very militaristic. As a six, seven year old, I paraded around in my father's World War I uniform in our back yard with a drum. From the time of my birth until 1930 we were under the French occupation of the Rhineland and that even aggravated our nationalistic feelings in the schoolyard, the public school in Gonsenheim which we shared with French kids. We regularly had fights with them and anybody who got friendly with the French was suspect as an informer. I imagine it was very similar to any occupied area anywhere in the world.

'I'm sure that if God had made me an 'Aryan,' my bones would be resting somewhere in Russia, like those of my friends with whom I grew up. There was a friend in Gonsenheim, I take it that he was killed in Russia as a tank commander. My attitude towards the Germans was one of very intense curiosity. I wondered what had happened to them since I left and how the Nazi thing had developed and what they were like. It wasn't hate exactly, but it wasn't that I was crazy about them. I was influenced by the propaganda and by the general tenor that was prevalent at that time. I hated Hitler personally and the krauts were the krauts.

'In 1930 we moved to Mainz and I went to the 'gymnasium' (high school) until I was kicked out in 1935 and we came to the United States. Those were very tough times. My father arrived in the United States in 1934 and my mother, brother and I followed in 1935. We left from Cherbourg on 28 May on the *'Aquitania'*. I grew up in Brooklyn and went to high school there and then City College. In 1941 I was in my senior year and I was working in the New York Public Library when the news of Pearl Harbor came. I immediately volunteered for the Navy. They turned me down because I was an enemy alien but I passed the Army physical and was inducted on 4 February 1942. I was sent to basic training and was picked for radio. I spoke fluent German and good French and the Army made me a radio operator. I served in the Military Police but I applied for the 309th Infantry of the 78th Division because I didn't want to be an MP. We had to go on thirty-mile hikes and had to do five miles in fifty minutes and all that stuff. I was eventually made a sergeant technician, fourth grade. Three stripes and a 'T.'

'In January 1944 I was charge of quarters when a teletype came in from division headquarters that radio operators were needed for a special assignment. I and another guy wanted to be radio chiefs of the regiment. We made a deal. He stayed and I was shipped out to some unit that was ready to go overseas. We were put on trains, shipped to Staten Island and before we knew it we were on a ship out in the narrows and in a huge convoy bound for Europe. There were small airplane carriers with planes on deck, troop ships and all sorts of other ships. We had daily lifeboat drills because of the submarine danger. We landed in Liverpool and were shipped by rail to Torquay, a lovely town on the south coast of Devon. We were billeted in private homes and I drew a lovely widow with two teenage daughters.

'We were not told anything, but we were trained for the invasion. In February and March we went on field exercises to acquaint ourselves with working the radios and learning our jobs. This outfit that I was with was the 293rd Joint Assault Signal Company. We had our insignia, a blue shield with the yellow anchor and Tommy gun through it. This logo had been the logo of the British amphibious troops that attacked Dieppe and the Americans copied it, just with different colours. We were attached to the 6th Engineer Special Brigade and our company consisted of three distinct, separate units; the Signal Corps, the Navy and the Air Corps. The Navy and Air Corps were radio coordinators, ground-to-air and ground-to-ground with the Navy gunfire during an amphibious attack. We had trained artillery observers and trained air spotters to guide air strikes. And in the Signal Corps, we had wiremen, telephone linemen, radio operators and message centre personnel trained in encoding and decoding messages. The radio operators were trained in radio nets and operated between the beach master and various sub-units. The linemen were laying telephone lines to various command posts, the beach master and the people who coordinated the supplies and troops. The beach master was the commander of the beach and coordinated troop movements and cargo, his word on the beach was law. He was the commander of the beach and we were his communications centre.

'We had to make a beach landing and to communicate with the beach master. Exactly the job we had to do later and these communications consisted in carrying radios and calling the beach master and reporting on troops status, stevedores status, freight status. We also learned about Bangalore torpedoes and cargo nets. In April we were put on LSTs and sent on exercise 'Tiger' at Slapton Sands. We didn't see any purpose in it. We were 21 year-old kids and it was just another piece of army chicken shit that we had to do. On this LST were about 300 guys and a radio room which was manned by one Navy petty officer, the only radio operator on this LST. The loudspeaker bellowed out that any radio operators were to report to the radio room. We reported and this petty officer showed us the speaking tube to the bridge and said, 'Listen, I want to get a night's sleep. You guys can keep watch, each of you two hours, until morning. If you hear anything, don't send or touch the radio - just notify the bridge.' We thought that was great because we were in a nice little room (the regular radio room in LSTs was a tiny little cubicle) and this guy had tons and tons of comic books. We read comic books all night.

'I went on watch and about an hour or so I heard 'Mayday! Mayday!' I thought; 'another piece of army exercise.' But it wasn't. I reported it to the bridge and I said, 'This is the radio room. I just got a Mayday call over the radio.' They said 'OK, thank you, that's it.' And I never heard anything more about it and I never thought about it again.'

Technical Sergeant Fritz Weinshank, 293rd Joint Assault Signal Company. 'After the war, I read that some American LSTs were apparently hit by German E-boats and a lot of GIs drowned'.

'On 28 April our captain received the signal to proceed to Slapton Sands where German E-boats had attacked a fleet of US landing craft who had been rehearsing for D-Day landings. I remember the dozens of corpses covered in fuel oil floating in the sea and our ship's boats being lowered to recover them. We had about 70 brought aboard, but only one was still alive and he died shortly afterwards. The flotilla returned to our base at Portland, where the dockland abounded with ambulances, but there was not much that could be done for the poor blokes.'

Ordinary Seaman Jack 'Buster' Brown aboard fleet minesweeper HMS *Kellett*.

'On the night of 28 April my landing craft berthed in Weymouth harbour and I was told to keep all sightseers away. Ships started to unload dead American soldiers on the quayside. The story was that there were three E-boats hiding under the cliffs when the US convoy went past. All they had to do was full steam into the convoy, fire their torpedoes and then head for home. That night US ambulances were taking the dead away, six to a van and it went on until four in the morning. All the ambulances left on the Weymouth to Dorchester road, so they went away from Slapton Sands. I read about it in the papers after the war - but the papers got it wrong. The stories said that the dead had been dragged up Slapton Sands and buried in nearby fields. That was all wrong. It was lies. There were no dead in them fields - the dead were treated with respect and they were all taken away in the correct manner.'

Ordinary Seaman Geoffrey Cassidy aboard HMS *Riou*.

'An American torpedo boat under the command of Commander Buckley had arrived at Dartmouth amidst talk of an operation to try out landing craft in advance of D-Day. Lots of officers had tried to give Buckley advice about how the German E-boat tactics worked but his attitude had been, 'Oh, we don't need that advice.' His skippers had wanted it - but he didn't. And then one night in April 1944, they carried out an operation called Operation Tiger. They were to do a landing at Slapton Sands - and Jerry sat out there and torpedoed these ships. It was exactly what we'd warned Buckley about. So this is one of those things - no matter who you are or where you are, it's foolish not to take any advice when it comes to enemy tactics. It was a tragedy that could have been averted if he'd only listened.'

Lieutenant Albert Morrow, Canadian officer commanding MTB 726 in British coastal waters.

'As I was passing the captain's door - BOOM! - followed rapidly by the sound of crunching metal, a painful landing on both of my knees on the steel deck, falling dust and rust - then darkness and silence - and aching knees and wondering, 'My God, what happened?'

'There was no electricity, but I had done my homework and knew where every battle lantern was located. One was by my right hand as I stood up, just across the passageway from the captain's door. With this first light, the rest were easily found and used. The force of the explosion had popped the first aid cabinet partly off the wall and it was leaning out about 30 degrees with its doors open and supplies all over the wardroom. Casualties came in slowly, some by themselves and some by litter, but most were half carried. There were only a few. One fellow sustained a broken thigh and we fixed him up with a splint. As more reports of the damage came in, we realised that the mid part of the ship was an inferno and no one could pass from one end of the ship to the other, either on the main deck or below. The flames and the heat were separating the front from the back. There were twenty-two DUKWS on board and the men had been sleeping in them and now they were ablaze... we could hear our small arms ammunition exploding and the men screaming. Navy regulations instruct you keep the integrity of the ship in any kind of an accident and you have to close the doors to all the compartments to maintain air tightness so that the ship can float... and then people can hang on to it to be rescued. So I did what I learned to do while training in the Navy, I closed all the hatches. I don't know how many people were in there. I couldn't get in and they couldn't get out... I could just hear them. Then we went up on deck and even though we had really thick-soled shoes on the heat was coming through the decks and it was like walking on hot tar. We were all jumping or climbing overboard by the time the skipper gave the order to abandon ship. I didn't want to jump, so I eased down the cargo nets into the cold water which was 44 degrees at the engine intake. The Channel's not the best place to swim - not out there in the middle. We were about twelve miles out from shore and we could see that the ship was burning brightly and you could see the explosions from the gas tanks and the trucks on top. We were all anxious to get away from the ship, because of the suction, of being drawn down. And then we'd heard that Germans often tried to save survivors, came back for them and that really scared us. We gathered round the life rafts and there were some floats around too, but pretty soon some of the guys started to lose consciousness and float away and I'd try to grab them, but I had no lines to hang on to, so they'd float away to nowhere. The water was so cold they were beginning to suffer from hypothermia. In the end I managed to get my hand round a rope that was on the side of the lifeboat, because I didn't want to drift off - and that's the last thing I remember... our ship had about 500 men aboard and we lost half...'

Lieutenant Eugene E. Eckstam, a doctor in civilian life, aboard LST 507.

'Night fell and our group of three LSTs from Brixham and Torquay joined up with five that had loaded in the port of Plymouth. The convoy proceeded onward and I turned in early to get some sleep in anticipation of the next morning's practice invasion. I was jarred awake around 01:30 by the sound of the ship's general alarm. Upon arriving in the wardroom a few minutes after hearing the general alarm I heard reports of some shooting outside. Just after two all hell broke loose... we saw astern a gigantic orange ball of flame and you could see bits of black blobs flying off and you knew that it was men and parts of the ship, it was the most awful sight I had ever seen... moments later we heard an explosion and we realized that the ship had been torpedoed. We'd never carried fuel on an exercise before... in fact most of the men thought that we were going to invade France because this time we were carrying live ammunition. All the men were carrying live ammunition and all the ships were carrying quantities of shells, fuel for the tanks and trucks and so on, so when the ship was hit, it just blew up like a fireball. Moments later we saw another explosion... we saw a sheet of flame, then a rumble and a couple of explosions and we realised that we'd been hit by a couple of torpedoes. By this time, the soldiers on the upper deck were getting hysterical... they were screaming... a lot of them were in open jeeps and half trucks and they were screaming 'Do something!' And there was nothing we could do. LCTs were not equipped to handle any sort of submarine or surface attack. We didn't know what to do... the sea was on fire, burning from the oil and the men were gone... there was no way we could get through that. We could see the bow wave with our naked eye... and a soldier with a heavy calibre machine-gun opened fire ...and the Captain hadn't given the order to fire but the whole starboard side of the ship opened fire, all the 20- and 40-millimetre guns. Everybody was cheering because they were hitting a target. But I found myself screaming at the Captain and all the men on the bridge, 'It's too high'. We were hitting something that was thirty feet off the water instead of the torpedo boats that were very low... we were hitting another LST, one of our own ships, the LST 511. There were a lot of casualties... we didn't go on about liberty after that, the men were so ashamed. It was one of those tragedies of war. The E-boats went on strafing us, you could hear them, but you couldn't see them, there were terrible swells that night. The captain said 'I'm getting the hell out of here...' and we headed for shore. The problem was we didn't know exactly where we were. We could have smashed into gigantic rocks ... but anything is better than being a sitting target... that's what we were. We were like a covered wagon going very slowly with the Indians riding around and just killing us...

'Nobody was killed on our ship... but we were numb with what we saw because washing in around the ship on to the beach were bodies. Some of the men didn't have a mark on them and they all hit the beach sitting up. They had their life preservers around their waists instead of under their arms and all these men had drowned sitting up. When they hit the beach depending on the force of the waves, some went on their face and a lot just fell back and they had their full packs on and it was the worst thing I've ever seen. In the sea it looked like seaweed, where groups of men - three or four were literally burned together, as far as the eye could see there were these bodies. It was the worst debacle, I think, that ever happened to the American Navy.'

Manny Rubin, US Navy Signalman, LST 496. On the night of 27/28 April two German E-boats found eight LSTs, sank two (LST 507 and 531) and damaged others. Altogether, 946 soldiers and sailors died. Three months later Rear Admiral Don Moon shot himself while the *Bayfield* was at Naples ready for the forthcoming landings in the south of France. Manny Rubin met an English girl after the war and she went to America. Manny wanted to live in England but she wanted to stay in the US but eventually they returned to the UK to live in Devon. Manny had nightmares for years. *'The sea was on fire, it was a surreal effect and you couldn't hear the men screaming out in the water, but you knew they were out there and the wind was howling through the flag hoist and the rigging - to me it was just like something out of Hell...'*

'We were housed in a British army barracks which was very cold and I developed a bad case of flu and spent about ten days in the station hospital in Exeter. I got back but our outfit had already returned to Torquay. So I was back with my widow and the two teenagers. Around four weeks before D-Day we left Torquay and moved into a huge assembly camp on the south shore of England. We moved into six-man tents and we were together with a mortuary outfit. This camp had been the barracks of a British motorized division before the war and it had stone buildings and parade grounds. These tents were erected over the parade ground and the whole place was surrounded by barbed wire and was guarded by British reservists. Nobody could get out except by the permission of the camp commander. It was starting to get very hush-hush.

'We were shown photos of 'Omaha' beach, which was sectionalized. In other words, we were taken in a long line and shown posted-up, magnified photos of the beach. And I remember seeing a house at the Vierville exit. This house was to be our landmark. When we got there, there wasn't any house. I remember seeing the bluffs, I remember seeing Germans walk on the beach, some P-38 pilot must have really taken his life in his hands taking these pictures. And we were shown that almost daily. And then, we were briefed on our part of the operation. Our platoon leader was Lieutenant Churan and the second in command was Lieutenant Vincent Fournier. Almost the entire outfit was ranked because it was so technical and it was difficult finding a guy to pull KP.

'Our destination was Easy Red on 'Omaha' Beach. We were behind the infantry of the 29th, the 116th Regimental Combat Team. We were supposed to immediately establish contact in a net with the beach master and other posts that we were supposed to operate. Before we left Torquay, we had to mark our helmets with a white half-crescent and our insignia in the middle. The non-coms had horizontal stripes on the

Time Line to D-Day

26 January 1942 Pfc Milburn Henke, of Hutchison, Minnesota is the first of 2 million American soldiers to arrive in Britain during the build-up to D-Day.

March 1942 BBC broadcasts a Royal Navy plea for holiday snaps of French coast to help map coastal areas. 30,000 letters arrive the following day.

19 August 1942 In a disastrous rehearsal for D-Day, of 6,100 men involved in the landings at Dieppe, France, only 2,500 return. One German Company repels three battalions of mainly Canadian troops, taking 2,000 prisoners and killing 1,000. Enemy losses are less than 600. The raid proves the need for overwhelming force and heavy bombardment and that a floating harbour would need to be provided.

June 1943 Americans are now living in 100,000 buildings in 1,100 locations in Britain. In December, 30,000 further acres of South Devon are taken over and 3,000 residents evicted from 750 properties. Landings are rehearsed in Devon's Bideford Bay, chosen for its similarity to the Normandy coast.

August 1943 During Churchill's voyage aboard the *Queen Mary* en route to Quebec for the summit with Roosevelt, Professor John Desmond Bernal, a scientific advisor, uses a loofah as a wave machine and 20 paper boats as the D-Day fleet. With the PM and aides looking on he proves success would depend on vast floating harbours - 'Mulberries' - represented by a Mae West life preserver. In Quebec the COSSAC plan to invade the continent in Normandy is approved by Churchill, Roosevelt and the Combined Chiefs of Staff. It is also agreed that the Supreme Commander should be American and that his deputy and three commanders-in-chief should be British and May 1944 fixed as the target date.

November 1943 Thirty directives for Overlord issued. At the Teheran Conference at the end of November, Stalin shows himself very impatient for the opening of the 'second front'. Roosevelt and Churchill promise him that the invasion will start in May 1944.

6 December 1943 General Dwight D. Eisenhower appointed to command landings in France.[1]

1 January 1944 General Montgomery relinquishes command of 8th Army in Italy and flies to England to set up his invasion HQ at his old school, St. Paul's, Hammersmith. Montgomery will remain in command of ground forces until September 1944 when General Eisenhower assumed direct control. For the purposes of Overlord, RAF Bomber Command and the Eighth US Air Force are placed under the operational direction of the Supreme Commander to add to the aircraft of the Allied Tactical Air Forces.

17 January Supreme Headquarters, Allied Expeditionary Force established in London.

21 January Generals Eisenhower and Montgomery agree changes to General Morgan's COSSAC plans which set the invasion date as 31 May, extending the landing area west across the Cotentin Peninsular towards Cherbourg and increase the initial seaborne force from three Divisions to five Divisions.

---

1   When General Montgomery was elevated to the rank of field marshal on 1 September 1944 (five star rank, which the US armed forces did not have) President Roosevelt created the US five-star ranks on 12 December and Eisenhower was one of the first recipients, being promoted to General of the Army on 20 December 1944. Following the war, Eisenhower ran for the US Presidency and served two terms in the White House 1953-1961.

1 February Revised 'Overlord' plan, 'Neptune', the sea transportation and landing phase of Overlord issued.

5 March Supreme Headquarters Allied Expeditionary Forces (SHAEF) moves from Grosvenor Gardens to former US 8th Air Force HQ at Bushey Park near Hampton Court, code name Widewing. Eisenhower lives nearby in Telegraph Cottage, Wan Road, Kingston upon Thames.

April All leave cancelled for troops destined for Overlord. Eighteen Allied air forces begin pre-invasion bombing of France. Ninth Air Force begins bombing targets in the Pas de Calais, railway marshalling yards and important bridges. ACM Sir Trafford Leigh-Mallory (younger brother of the noted climber George Mallory, who died on Everest in 1924) remarks that the 9th Air Force is by far the most effective force in knocking out these types of target. On 15 November 1943 Leigh-Mallory had been appointed Air C-in-C of the Allied Expeditionary Air Force consisting of the Second Tactical Air Force (RAF), Fighter Command and the US Ninth (Tactical) Air Force. (From the beginning of May the 9th dispatches more than a thousand aircraft each day, weather permitting, against targets in Normandy and the Pas de Calais).

10 April Naval Commander in Chief, Admiral Sir Bertram Ramsay, responsible for 'Neptune' issues orders for the naval involvement on D-Day. Document stretches to 1,100 pages.

22-29 April Operation 'Tiger', realistic US rehearsal for Overlord at Slapton Sands between Plymouth and Dartmouth. On the night of 27/28 April two German E-boats in the English Channel sink two LSTs and damage others. 946 men are killed.[2]

1 May Eisenhower and Admiral Ramsay, aware Feldmarschall Erwin Rommel is strengthening the Atlantic Wall (by D-Day 6½ million mines are laid along the approaches) and covering the beaches with below the water obstacles, decide that the landings will be in daylight and at low tide, so that the obstacles will be visible. A daylight landing also increases the accuracy of air and naval bombardment.

2-6 May Operation 'Fabius', final rehearsal for Overlord at Slapton Sands.

8 May SHAEF selects 5 June as D-Day. HM The King, General Eisenhower, Field Marshal Smuts and others attend conference at General Montgomery's St. Paul's HQ to review the final plans for Overlord. The experienced US 1st Division - the 'Big Red One' - is selected to lead a beach assault; a major assessment report rates almost every other American formation allocated to the invasion as 'unsatisfactory'.

18 May German radio broadcast that 'the invasion will come any day'.

23 May Camps containing the soldiers who will land on D-Day are sealed with barbed wire. Senior Commanders told that D-Day is 5 June. Detailed briefings begin.

28 May Time the leading troops are to land ('H Hour') is set at a few minutes before 0600 hours and after 0700 hours. Americans are to land first on 'Utah' and 'Omaha' then minutes later, to allow for the difference in the time of low tide, the British and Canadians agree to land on 'Gold', 'Sword' and 'Juno' (originally named 'Jelly' but changed to 'Juno' by Churchill who disapproved of 'Jelly'). 'Omaha' and 'Utah', supposedly named after the respective birthplaces of the US V and VII Corps' commanders, General Leonard T. 'Gee' Gerow and Major General Lawton L. Collins. (However, Collins, a dynamic leader known to his men as 'Lightning Joe', came from Louisiana and Gerow was from Virginia). Also, 'Band' a little-known sixth beach to

---

2   See *The Forgotten Dead* by Ken Small (Bloomsbury, 1988).

the east of the Orne River is possibly for use if a disaster occurs on any of the other beaches, as had been the case during the Sicily campaign.

Eisenhower and Montgomery move elements of their HQs to Southwick House, near Portsmouth to be near the embarkation ports.

31 May Group Captain John Stagg, Chief Met Officer, warns Eisenhower to expect stormy weather for several days to come.

1 June Admiral Ramsay takes command of the immense armada of ships for Operation 'Neptune', the naval part of 'Overlord'. First regular morning and evening meetings begun between senior commanders at Southwick House, principally to discuss deteriorating weather conditions in the Channel. Eisenhower begins a daily shuttle between his forward HQ at Southwick, Bushey Park his main HQ and Stanmore where SHAEF Air Forces HQ is located. Weather forecast is poor.

Sunday 4 June At Southwick House Stagg meets commanders at 0415 hours. The forecast is a rising wind and thicker cloud. Eisenhower orders twice-daily meetings of SHAEF. Only nine men are present at the meetings and even the most junior of them carries a fearful responsibility. Nobody is there as an observer. The men are General Eisenhower, Air Chief Marshal Tedder, Admiral Ramsay, General Montgomery and Air Chief Marshal Leigh-Mallory; and the four chiefs of staff, Lieutenant General Walter Bedell Smith, Rear Admiral George Creasy, Major General Sir Francis 'Freddie' de Guingand and Air Vice Marshal James M. Robb. Stagg's report at 1630 hours is no better: Montgomery is prepared to go despite the weather but Air Chief Marshal Sir Trafford Leigh-Mallory, concerned about the very real threat that a 1,000-foot cloud ceiling and gale-force winds pose to the air forces, is not in favour and urges a postponement. Initially Montgomery disagrees, but when Ramsay points out that the Commanders have to make up their minds within half an hour or it would be too late and the main naval force would have set off, he concurs. With so much depending upon air superiority Eisenhower has no choice but to postpone the landings, scheduled for 4/5 June, for 24 hours. All convoys at sea have to reverse their courses and the pre-arranged signals for delay are sent: 'Bowsprit' to all naval forces and 'Ripcord Plus 24' to the airborne divisions. The fleet of big ships steaming south down the Irish Sea turn about, to steam north for 12 hours. A flotilla of minesweepers is only 35 miles from the Normandy coast when it gets the order to return. The landing craft from Devon, which are off the Isle of Wight, put back towards harbours which are already full. At Portland, there is the most tremendous traffic jam in maritime history. During the morning, in rising wind, it seems that the landing craft will have to go back to Devon to sort themselves out and start again and if they had, they would not be ready for at least two days. But order is restored, in a struggle which lasts all day and not very much damage is done except that one tank landing craft drifts into the tide race off Portland Bill and founders.

A convoy of 138 ships carrying the US 4th Infantry Division on its way to 'Utah' Beach does not acknowledge that they had received the order to stand down and ploughs on towards the rendezvous point south of the Isle of Wight. Destroyers are sent to turn the errant convoy back, but it cannot be found.

'In the early hours of 4 June I got a signal to send out in cypher giving a twenty-four hour postponement of the Operation. I sent that off, but we didn't know whether it had got through to everyone. They couldn't answer back because of radio silence and we could not guarantee that they had received the signal. So we had to send out Walrus amphibian aircraft flying low over the sea to make sure that they had come back.' Captain Richard Courage RN.

In desperation when its radio signals are not acknowledged, that morning at 0900 the Walrus sent out by Coastal Command, drops a canister on the deck. The task force turns back, narrowly averting compromising the success of the whole operation but two British midget submarines continue and just before midnight took up their positions off the beaches to act as markers for the invasion army when it arrives. Feldmarschall Rommel, convinced an invasion is not imminent, decides to leave the Normandy coast for Germany.

Monday 5 June At the morning conference Stagg predicts 36 hours of relatively clear weather with moderate winds; a cold front is advancing from Ireland. Sea would be moderate and it was even likely that the cloud cover would lift and the wind would drop. With no basic changes to the weather pattern described the previous day, Eisenhower turns to General Montgomery and asks whether he could see any reason for not going on Tuesday, to which Montgomery replies, 'I would say - Go!' Ramsay agrees; Leigh-Mallory and Tedder are more circumspect but Bedell Smith says: 'It's a helluva gamble, but it's the best possible gamble.' 'OK' says Eisenhower; 'We'll go'. SS-Obersturmführer Rudolf von Ribbentrop, the son of Joachim von Ribbentrop, Hitler's foreign minister, returning from a 12th SS Panzer-Division exercise when his vehicle is machine-gunned by an Allied fighter is visited in hospital by a member of the German embassy in Paris who says that, according to a report, the invasion is due to start. 'Well, another false alarm,' Ribbentrop replies.

'The fifth of June is not quite over yet,' his visitor says. [3]

A coded wireless message sent out by the BBC instructs the French Resistance to cut railway lines throughout France. German intelligence, which had partially broken the code, warns Rommel's HQ at Château de la Roche-Guyon but in his absence it seems to have been ignored.

---

back of their helmets, the officers had vertical stripes. And the whole thing was a joke because we said that only the Army could mark helmets as an aim for enemy gunners right in the middle of our brains. And we also had to waterproof our radio sets, the SCR 245s. They were big boxes and kind of heavy and they had batteries, but the sending units operated by a dynamo that was hand-cranked on a little horse, like an exercise horse. Some of us learned how to operate this thing cranking and sending at the same time, this was a fine art. Ordinarily, you needed two guys to operate the radio, but we got it down to a science. We spent a lot of time in Torquay putting pitch around the covers to get it waterproof. In one of those pitch sessions, Ike came to inspect us. Our company commander was bowing and fawning and Ike looked around and walked around and was very interested and he looked at all this pitch and he left, well I don't know what he thought [laughter].

'We saddled up and moved to an embarkation point at Bournemouth. We unloaded and we took it all on the boat. During one of the last days in that assembly area I was in our tent and there was chow call. I was so anxious to go to the chow line that I tripped between two ropes that were crosswise between two tents. I tore a ligament and I suffer

3   *D-Day: The Battle for Normandy* by Antony Beevor (Viking 2009).

limping and my greatest fear was that they would leave me behind, so I just smiled and said 'Absolutely perfect' and whenever he was around, I hid it.

'Not only did I have to carry my radio, but I had to help these God damn wiremen with their wire reels, which we cursed them…a lot of four-letter words. They had a lot of the stuff, switchboards and wire reels and we had to help them. And I was overloaded with this stuff and when we finally got on the boat, my shin was swollen up and I remember that. And I dressed it and I spent a lot of time flat, so that it would go down. 'The boat that we were on was an LCI (Landing Ship. Infantry) and it was the famous LCI 92. We spent about four or five days on this boat, lying in that harbour, a typical Army 'hurry up and wait' operation. We had to line up to get chow; we only got it two times a day. We had to do calisthenics on the dock and more briefings. We were bored and we wanted the show to get underway.

'On the evening of 5 June they let go of the lines and the engines started going and we left, without fanfare just one after the other slipped out. We were then strung out in a long line of troop ships, all of them with large balloons up. Lieutenant Churan handed out the leaflets of Ike, 'Soldiers, Sailors and Airmen, you are about to embark on a Great Crusade.' I did not take it as a monumental thing, something that the entire world would be watching. Quite on the contrary. We were concerned with the thing at hand and we didn't give it a second thought. Due to the fact that we had so much equipment and we couldn't carry it all, Lieutenant Churan and the brains trust in the platoon devised a method. We took a rubber boat and we filled it with the equipment and a number of guys were going to drag this boat ashore so that we wouldn't have to carry it ashore. I was one of the guys who was the first to man this pontoon; get it off the deck. During the night it started to get stormy and the boat started to rock. I and a few other guys lashed the thing down on deck so it wouldn't float around and fastened rubber tarps over it so it shouldn't get wet. It was one of those miserable sea voyages that we had already gotten used to too some extent.'
Technical Sergeant Fritz Weinshank.

'The third battalion of the 508th boarded the buses, with full combat equipment and were driven to the airfield at Folkingham. It was just a short ride to the hangars and when the buses stopped we assembled and marched inside, where we were assigned an army cot. I put my rifle and combat gear beneath the cot and lay down, closing my eyes. I thought to myself, 'This is it, just a matter of time and I will be in combat. Wonder what my folks are doing at home? Are they thinking about the invasion? What would they think if they knew at this moment we were preparing ourselves for the invasion?' 'Chow time!'

'Those words interrupted my thoughts. The men seemed to be taking their time lining up. It was by contrast a strange sight to see, for when at base camp there was always a race to be first on line. To me, it appeared that the troopers were in no hurry.'
Private Thomas W. Porcella, a tough little New Yorker in Company 'H', 508th Parachute Infantry Regiment, 82nd Airborne, Sunday, 28 May.

'We listened to the radio for messages all the time. The men could not, of course. It fell to the people who were in the home - whether it was grandma or children - everyone contributed to try and listen in. The main times were the six and nine o'clock broadcasts from the BBC. One day we had a message, which said 'Listen in to the broadcasts twenty-four hours a day,' so the boss and I installed a little set in the hay up in a loft outside the farm and we listened. We were told it might happen any time, 'You must listen in, you might hear your message. Get yourselves ready, put on the clothes you will wear for work when you go away and make all arrangements for those who stay at home looking after the animals, that they have food.' Then finally the message came through that the armada had sailed and there was terrific rejoicing and a little crowd came up to our village during the night. We had been up all the time, cleaning what weapons we had. They had been hidden in the beehives. Then by morning, the others had turned up and we allocated them to various people in the village we knew we could trust. They went out, despite the fact that they'd only had about five hours' sleep - they went out as soon as possible to blow up the railways and bridges - get trees knocked down so as to block the roads - the bigger the tree the better.'

Yvonne Cormeau Agent, 'F' Section, Special Operations Executive (SOE) working with the French Resistance. SHAEF estimated that about 16,000 Frenchmen and women were under arms and their participation in the run-up to D-Day was crucial - and dangerous. 1,500 resistants were betrayed by their countrymen or the Milice (pro-Nazi French militia) or were intercepted by the Gestapo. About a week before D-Day, immediately following the 7pm and 9pm news broadcasts, 'The Voice of SHAEF' on the BBC French service began to broadcast, in deadpan tones, a series of Code B messages prepared by the SOE instructing the Resistance to cut railway lines throughout France. On the night of June 5-6, the exercise was repeated:

'I am looking for four-leafed clovers.' 'The tomatoes should be picked.' 'The dice are on the table.' 'It is hot in Suez.' 'The children are bored on Sundays.'

Each message was aimed at a specific group; the second half confirmed that it should now execute a predetermined act of sabotage to distract and impede the Germans as the invasion began. Of 1,050 planned breaches of rail lines by the Resistance, 950 were carried out. In southern France the 'Piemento' circuit halted the movement by rail of the 15,000-strong Second SS Panzer Division Das Reich between Toulouse and Montauban when two French teenage sisters, the elder was 16, the younger, 14, siphoned off all the axle oil from the tank transporter cars and replaced it with ground carborundum, parachuted in by SOE. The abrasive grease ensured that when the division received a warning order on 7 June to stand by to move to Normandy 450-miles distant, every tank transporter car seized up after loading at Montauban. It was a week before the division found alternative cars and it was not until D+17 that it saw action in Normandy.[4] The 'Jockey' circuit made sure that every train leaving Marseilles for Lyon after D-Day was derailed at least once in its journey. The 'Farmer' circuit ensured that the railway junctions around Lille and Tourcoing were cut within two nights of D-Day and kept cut until the end of the month.

'Le champ du laboureur dans le matin brumeux' instructed the Resistance to fell trees and scatter nails in the path of advancing German reinforcements. Fifteenth Army HQ near the Belgian frontier heard the most important signal of all - from 'Ode to Autumn' - the couplet by the poet Paul Verlaine whose first line indicated that the

---

4   In retaliation for the killing of 40 German soldiers in one incident, SS Das Reich Panzer murdered 100 men seized at random in the town of Tulle in the Correze. Children and wives were forced to watch while they strung them up to the lamp-posts and balconies outside their own homes. The next morning at the small village of Oradour-sur-Glane Major Adolf Diekmann's unit murdered 642 people, including 190 schoolchildren; the men were shot, the women and children were burnt alive in the church and the village was razed.

invasion was about a week ahead; the second, that it would begin that night:

Les sanglots longs des violons de l'automne

Blessent mon cœur d'une langueur monotone.

[The heavy sobs of autumnal violins/Soothe my heart with a dull languor] [5]

Normally 'The Voice of SHAEF' broadcast lasted five to ten minutes but on this night it ran on for twenty and during it the spokesman 'declared, *'To-day the Supreme Commander directs me to say this: In due course instructions of great importance will be given to you through this channel, but it will not be possible always to give these instructions at a previously announced time. Therefore you must get into the habit of listening at all hours.'* When this was monitored the German wireless interception station in Paris alerted von Salmuth's 15th Army in the Pas de Calais and the 7th in Normandy. Fifteenth Army HQ implemented Alarmstufe II (level II alert), signalling to all German units between the Orne and the Scheldt that invasion was about to start and troops were put on full alert. But at the Château de la Roche-Guyon where Generalmajor Hans Speidel, Rommel's Chief of Staff and Admiral Ruge had guests to dinner, Speidel, in Rommel's absence, was not sure that the landings had taken place. As one officer commented, *'Does anyone really think the enemy is stupid enough to announce its arrival over the radio?'* (Speidel was about to go to bed at 0100 hours on 6 June when the first reports came in of airborne landings). Feldmarschall Gerd von Rundstedt, Commander- in-Chief West who was in the middle of his dinner at his HQ at Ste-Germain-en-Laye outside Paris, also dismissed it as a false alarm when a general warning only arrived at 2115 hours. von Rundstedt's Chief of Staff, Generalmajor Günther Blumentritt discounted the suggestion that this was the start of the invasion and no special precautions were ordered by C-in-C West.

'At four o'clock in the morning, three hours after I received the first reports of the invasion, I decided that these landings in Normandy had to be dealt with. I asked the Supreme Command in Berlin for authority to commit these two divisions into the battle. Although Panzer Lehr and the 12th SS Panzer Divisions were under my command, I could not move them until I had received permission from Berlin. Berlin replied that it was still uncertain as to whether or not these first assaults were the main Allied efforts or merely a diversion.'

Feldmarschall Gerd von Rundstedt, who had already been told by his naval advisers that the Channel was far too rough for an invasion and the Kriegsmarine had decided that it was not worth sending out naval patrols into the Channel that night. At Cherbourg, German Naval HQ entered the 15th Army signal on its record with a comment; 'Of course, nothing *will* happen.'

'...The Century network created a living map of Normandy. Each square mile became the responsibility of separate cells; clandestine photos of positions, stolen blueprints of bunkers and details leaked by drunken Germans all formed part of the overall picture... Agents included the Grandcamp café proprietor Andre Farine, who recorded the barbed-wire fences of the Pointe-du-Hoc battery with binoculars from a nearby church tower, supplemented by titbits overheard in his cafe. The Port-en-Bessin music teacher Arthur Poitevin was allowed to walk the cliff tops because he was blind; he used the opportunity to pace out every defensive perimeter, committing the figures to his sharpened memory. Jacques Sustendal used his position as the doctor of Luc-sur-Mer to visit perfectly fit patients

5   It is immortalized in the film *The Longest Day* but is misquoted - 'Pierce my heart with a dull langour.'

details of concrete thickness, gun calibres, minefields and leave rosters.'[6]

Tactical intelligence-gathering undertaken by 7,000 very brave men and women of the Resistance was directed from London via field offices in Paris and Caen. Resistance groups were kept supplied and reinforced with specialist troops by the RAF Special Duty squadrons and the American 'Carpetbaggers'. Just prior to and shortly after D-Day an increased number of OSS Joes (agents), SOE operatives and three-man 'Jedburgh' sabotage teams were dropped into France by specially modified B-24 blacked painted Liberators from Harrington and RAF Special Duty units at Tempsford. On the night of 3/4 June 23 'Carpetbagger' B-24s were dispatched. On 4/5 June a Carpetbagger B-24 taxied out at Tempsford carrying four agents who were to be dropped into the Limoges area. Among them was 22 year-old SOE agent Violette Szabo, known to the Resistance as 'Corrine'. The B-24 pilot received word that the weather up ahead was bad and aborted the mission right there on the runway. The Joes returned to Hassell's Hall, the lovely Georgian house at Sandy concealed in woods, which was used as a club house and dormitory by the agents. On the night of 5/6 June 11 Liberators were dispatched to drop zones and the 'Carpetbagger' Liberator carrying Violette Szabo passed over the invasion fleet heading for Normandy. At the drop area the Maquis failed to flash their reception lights and caused the mission to be aborted. (Finally, on the night of 7/8 June, Violette and her three companions were successfully dropped in France but on 10 June she was captured and in January 1945 was executed in Ravensbrück concentration camp). British, French and American nationalities were all represented and they added greatly to the successful D-Day assaults. Four Hudsons of 161 Squadron at Tempsford flew 22 sorties making radio contact with Resistance groups on D-Day.

The part played by the RAF, mainly 38 Group, sometimes 46 Group and also RAF Tempsford was crucial to the success of SAS operations. Two methods were employed to get them in. The first was to work in conjunction with 'Jedburgh' teams, which consisted of guides provided by Special Forces HQ. These would organize the local forces, supply them with arms and arrange Dropping Zones and so on. The other method was to drop blind in a selected area. The SAS required the close co-operation and advice of local resistance forces and others. From this base other expeditions could be launched. There were 43 operations carried out in the four months after D-Day and this figure was soon stepped up.

'I joined the Army at the age of 19 and I ended up in the Royal Corps of Signals. After training as a wireless operator I was posted to a regiment that became known as Phantom. Then 90 of us were posted to Scotland to join the Special Air Service, which was re-forming after returning from the Western Desert. I became part of the Phantom patrol with the 1st SAS Regiment. The training was tough. Our task a secret. No one knew what we were doing. We were to roam the battlefields, gathering intelligence and information that was sent back to senior commanders. We were to sabotage enemy supply lines and disrupt German attempts to reinforce troops battling against the invasion forces in Normandy. We wore a letter P on our sleeves and we were ordered never to reveal what it stood for. Many other soldiers thought it indicated we were Polish. After commando and parachute training, we were ready to be dropped into

6 *Ten Thousand Eyes*, Richard Collier / *Monty And Rommel: Parallel Lives* by Peter Caddick-Adams (Preface Publishing 2011).

occupied France. A fortnight before D-Day we travelled to Fairford aerodrome in Gloucestershire. There, sealed off from the outside world and surrounded by barbed wire and sentries, we received detailed instructions.

'I flew in with an advance party of Operation 'Houndsworth'[7] and our task was to set up a camp and then signal back to England to bring in the rest of the squadron. Trouble was, the weather was so bad that the aircraft crew couldn't find the dropping zone. Nearly a week was lost before we jumped, in terrible weather and ended up scattered over a wide area about 150 miles south of Paris. We didn't know who or what we were going to meet on the ground, but we had a job to do and were determined to do it. What we did know was that in 1942 Hitler had ordered that captured commandos or similar troops operating behind enemy lines should be executed if captured.

'We were on our own for about six days before we eventually met up with a peasant farmer who put us in touch with the underground Resistance. Then one of them told us that Rommel had taken over a nearby château [Château de la Roche-Guyon] as his headquarters. Our commander, Major Bill Fraser, wanted us to capture him. The plan was to call a diversionary air raid. During the confusion, two jeep-loads of men would go in and capture Rommel. As wireless operator I was to go in with them. This sounded good but when our commander put it to the powers-that-be they said it would be suicide and we were ordered to call it off. The bombing raid did go ahead but Rommel wasn't there at the time.

'During one operation, called 'Bullbasket',[8] 20 soldiers were betrayed to the Germans and captured. The body of one of my friends, a sergeant, was found half-buried. They had tried to burn his body to hide the fact he had been tortured. Our Sergeant-Major, Reg Seekings, was shot in the head. I remember him with a bullet lodged in his head, walking into camp with the back of his battledress soaked in blood. They couldn't operate on him in case it did more damage, so he carried the bullet in his head right through our missions. He did survive. Two SAS soldiers, including Captain Roy Bradford, were killed after driving round a corner meeting a German convoy. Three others escaped. One operation did end in tragedy. A large unit of Russian PoWs who had volunteered to serve their captors, had been burning houses and taking Resistance sympathisers hostage. After a

7 'Houndsworth' near Dijon was a highly successful beginning to SAS operations in France. It began on 6 June and continued until 6 September, during which time the party of 18 officers and 126 soldiers from 1 SAS blew up the railway lines Lyons-Châlons-sur- Saone-Dijon-Paris and Le Creusot-Nevers 22 times. It also took 132 prisoners, killed or wounded 220 Germans and reported 30 bombing targets to the RAF. *The Special Air Service* by Philip Warner (William Kimber & Co. Ltd, 1971).

8 'Bulbasket', commanded by Captain John Tonkin was composed of 43 men from 'B' Squadron 1 SAS and 12 from 3 Patrol Phantom. It was launched on 5/6 June for the area south-west of Châteauroux to harass the 2nd SS Panzer Division on its move from Toulouse to Normandy. They attacked the railway lines Limoges-Vierzon-Poitiers-Tours, cut the railway 12 times and inflicted 20 enemy casualties besides sending vital information to the RAF. The main party was dropped on 11/12 June and joined up with the Maquis. On 3 July their main camp in the Fôret de Verrieres was attacked by German troops. Nine SAS members got away but 31 SAS and Lieutenant Tom Stevens, a USAAF evader who had joined them were taken prisoner. One officer was wounded before capture and was tied to a tree and publicly beaten to death in Verrieres. Three SAS prisoners were also wounded and taken to hospital in Poitiers, where they were given lethal injections. The remainder, including the American and two other SAS captured previous to this engagement, were shot in the Fôret de Saint Sauvant near the village of Rom. The German unit responsible for this atrocity was believed to be the 158th Security Regiment from Poitiers. The SAS survivors signalled the UK with the information of their disaster and that the unit responsible was billeted at Bonneuil Matours. This was flattened by 2nd TAF on 14 July, Bastille Day when FB.VI Mosquitoes in shallow

successful operation to free the hostages, which left dozens of Russians dead, half of the village of Montsauche was burned and 13 villagers shot.'

20-year old Arthur 'Chippy' Wood who was awarded the French Croix de Guerre with Silver Star and a Mention In Despatches.

'We were given Armoured Vehicle Royal Engineers (AVREs) equipped with improvisations for getting over or through any obstacle we might meet on D-Day. These included fascines, which were huge bundles of chestnut paling about 12 feet across which were held on a little ramp which could be released to fill up a ditch. There was an assault bridge, which could be dropped. The tank didn't have the ordinary gun. It had a thing called a 'Petard', which was a codename for a Spigot Mortar that fired a charge of about 25 pounds of explosive a limited distance, I think about 50 yards was the maximum range. The object of this was to break up concrete so that if, for instance, you met a wall and you couldn't get over it any other way, you could smash it down. We also had a lot of shaped charges called 'General Wades'. They each weighed about 25 or 30 pounds and they could be placed on concrete to smash it up - but you had to get out of the tank, clamp them on to the concrete, get back in, pull the string and there'd be a terrific bang and with a bit of luck, the concrete would fall to pieces and you could climb over it.'

Lieutenant Colonel Allan Younger, 26th Assault Squadron, Royal Engineers.

'I remember seeing all these enormous tins, enormous piles of Compound 219. This was simply grease with lots of fibre in it - a bit like putty - which you applied around any particular crack or crevice in the Sherman tank to make it waterproof for the beach landings. Sherman tanks had an escape hatch in the floor of the tank through which the driver and co-driver could escape. Obviously it wasn't water-proofed so that was where the Compound 219 was placed. The engine inspection doors were also sealed with it. As you went up the hull, the turret ring was sealed with a type of plastic covering and tape. The gun mantlet was sealed and of course the gun barrel was sealed and these seals had little explosive charges attached to them which ran back inside the tank, the theory being that as the tank came off the landing craft and rolled up the beach, the gunner or

---

dives dropped nine tons of bombs on the barracks while the 158th Security Regiment were eating dinner. On 30 July the SAS learned that 2,000-3,000 Germans were massing for an anti-Maquis/SAS sweep and the majority was billeted in the Caserne des Dunes barracks at Poitiers. This resulted in a raid by 24 FB.VI Mosquitoes escorted by Mustangs on 1 August. Meanwhile, the SAS learned that the survivors of the 158th Regiment were now in the Château de Fou, an SS police HQ south of Châtellerault. This and Château Maulny, a saboteur school was attacked by 23 Mosquito FB.VIs on Sunday 2 August. It is estimated that 80 per cent of the regiment were killed, so that unit paid dearly for its actions. It was decided that the remainder of the SAS, after losing 36 out of the original total, would be evacuated by air; this was done at the beginning of August by Hudsons and Dakotas. See *Mosquito Menacing The Reich* by Martin W. Bowman (Pen & 'Sword', 2008).

Operation 'Samwest' was also launched on the night of 5/6 June. It totalled 145 including 30 locally recruited French Resistance fighters. As originally conceived it was a disaster, for the local recruits turned out to belong to different groups who hated each other nearly as much as they hated the Germans. Furthermore, some of the SAS personnel were a little too slap-happy and started having meals in local restaurants. Eventually the Germans put in a full-scale attack and inflicted 32 casualties, but their own casualties amounted to 155. Thirty SAS members stayed with the local resistance and organised them into a most effective unit. Other survivors of 'Samwest' linked up with 'Dingson' which had been established near Vannes and was on a much larger scale. Once the invasion force was established and the Germans began to withdraw the SAS undertook a series of harassing operations. *The Special Air Service* by Philip Warner (William Kimber & Co. Ltd, 1971).

No.10 (Inter-Allied) Commando

One of the Allies' most secret elite units which played a crucial and unsung role in preparations for D-Day was formed in July 1942. It consisted entirely of foreign commandos - most were Jewish refugees from Germany, Austria, Czechoslovakia and Hungary. They knew about Hitler's order that captured commandos or similar troops operating behind enemy lines were to be executed and those who were Jewish, knew also that their families still in occupied Europe would be tortured and killed, so they took English-sounding 'nommes de guerres' and if caught tried to bluff their way out of trouble. Many of their details were known to the Gestapo and so they were given false personal histories, regiments and next-of-kin. They became experts in handling explosives, parachuting, using small boats, night-time reconnaissance, climbing and lock-picking and were used for daring and dangerous secret missions. The unit was formed with just eight recruits and trained in North Wales by a tough Welshman, Captain (later Major) Bryan Hilton-Jones. Volunteers reported to the Grand Central Hotel in Marylebone, London, for selection. In all, about 160 men were chosen. One of them was 29-year old Georgi Lanyi, a Hungarian, whose nationality barred him from serving in a British infantry regiment. In the 1930s he had been an Olympic water-polo player and he had studied at Oxford University before becoming a journalist. Sergeant (later Second Lieutenant) Lanyi, who became 'George Lane', took part in Operation 'Tarbrush', a series of secretive and daring raids on the French coast in the weeks before D-Day.

In mid-May 1944 he was briefed by superiors about a potential new type of German mine which could frustrate the D-Day landings. He and his men made several trips in an MTB across the Channel under cover of darkness and on 17 May he was instructed to return to Onival, his third raid in three nights. On board the MTB was Major Hilton-Jones and a dinghy party consisting of Lane, a coxswain called Private 'Davies' (a Dane) and the signaller, Corporal King, Royal Marines. The sappers, Lieutenant Roy Wooldridge, a volunteer from Royal Engineers and Sergeant E. Bluff, were equipped with an infrared camera to take photographs of Element-C,[9] known from air photographs to be near Ault, to the south-west. At about 01:40 hours Lane and Wooldridge set out alone to search for an Element-C, leaving instructions that if they were not back by 03:00 then the others were to return to the MTB. By about 02:15, still some distance from Ault and with dawn not far off, Lane and Wooldridge decided to return to the dinghy but the dinghy party had come under fire and had finally been forced to return to the MTB as agreed. The MTB could not wait beyond 0415 and left for Dover and both the officers were posted as missing.

Lane and Wooldridge had reached Houlgate beach and with no response they walked the beach and found a dinghy which they launched with sunrise only 30 minutes over the horizon. By dawn, when they were a mile offshore, a German motorboat approached from Cayeaux and they were captured. At Cayeaux both men were interrogated for two days before being driven, blindfolded, the Château de la Roche-Guyon near Vernon, Rommel's HQ Heeresgruppe (Army Group) B which comprised the Wehrmacht armies in northern France, Belgium and the Netherlands. The seat of the Rochefoucauld family, where the current Duke and his relations kept

---

9   Large, fence-like structures developed by the French in 1933, used as beach obstacles. Also known as 'Belgian gates'.

apartments on the upper floor, at Ile-de-France near Grasny, lay on a great bend of the River Seine, which marked the boundary between Rommel's two armies; 7th Army west of the River Orne and 15th Army east of the river. With chalk cliffs behind it looks down across the parterres of a famous herb garden to the great river below. Rommel seldom spent daylight hours at the château, choosing instead to inspect his troops in his Horch staff car accompanied by no more than two officers. Lane was marched off to see Rommel in the grand salon with its magnificent Gobelin tapestries where the 'Desert Fox' sat behind a desk on which the revocation of the Edict of Nantes had been signed in 1685. Lane was brought before Rommel and his interpreter in the château library. Lane spoke in a Welsh accent to disguise his Hungarian origin. He told the interpreter that Rommel would not have invited him to talk if he was seriously regarded as a saboteur. Rommel laughed and replied 'You regard this as an invitation?' Lane said 'certainly and a great honour.' When Rommel asked Lane about the invasion the Hungarian said that he knew only what he had read in The Times. Rommel replied that he already had that information; he received a copy of The Times every day from Lisbon. Wooldridge was also brought before Rommel but gave nothing more than his name, rank and serial number. Both men were transferred to Fresnes Prison in Paris where the Gestapo interrogations were not as brutal as expected because Rommel had ordered that they be treated as prisoners of war. Lane later escaped from Oflag IXA at Spangenberg and returned to England where he was awarded the Military Cross.[10]

the crew inside could activate these charges and blow away the waterproofing membranes so that the turret would be able to rotate freely.'
Sergeant Anthony Bashford, 44th Royal Tank Regiment, 4th Armoured Brigade.

'On exercise at Hayling Island, we were landed in water up to our waists and by the time the soldiers had marched 12 miles inland with wet trousers, they had become very raw in the crotch. It was decided therefore to issue oilskin trousers, which were part of the anti-gas equipment, which sat over the boots and high up the waist so that everybody would land with dry trousers and would not become all raw and red by the time they reached the objective.'
Major Peter Martin 2nd Battalion, Cheshire Regiment.

'I was 20 years old in 1944. We were farmers and lived at Houesville in the region called the Manche. Living conditions were difficult. We had some cows that gave us milk and we made butter that we traded the nearby baker for bread. We traded for all sorts of things and this is how we survived. Since 1942 I was recruited to work for the Todt Organization on the construction of German bunkers at Cherbourg. The city was bombarded and I ran away one time, but the Germans arrested my father. I returned to Cherbourg and was made to sign a document that stated that I was a deserter of the German Army. Initially, they thought of sending me to work in Germany, but finally, I was sent to Fort Roule, where we dug a tunnel which housed large artillery guns that moved on rails so that they could be used when needed. We were paid 48 Francs per day, also receiving a small portion of bread, 40 grams of sausage and 40 grams of butter

10   See *Commandos In Exile; The story of 10 (Inter-Allied) Command 1942-1945* by Nick van der Bijl BEM (Pen & 'Sword' 2008).

and stayed in the 'South America' Hotel in Cherbourg, in which 40 workers shared one room, sleeping on bunk beds. There were also some Russian women who worked with us. They were at the coastal train station to unload cement from the arriving trains. In the evening, they made the crossing between the train station and the hotel escorted by German guards. They were required to carry a stone on their heads and were not allowed to speak. Towards the end of May, the bombings intensified and this made things very unpleasant. The planes flew low over Cherbourg and strafed the city, while the German flak guns blazed away. In some cases, the flak guns mounted up on the mountains did more damage to the houses and chimneys than to the planes. I fled a second time and this time they didn't find me. I fled with a friend and we spent nine hours on foot to go from Cherbourg to Houesville, taking only the back roads. I hid near our farm and the Germans never returned to get me. At the beginning of June there was an increase in aerial activity and we saw numerous observation aircraft. I thought that something was brewing, but did not know precisely what. My uncle said to me, 'if ever there is an invasion by the English here, say to them: Be Welcome'. I have always remembered these words.'

Roger Lecheminant.

'We had to do training for stand up tank battles and we were fairly good after all this. We trained harder than anyone else, as most of the boys were green troops (green being not battle experienced). Recce Troop was told by Major General P. C. S. Hobart, who commanded the 79th Special Armoured Division, 'A good recce gives a successful victory'. The 79th Armoured Division was special in as much as they had flamethrowers, which threw a flame approximately 200-300 yards and God help you if you were on the receiving end. Bobbins with chains were fixed in front of a Sherman tank. The chains whirled round and blew up mines in front. There were also bridge layers and buffaloes (Amphibians).'

Corporal Walter William Oliver, Reconnaissance Troop, Staffordshire Yeomanry.

'The Crocodile flame-thrower was very secret... the people who were trained on it in England before D-Day were kept away from the rest of the regiment. When I first saw it I found it very impressive. It was clearly a very destructive weapon and one way of dealing with things. What I was chiefly worried about was that it only had a range with the wind behind it of 150 yards and for effective purposes 800 yards downwards. So you had to get very, very, close to the enemy and therefore you stood a much better chance of being knocked out by a bazooka or something like that. They were usually used in set-piece attacks. You knew your objective before you started, so you had a plan and the most important thing was to keep the enemy quiet while you were actually giving directions to the flame-thrower gunner. You had to be very careful because he couldn't see after the first shot, he'd be obscured. So it became a very desirable thing to keep as far away from the enemy as possible and be supported by other tanks so that you couldn't be knocked off course while you were concentrating on flame throwing. If you fired into a house, the house went on fire. If you fired through the slot in the pill box it would probably destroy the oxygen in there and suffocate the people. No one set out to set people on fire. The hope was that they would surrender before you did that. I don't think that anybody wanted to flame Germans in particular. It was a rather repugnant job, but it had to be done.'

Lieutenant Kenneth Macksey, 141st Regiment, Royal Armoured Corps.

Hobart's 'Funnies'

In March 1943 the irascible, bullying Major-General Sir Percy 'Hobo' Hobart, a pioneer of tank warfare who created the original tank brigade in 1934, was called from his post as a corporal in the Home Guard by Winston Churchill to develop armoured tanks for use in the coming invasion. Hobart, who had originally served as a Royal Engineer but had transferred to the Tank Corps in 1923, developed tactics and doctrines of tank warfare which the Germans had promptly applied in the development of their armoured formations. But in Britain, Hobart's ideas were considered too unorthodox in some quarters of the Army and in 1938 he was shunted off to Egypt where, out of a scratch formation, he created the famous 7th Armoured Division (the famous 'Desert Rats'). Hobart was forced in 1940 to retire prematurely and was relieved of command. After the disaster at Dieppe on 19 August 1942 a whole gamut of brutal new weaponry was devised (some by Churchill himself) specifically to break through concrete, wire and minefields along the French coast. In 1943 Major General Hobart formed in secret, the 79th Armoured Division and then trained the division for operations on D-Day and after wherever it was necessary to overcome enemy tank obstacles.

Hobart and his staff prepared a remarkable variety of uniquely armoured vehicles from bulldozer tanks to clear away beach obstacles; 'flail tanks' to beat pathways through minefields; tanks which could hurl explosive charges against concrete fortifications; turret-less tanks which were in effect self-propelled ramps, over which other tanks could scale sea-walls; tanks carrying bridges to span craters and ditches; flame-throwing tanks to deal with pill-boxes and, most important of all, amphibious or DD (Duplex-Drive) tanks which could swim ashore under their own power. The 'flails' and DD tanks had been devised before Hobart began his experiments, but they were only in the first stages of development. The DD tank was the invention of a Hungarian-born engineer, Nicholas Straussler, who had succeeded in selling the idea to the War Office in spite of opposition from the Admiralty. Naval experts had declared that these tanks would never be able to swim in the open sea and could not be launched from landing-craft and denounced them as unseaworthy, mainly because they did not have a rudder! The five DD tanks which Hobart took over were obsolete Valentines, but he was able to adapt the equipment to the American Sherman. In July 1943 orders were placed for the conversion of 900 Shermans but the output was so small that six months' later Hobart doubted whether these tanks would be available in sufficient numbers to permit their mass employment on D-Day. Then on 27 January 1944 the DD tank was demonstrated to Eisenhower for the first time, a British engineer was sent by air to Washington with the blue-prints and within two months 300 Shermans had been converted and were on their way to England.

General Montgomery (Hobart happened to be his brother-in-law) adopted a suggestion of Hobart's for placing armour in the vanguard of the assault on the invasion beaches. If the first assault waves were to touch-down at high-tide, as had been planned, large numbers of landing-craft would be wrecked by Rommelspargeln ('Rommel's asparagus' - an obstacle consisting of two pieces of steel or timber in the shape of a diagonal cross with an upright pole to stabilise them with a Tellermine

(Plate mine) on top and designed to destroy ships at low tide).[11] Alternatively, if the landings were to be made at low-tide, leaving the maximum time for clearing the obstructions, the infantry would have to cross several hundred yards of open, fire-swept beach. Either way casualties would be severe. Montgomery decided that the first troops would land short of the main belt of obstacles at half-tide, or earlier, if necessary, three or four hours before high-water, to greatly reduce the danger to the assault-craft. It would also give the engineers time to clear lanes for the follow-up craft before the incoming sea interrupted their work. This would expose the infantry to considerable fire before they could bring their own weapons to bear against the defences so Monty decided he would land the DD tanks in the first wave, the specialised arm in the next and the infantry in the third. But because the beaches were mined, Hobart proposed using 'flails' to clear the way for the DD tanks and other armoured devices. Some of the beaches had treacherous patches of soft clay below high-water mark so Hobart produced a 'bobbin' tank that could lay a carpet of matting in its own path and leave it there as a roadway across the clay for others to follow. The loading tables were so adjusted that in every LCT which was due to touch-down opposite a clay patch, the first tank out would be a 'bobbin'. [12]

When Montgomery first saw Hobart's 'funnies' he ordered him to make one-third of it available to the Americans and set himself to interest Eisenhower and Bradley in its revolutionary employment. Hobart was to recall that 'Montgomery was most inquisitive. After thorough tests and searching questions he said in effect: 'I'll have this and this and this; but I don't want that or that.' Eisenhower was equally enthusiastic but not so discriminating. His response was, 'We'll take everything you can give us.' Bradley appeared to be interested but, when asked what he wanted, replied, 'I'll have to consult my staff.'[14] Bradley eventually accepted the DDs but did not take up the offer of 'Crabs', 'Crocodiles', 'AVRE's and the rest of Hobart's menagerie. Their official reason was that there was no time to train American crews to handle the Churchill tanks in which most of the special British equipment was installed, but their fundamental scepticism about its value was shown when they rejected even the 'Crabs' which offered few training difficulties, since the 'flail' device was fitted to the standard Sherman tank. [15]

11 'Rommel's Asparagus' was so-called because his sketches of his obstacles made the beaches look like vegetable gardens. Rommel also ordered that the low-lying areas behind the coast be flooded to turn them into inaccessible marsh-land.

12 This information came from one of Montgomery's scientific advisers who had spent a holiday on the Bay of the Seine before the war and had noted the presence of clay. The patches were located from aerial photographs and commandos brought back samples which showed that the warning was well-founded. At Brancaster in Norfolk geologists discovered a beach with similar patches, and when tanks were tested there they became bogged. 'The Struggle For Europe' by Chester Wilmot.

14   This account was given to Chester Wilmot by General Hobart on 10 November 1946.

15 'The terrible consequences of this short-sightedness were only too apparent on 'Omaha' on D-Day. The failure of the bombardment and the non-appearance of the DD tanks left the infantry at the mercy of the strong-points which they were required to take by storm. Where tanks were available, landed direct from LCTs, they proved invaluable, but they were too few and too dispersed and they found great difficulty in manoeuvring because of the congestion of vehicles on the foreshore. This congestion was chiefly due to the absence of specialised armour capable of dealing with the natural obstacles and fixed defences. The British had learned from the Dieppe Raid that engineers cannot consistently perform under fire the deliberate tasks required of them unless they are given armoured protection. No such protection was available on 'Omaha'. Apart from lightly armoured bulldozers the Americans had no mechanised equipment for dealing with the obstructions and fortifications. They were expected by their commanders to attack pillboxes with pole-charges and man-pack flame-throwers, to clear barbed wire entanglements and concrete walls with explosives manually placed and to lift mines by hand, all under fire. That they often failed is not surprising.' 'The Struggle For Europe' by Chester Wilmot.

All Hobart's tank-based secret weapons, usually with animal names (Crab, Crocodile etc.), supported every British and Canadian army formation and many American units in the eleven months of fighting in NW Europe in 1944-45. During this time 79th Armoured Division was by far the largest formation in the British Army. Although it never fought as a division or a brigade and rarely as a regiment in vital 'penny pockets' of AVRE's, flails, flame-throwers, or armoured troop carriers, they were indispensable. They were unique and every fighting formation in NW Europe was grateful for Hobart's Zoo.

'The Dragoons were originally a cavalry regiment way back before Napoleonic times but had been reformed late in 1940 as a cruiser tank regiment and we were all raring to go, scorching across the French countryside, or wherever we were sent. And then one day we had a visit at Stow-on-the-Wold from Major General Percy Hobart, who was the 79th Armoured Division's GOC and who thought up the canvas flotation collar, which displaced enough water to keep the tank from sinking after it left the landing craft. He gathered everybody round him and said, 'I have some news for you. You have heard of the Lord Mayor's Show?' And everybody's heart stopped beating. 'You know that people come round afterwards to clear up the mess? Well, your job is going to be the very opposite. You're going in front, to clear up the mess. You are going to be mine-clearers: flails.' Nobody had ever heard of them. The bottom dropped out of their world. They were stunned, absolutely stunned. They'd all been trained to go dashing across the countryside, whereas I'd had my training on infantry tanks, which were much slower-moving things.

'To find out how these things worked, I was sent back to my old battalion in Suffolk, who were experimenting with flails, Snakes and Scorpions and all the other strange menagerie of things, in the Orford training area, a part of Suffolk that was sealed off, highly secret. Some of the villages were evacuated, boarded up and there they'd built replicas of the Atlantic Wall - pillboxes, bunkers, walls, minefields, wire, anti-tank ditches, the lot, full-sized - and we practised breaching them.

'The Crabs were the flail tanks. The flail consisted of a number of chains offset around a long cylinder which was mounted on a jib on the front of the tank and driven direct from the tank engine. The jib could be raised or lowered by hydraulics and the driver had control of that and at either end of the flail rotor were cutter blades for cutting through barbed wire. The chains we used to start with were rigid chains like a motorcycle chain ending in a broad chain end, so it gave it weight. That was later changed to oval chains with a heavy ball on the end. When you blew mines you might blow half a dozen before you blew the ends off the chains and then you had to stop and change them. They were simply fixed with a bolt and a split pin and we carried spare chains on the outside of the tank.

'The flail beat a path through minefields about nine feet wide, which is not wide enough for practical purposes for another tank to follow through, so the idea was that you had at least two, possibly three, in echelon, with the driver putting the nearside track in the offside track mark of the tank in front, or the other way round, depending. 'We'd have a weekly meeting of each troop and the men were encouraged to put forward ideas as to how these machines could be used and whether there were any problems that we saw that could be overcome... of course no one was ever very happy at the idea of travelling at one and a half miles an hour through a mine field which has been put there specifically to enable enemy anti-tank gunners to more easily engage a target; it's not a very happy-making thought. But we had a job to do and somebody had to do it and we did it to the best of our ability.

'At first we practised at Alford in Lincolnshire where they'd built full-scale replicas of parts of the Atlantic Wall with concrete bunkers and mine fields and wire entanglements, for which the crab was ideally suited, because of the cutters on the end of the drum which proved to be extremely useful. The only level ground in Stow-on-the-Wold where we could practise was the cricket pitch and much to the annoyance of the city fathers, I'm afraid we chewed that up rather badly.'

Lieutenant (later Major) Ian Hammerton, Sherman Crab flail tank commander, 1st Troop B Squadron, 22nd Dragoons. Each troop had five Sherman Crab tanks.

'In the winter of 1943 we were taken to a cinema in Keighley, near Bradford in Yorkshire where I was stationed. It was heavily guarded. We had to identify the men on each side of us before we were let in. And then they told us that we were going to be at the sharp end; we were going to be trained on a secret weapon. It wasn't good news. We were in Keighley and we were enjoying ourselves, we were in a town where you could go out and meet girls and go to pubs, we were having a good time and all of a sudden the war was being pushed at us very hard. We were to go down south and start training. It was on the cards that we were going to work with 'swimming tanks'. We were lined up and asked if we had any seafaring experience. But only one man did, he'd once been on a trawler. But none of the rest of us had any experience of the sea at all.

'We went down to Suffolk and here we learned how to breathe under water wearing submarine escape equipment. Then we were taken to a local lake where the tanks were. We were shocked, horrified when we first saw the floating tanks. They looked so crude as if they'd been knocked together like Meccano... but they worked. We lifted up the screen and the tank floated. It was good fun, we played around with them. It became a lark.'

Jack Thornton, a tank driver in the 4th/7th Royal Dragoon Guards, who trained on the early Valentine DD tank, which was 'quite useless for battle'. They went on to the Sherman which was 'much better equipped' and 'much tougher.'

'If you get a heavy stone and put it in a canvas bucket and put this canvas bucket in water, the bucket will go down a bit, but then it will float, so they figured that if they built a canvas bucket - a screen - around a thirty-two-ton tank which could be inflated, then when the screen stood up the tank would float in the water.'

Lance Corporal Patrick L. M. Hennessey, DD tank commander, 4 Troop, A Squadron, 13th/18th Royal Hussars.

'The ramps went down on the Landing Craft and we inflated the screen on the tank and went into the water. We formed up and headed for land. I was the lead tank. But within minutes, out of nowhere a storm suddenly sprang up and the waves got bigger and bigger and they started to slop over the screen into the tank and as the tank started to fill with water it sank lower into the water, so more water came in and we were gradually sinking. I managed to get my escape apparatus on and breathe oxygen and got to the beach where I deflated the screen. I looked behind and there was no one following. The tanks behind had all disappeared. But before I could do anything the CO drove past in a jeep and told my sergeant, who was still in the turret, to put me on a charge for not wearing my tin hat, that's all he was concerned about. We lost the two tanks behind me and all the men out there. A tank crew's like a close-knit family, really. There were five of us in a tank. The men were my friends and my particular friend was Corporal Park who lived just outside Lancaster. He'd died and I was given the task of sorting out all his possessions, so I bundled them up and I was put on a train to Lancaster and I had tell his wife that her husband was dead - drowned. But I couldn't tell her how he'd drowned. I couldn't tell her that he was in a DD tank that had gone down, that was still top secret. All I could say was, 'I'm sorry, Arthur's been drowned on an exercise.' That was it. And I kept thinking about the driver, Trooper Petty, because when the screen collapses with the pressure of water it collapses inwards so the driver is really trapped and the tank sinks to the bottom and the driver puts on his mask and he's breathing the oxygen and it'll only last him about thirty minutes. Did he have to sit there breathing, struggling to get free for thirty minutes? I often think about that, it really upsets me.'

Jack Thornton, when his DD tank sank on the exercise in Studland Bay on 4 April 1944.

'We were summoned to a cinema in Portsmouth. There were about 400 officers there and redcap police all round the place, it was all very secret and we sat down in this cinema and Monty came in. He told us something about the plans for the invasion. He said this is what we're going to do, this is what we expect the Germans to do - and this is what I'll do to the Germans. It was terribly inspiring, because I'd been planning my own little corner of the invasion, getting more and more puzzled, not knowing quite where it fitted in and he suddenly put everything into perspective and I can only say that he raised my morale just like that. He was a leader and I would have followed him to hell.'

Brigadier Arthur Walter, Director of Ports and Inland Water Transport.

'Eisenhower came to have a chat with everybody. He was great. The finest general there's ever been. We formed a whole square right round this great big field. And he walked into the middle of the field and he said, 'Righto, gentlemen. When I give the signal, all come in and sit down. Never mind the officers; they'll walk in with the men. I want everyone to hear what I have to say.' That pleased everybody. There was no bullshit about him. He was immaculate. He could have been cut out of chocolate. He said he'd heard all about us down in Southampton, how we'd been living it up and now the time had come to get aboard ships and fight alongside each other. He did more to lift the morale - certainly my morale - than anything else.'

Sergeant Major William 'Bill' Brown Company 'D', 8th Battalion, Durham Light Infantry. This was in sharp contrast to a visit by General Montgomery in February who told the Durhams that they were to be in the first wave of the invasion. They had only recently returned from fighting in the Mediterranean and had received little home leave. 'The Bloody Durhams again' was the reaction.

'When we moved to a camp near Romsey we had battles with the Yanks nearly every night in Southampton. The cause of the friction was money and their arrogant behaviour. Eisenhower came to see us and gave us a lecture about the American soldier. He agreed they were overpaid, oversexed and over here - but when they got over the other side, they would show us the road home - how to fight. That was

the worst thing he could have said. That night the blood flowed in Southampton.'
Sergeant George Self, 8th Battalion, Durham Light Infantry.

'During the physical training we focused on four objectives: speed, control, simplicity and fire effect. As parachutists we didn't carry much equipment and we had to make use of this advantage to achieve great speed. If you could give orders twice as fast as anyone else you could gain ten minutes on the enemy. Coupled with speed was control - it was no good having expensive paratroops if they weren't under control. Simplicity was vital - the simpler things were, the fewer mistakes were made. Fire effect was essential because we didn't carry much ammunition, so every shot had to count. In order to achieve these four objectives we had to become amazingly fit. The initial training was extremely hard and many of the volunteers left - they simply couldn't stand the pace of the training. We knew we would have to fight at night so we spent a great deal of time doing night-time training. For one week every month my brigade used to operate at night, sleeping during the daytime. Of course that was marvellous for all the chaps, but the poor brigade commander still had to spend the day doing administrative work!

'I was always keen for my brigade headquarters to do just as well as the chaps of the battalions, so on one occasion I took them for a two-hour march carrying 60 pounds of equipment. This of course included the clerks and the telephone operators! As we were staggering into the town of Bulford I was cheering them on, as you do, so that they would get to the end within the two hours. On the following Monday I received a notice saying that a deputation from the local Women's Institute wanted to see the brigade commander. They had come to complain about the way I had shouted at the chaps to finish - they thought it had been cruel and brutal. That rather amused me!

'Napoleon said that 'the morale is to the physical as two is to one'. I found that if you are very fit, your morale is automatically good and I put an awful lot of effort into getting the chaps extremely fit. It's amazing what a fit young body can take in the way of wounds and survive. The other thing that is important for morale is to be fighting a noble cause. I could not have fought for six years if I hadn't believed our cause to be completely right. I was asking those chaps to possibly die for the cause. I had to believe the cause to be true. I loved the men of my brigade and if you love people they'll love you too, they'll follow you and they'll have respect for you.

'At that time there were two fighter pilots who became known for being highly successful at shooting the enemy down at night - Cat's Eyes Cunningham and a chap called Wight-Boycott, who had been at school with me.[16] Rumour was that they were so good at night fighting because they ate a lot of carrots and so we also ate carrots until we were quite sick of the things. In fact the carrot story was just a ruse to prevent the enemy from finding out that they were equipped with the very latest form of radar.

'As the great day was arriving, all my battalions were penned in their camps - which they weren't allowed to leave. This period was very interesting to me. All day long the Canadians, with whom I'd pitched my tent, were playing games - baseball, throwing balls about - and I thought what tremendous vitality these Canadians had got. Then in

16 Wing Commander John 'Cats Eyes' Cunningham DSO* DFC* destroyed twenty enemy aircraft at night flying Beaufighters and Mosquitoes. Wing Commander Cathcart Michael Wight-Boycott DSO who commanded 29 and 25 Squadrons in 1942 and 1943, destroyed seven enemy aircraft at night and two V-1s flying Beaufighters and Mosquitoes. He had attended Cambridge University.

the afternoon I would visit my English battalions and find half a dozen chaps desultorily kicking a football and the rest asleep. I thought to myself, here is the difference between the Old World and the New - the élan and joie de vivre of the New World of the Canadian - and the maturity and the not worrying, not bothering and having a good nap while you can, of the British.'

Brigadier James Hill, commanding 3rd Parachute Brigade, born in 1911 and who went to Sandhurst in 1929. After a spell as an army officer he went into the family business, but he was called up for duty when war broke out in 1939. The brigade had been formed in the beginning of 1943 with the sole purpose of taking part in the Normandy landings. The brigade was made up of three county battalions, who were 'invited' to join the parachute brigade and they volunteered to a man.

Nations Represented On D-Day

Australia

Virtually all 11,000 Australian aircrew participate in Overlord. Most of the 1,100 officers and men of the Royal Australian Volunteer Naval Reserve (RANVR) serve aboard British cruisers, HMS *Ajax* of 'Battle of the River Plate' fame, *Enterprise, Glasgow* and *Scylla*, or as commanders of several flotillas of landing craft and MTBs. On *Ajax*, a RANVR officer commands the 6-inch gun bombardment of the German Naval Battery at Longues-sur-Mer on cliffs 200 feet above 'Gold' Beach. Australians also serve aboard destroyers HMS *Ashanti, Eskimo* and *Mackay*. Two members of the Royal Australian Navy are known to have died on D-Day operations.

As late as June 1944 11,000 RAAF officers and men were serving with the RAF or the ten RAAF squadrons. Australia also provided 168 of the 1,136 aircraft committed by Bomber Command, almost 15 per cent of the total. RAAF pilots flew six Lancasters of 617 'Dam Busters' Squadron in a deception operation on 5/6 June and five more flew Stirlings of 199 Squadron in their deception operation. In the attack on coastal batteries on 5/6 June RAAF Lancasters flew 67 sorties, the majority of them against German gun emplacements at Pointe-du-Hoc. Just after midnight RAAF officers piloted 41 transports of the ten squadrons of 38 Group for the drop of the British 6th Airborne Division, the RAAF providing about one on seven of the pilots. On D-Day the Mosquitoes of 464 Squadron RAAF attacked transport further east across the Seine. One Mosquito was brought down. Flight Lieutenant D. M. Shanks, navigator, survived and remained hidden until August. Australian piloted Typhoons of 121 and 247 Squadrons made ground attacks south of Caen amid heavy anti-aircraft fire. Three Australian Typhoons were shot down although Warrant Officer G. K. E. Martin, who had severe burns and a broken leg, evaded capture and reached the beachhead. In the week following D-Day 460 Squadron RAAF flew on five of the seven nights and flew 107 sorties. Each of the three other RAAF bomber squadrons operated on four nights.

One of the last Australian bomber crews out early on the morning of June 6 was a Lancaster crew captained by Flight Lieutenant F. L. Merrill DFC RAAF. To his crew it had been just another sortie in the pre-invasion softening-up when they took off in the small hours to attack a coastal gun battery. They were scheduled to be among the last of the night bombers to bomb that night and thus were among the first to see the invasion begin. They came down below the clouds on the way back, rounded the south-western side of the Cherbourg Peninsula, passed over a then seemingly empty

French coast and set course for home. Nearing Alderney off the tip of the peninsula the whole island seemed suddenly to burst into flame as the anti-aircraft defences opened up - unsuccessfully - on the Lancaster ahead. A few minutes later the invasion fleet came into view, filling the scene as far as eye could reach as ships of every kind moved across to Normandy.

Just before the landing of the troops and the establishment of the beachhead, the airborne men went over in the early hours. Australians helped man many of the four-engined aircraft which carried them and their weapons and supplies. Some of them, flying in Halifax bombers, towed Horsa gliders carrying men of the 6th Airborne Division to the Orne area at H-Hour and returned in the afternoon towing Hamilcars containing the new seven-ton tanks. Flight Sergeant W. Q. McGeachin, a navigator, was one of the Australians who had narrow escapes on the glider towing operations that morning. He stood up from his chart table for a moment to watch one of his instruments. At that instant a piece of flak came through the chart table, tore through his maps and went past where his head had been as he bent over his table a split second earlier.

To the RAAF Sunderland squadrons Nos. 10 and 461 fell part of Coastal Command's invasion task of sinking the U-boats, guarding the convoys. During the terrible weather that came in June after the invasion had begun, the Coastal squadrons carried on with their task and won high praise for their willingness to fly in the face of Coastal Command's dangerous enemy, the weather. In that invasion month, despite the weather adversary 10 Squadron put in more than 1,700 hours' flying on operations, breaking its own and all records for Sunderlands. The Australian Beaufighters of 455 Squadron were operating off the Boulogne-Fecamp area on D-Day and attacked eight E-boats, the type of operation which had engaged so much of their attention in the weeks before the invasion.

When the landing in Normandy began, the Australian Spitfires of 453 Squadron flew 47 sorties to provide low cover for the troops; on the night of June 6 the Australian Mosquito night fighters of 456 Squadron destroyed four enemy aircraft and the Australian Mosquito fighter bombers of 464 Squadron made 27 sorties to attack road and rail junctions and bomb enemy troop concentrations in advance of the land forces.

The enemy made repeated efforts to attack the Allied invasion shipping from the air and 456, led by Wing Commander Keith Hampshire DSO DFC was among the defenders in the air. The unit had had a remarkable run of 'kills' against the Luftwaffe earlier in the year and it went on to add more after D-Day. After the four enemy aircraft destroyed on the night of D-Day, it went on to shoot down three more next night.

The Roll of Honour lists 12 members of the RAAF who died on D-Day. Casualties continued to mount as the air forces supported the advance. The largest single crew loss of Australians in operations relating to Normandy was on 7 June when a Liberator on 224 Squadron in RAF Coastal Command, searching for German submarines, crashed into the English Channel with eight Australians lost in this incident. More than 200 other Australian airmen were killed during June and July on operations relating to the seven-week battle for Normandy.

The Australian Army contingent to Normandy was small. Up to 25 Australian officers who had been seconded to the British Army for experience or to assist in the training of amphibious troops - Australians had experience of amphibious landings in New Guinea - were involved in the Normandy operations. Those who took part mostly were serving in various divisional headquarters as staff officers responsible for planning and administration - key roles in any force. A handful fought in infantry and tank battalions, engaging the enemy. No members of the Australian Army died in D-Day operations.

Behind enemy lines, a small number of expatriate Australians were involved in French Resistance activities. Most famous was Nancy Wake, a member of the Special Operations Executive who had been parachuted back into France to plan resistance activities in her area as the invasion loomed. A few others, including airmen who had been shot down behind enemy lines, either assisted the Resistance or were hidden by them until Allied forces could advance and rescue them.

Belgium

Two corvettes, three merchant ships and three Congo boats. 350 Squadron participate in aerial defence of 'Gold' and 'Sword' Beaches. 349 Squadron provide covering fire for US 82nd Airborne Division.

Canada

Of the 39 divisions involved in Operation Overlord, three were Canadian (100,000 men). About 15,000 troops of the 3rd Canadian Division commanded by Major General Rodney Keller were deployed on 'Juno' Beach. RCAF committed 39 strategic and tactical squadrons, who flew 230 sorties of the 1,200 mounted by Bomber Command. Nearly 10,000 officers and men aboard 126 Canadian fighting ships and 44 landing craft among them. The 1st Canadian Parachute Battalion, formed and trained during two years' hard work beginning in August 1942, dropped in the general area round the villages of Varaville and Robehomme on the River Dives. On 23 July 1944 the three Canadian divisions (together with the Polish 1st Armoured Division and a Canadian tank brigade) formed the separate 1st Canadian Army.

Czechoslovakia

310, 312 and 313 Squadrons (Spitfire IXs), 134 Wing, 84 Group, 2nd TAF and 311 Squadron (Liberator Vs), 19 Group, RAF Coastal Command.

Denmark

800 Danes mostly served aboard ships.

France

France contributed one Division to D-Day. 329, 340 and 341 Squadrons, 145 Wing (Spitfire IXs) and 88 and 342 Squadrons, 2 Group (Boston IIIAs) in 2nd TAF, Allied Expeditionary Air Force and 345 Squadron (Spitfires) in 11 Group, ADGB. Light cruisers *Montcalm* and *Georges Leygues* in the Western Task Force off Port-en-Bessin and the destroyer *La Combattante*, Eastern Task Force off the coast of the oyster port of Courseulles-sur-Mer, took part in the naval bombardment. Five frigates (*La Decouverte, L'Adventure, La Surprise* and *L'Escaramouche*), two corvettes (*Aconit* and *Renoncule*) and four submarine chasers performed escort duty. The elderly battleship *Courbet* was towed across the Channel and sunk off Ouistreham to act as a breakwater for the 'Mulberry' harbour at Arromanches-les-Bains on the Calvados coast.

Great Britain

Britain contributed fourteen Divisions to D-Day. Second Army composed of two corps (including three British divisions with auxiliary units and services - some 62,000 men). Provided about 80 percent of the warships. RAF flew 5,656 sorties.

Greece

Two Royal Hellenic Navy corvettes *Kriezis* and *Tompazis* escorted convoys to 'Juno', 'Gold' and 'Sword'. A number of Greek soldiers, sailors and airmen served in Allied Forces.

Norway

Ten warships, including the destroyers *Glaisdale, Stord* and *Svenner*, of the Royal Norwegian Navy in exile and 43 ships of the Norwegian Merchant Navy (two of the cargo ships were scuttled to create a breakwater for landing craft) and three fighter squadrons - 66, 331 and 332, 132 Wing, 2nd TAF, flying Spitfire IXs.

Netherlands

Cruiser, *HMNS Sumatra* and two sloops, *Flores* and *Soemba*, (The latter two fire in support of the landings on 'Gold' and 'Utah' respectively. On D+3 *Sumatra*, its armour dismantled, was intentionally scuttled near the shore to form part of the breakwater for 'Mulberry' harbour. Nos. 98, 180 and 320 Squadrons, 139 Wing (Mitchell IIs), 2 Group and 322 Squadron (Spitfire XIVs), 141 Wing, all from 2nd TAF.

New Zealand

By June 1944 more than one third of New Zealand's overseas manpower - about 35,000 men - were serving in Britain. Of these, about 30,000 were in the RAF or in the six RNZAF Squadrons and they took part in every phase of the operation. 4,000 officers and men of the Royal New Zealand Naval Volunteer Reserve were in the Royal Navy. Junior officers of the RNZNVR command scores of landing craft and flotillas of New-Zealand-manned MTBs. In May and early June RNZAF fighter and bomber squadrons were heavily involved in operations in support of Overlord. Tempests of 486 Squadron and Mosquito Intruders of 487 Squadron attacked the railway system of northern France. On D-Day 489 Squadron RNZAF Beaufighters patrolled along the invasion coast and in the week after the landings made 34 separate attacks on E-boats and R-boats.

After dusk on D-Day Mosquitoes of 488 Squadron RNZAF took over patrol duty and intercepted several Luftwaffe raids against the beachhead and claims for 20 bombers shot down in the first week were recorded. Lancasters of 75 Squadron RNZAF were among those who bombed Ouistreham on 5/6 June and who participated in other raids in the Normandy area on four of the six succeeding nights.

Poland

Poland contributed one Division to D-Day. 302, 308 and 317 Squadrons, 131 Wing, 84 Group (Spitfire IXs) and 306 and 315 Squadrons, (Mustang IIIs) 133 Wing, (all from 2nd TAF) and Lancasters of 300 (Polish) Squadron, 1 Group, RAF Bomber Command. Destroyers ORP *Krakowiak* and ORP *Slazak* took part in the Eastern Task Force's naval bombardment of the coast. Four other Polish warships including the destroyers ORP *Blyskewica* and *Piorun* and the cruiser *ORP Dragon* and eight merchant ships played various roles.

United States

The US contributed twenty Divisions to D-Day. First Army composed of two corps (five divisions with auxiliary units and services - about 73,000 troops). Navy provided 16.5 percent of the Allied warships and hundreds of landing vessels. 8th and 9th Air Forces (6,080 tactical and strategic aircraft) in Allied Expeditionary Air Force.

'The camp was hidden away in the grounds of a big English country house, Here, in tents screened by trees, were several thousand troops, concentrated for" D "Day. The big house itself was used as offices by an armaments firm.

An exciting situation.

But however anxious you may be to liberate Europe or to get there and fight, you can't remain tense with purpose indefinitely. After waiting for a week or two something sags. The tense becomes past.

The men in the Armoured Brigade were lucky. They hadn't been in the camp more than 10 days and they had the absorbing job of looking after their fled of' tanks. But many of the troops had been in the camp for a number of weeks. In the last week or two there had been nothing much to do. Practically no training was possible because every man had been stripped down to what he would carry with him on the assault and most of this had been taken for loading elsewhere. Everyone and everything not needed in the first assault wave had been sent away.

The infantry went for route marches. "Send men to bed tired and you've got a happy battalion," said the officers; particularly the ones who didn't have to go on the marches. Other units went for slightly shorter marches. It was difficult for anyone to avoid doing P.T. Last minute inoculations were performed, equipment deficiencies were made up, kit inspections were held. But in spite of all the wonderful, unsuspected ways there are in the British Army of using time, the days were pretty empty. Even when you counted the hours spent queuing for meals.

It was pleasant enough to sit in the sun listening to the amplified radio, echoing across the fields. Or to sit in the coolness of the tent, contemplating patches of sunlight on the ground between the trees, deciding whether to wash one's clothes or get one's hair cut.

The idea that a considerable proportion of the men in the camp were likely to be killed or wounded during the next few days didn't really seem likely; One accepted it as an intellectual proposition, but no more.

It wasn't all sitting in the sun. There was also a lot of queuing in the NAAFI and being Turkish-bathed in the camp cinemas. The recreational facilities were greatly overcrowded. Above all there was no leave. 'No leave, no second front,' wrote the washhouse wall commentators. The camp staff tried to secure 400 extra rat-traps, one trap having caught six in an afternoon.

Now was the time for unit commanders to take another look at the Administrative Questionnaire, which had been issued a month before.

Have you disposed of all surplus forms, manuals, pamphlets, stationery?

Are all men in possession of first field dressing?

Have you disposed of surplus baggage?

Are your camouflage nets in good repair?

Have all ranks been warned to take with them matches or a lighter?

Have you warned every man to carry sufficient razor blades, soap, tooth paste, etc., for seven days?

Have you indented for rum: on the scale of two measures per man?

Are you arranging to take overseas two weeks supply of disinfectant?

Do you hold water containers to scale?

When did you last have your ammunition inspected? To whom have you submitted deficiencies (if any).

Have you arranged to leave to the last minute paint (all colours), brushes and stencils?

The list of questions went on for a long time like this. But, on the whole, the unit commanders didn't seem as bogged down by their responsibilities as they might have been. Administratively it was a wonderful opportunity to get all sorts of things for nothing, to tear up embarrassing, correspondence; to abandon courts of inquiry, to indent forthings and, miraculously, get them.

All the things which had never been available were now suddenly available for the asking. And through all, these transactions there ran a stimulating sense of impunity, summarised in the current tag, "They can't touch you now." It didn't matter much what you did, they wouldn't leave you behind.

Under these circumstances how did men feel? What did they talk about?

In the first place they nearly all expected that the assault would be a bloody and costly affair. There were optimists who thought that it wouldn't last long, that, once we got ashore and broke the initial resistance, it would be simply a question of chasing the Germans home.

But even the optimists expected that the first few days would see a terrific battle, and everyone in this camp was going to be landed during the first few hours. Whatever might be in store was in store for them.

But you wouldn't have thought so from talking and listening about the camp. Those who aren't personally exposed to the dangers of war often talk as if they were. Here it was the same story in reverse. Men talked about the forthcoming battle as a general problem, not as a personal one. They talked about the landing with the detachment of newspaper readers. In general terms they talked about the prospects a good deal; mainly how long it would last.

Perhaps half the men in this camp had been in action before the estimate is a rough one. Is a man's morale strengthened by previous battle experience? Presumably: so, but he doesn't always think so. The man who has never been in a battle finds it easier to visualise a pleasantly film story immunity from shot and shell. That is, in his optimistic moments.

At other times, inexperience isn't so comforting. The inexperienced man can't help wondering sometimes whether he can take it. He can't tell himself that he has done it once.

I asked experienced men what advice they would give, say, a younger brother who was going into action for the first time. The question was put to a number of men in the Armoured Brigade. The first man was 42. Life begins at forty and there are thousands of men aged 42 in the British Army, but not many of them are acting as the crew commander of a Sherman tank. And, this corporal had been pensioned off from his job as police superintendent of Stratford-on-Avon on the grounds that his health couldn't stand it. He was told that on no account must he take any risks. He went into the Army at the beginning of 1942, joined his unit just before El Alamein and went with it right across North Africa. It must have done his health a world of good because he now looked like a heart of oak. He had no theories about the Second Front. "I don't think about it much. The only part I don't like is crossing water. Rather stupid, but most of our men feel that way. I know I shall feel much safer when I get on land again."

In a nice battle.

The ex-policeman continued. He spoke with the measured tread of that splendid body of men.

"Noise is the most alarming thing. Cut out the noise, find battle wouldn't worry me a bit. Probably seem quite a tame sort of affair...

"At Alamein we had to sleep night after night in front of a lot of 25-pounders. I found it wore me down much worse than fighting in a tank. The important thing is to learn some way of cutting it out of your mind's attention."

The same question - what would you tell a novice? - was put to another tank crew commander. He said:

"I'd tell him never to worry about being called 'windy' because he got under cover and wore his tin hat.

"The officers are the worst offenders; not bolting for cover quick enough. We've had two colonels killed from it; one of them would be alive to-day if he'd got down quick. They say it's not a good example. I think it is a good example - to keep yourself alive and not get hurt."

The third man questioned said:

"Keep the sweating parts clean. Shave and keep the mouth clean.

It makes all the-difference to how you feel and you don't get lousy."

A transport sergeant said:

"This waiting is the worst. Gets you worrying about home. Once you're in action you forget all about your wife. I was seventeen when I joined the Army. It's taught me two things - to appreciate my home and to look after myself. Some men look after themselves better than others. One man digs a slit trench; the other don't. The digger lives."

One of the transport drivers said:

"The first action I was scared stiff - saw a lot of our tanks go up in flames. Afterwards it seemed to grow on me - I never bothered. Then one fine morning, after a move by road to a new camp - this time in the marshalling area -we woke up to find the camp sealed. That means no one allowed out and a diminished number allowed in; Redoubled guards on the gates and guards patrolling the barbed wire perimeter of the camp.

This meant briefings. Directly there is any briefing in a camp; no one is allowed out except for a very few privileged pass-holders. Telephone communication with the outside world is abolished except for essential calls and these are monitored.

Briefing proceeds in a series of ripples, starting at unit and sub-unit commander level and expanding until the last private knows exactly where to go and what to do. I attended the briefing of unit commanders of the Beach Group, whose personnel formed a large proportion of the population of the camp.

A Beach Group is built around an infantry battalion, whose CO acts as Beach Group Commander.

This particular Group was born in July 1943 when the officers went on a two weeks' course. Since then they had had a thorough training in combined operation increasingly realistic in scope and atmosphere, including a number of full-scale landing exercises and endless subsidiary landing exercises...

The Group had grown until it was now comparable to a Brigade in size. It included sub-units of nearly all the supporting arms, Royal Engineers, Royal Signals, RASC, RAOC, REME, extensive RAMC activity, a Pro. Company., a Pioneer Company, a Camouflage Section, a special team for landing RAF stores; and the Balloon Barrage.

The briefing started at 9.30 am in a hut standing in a wired enclosure guarded by military police. There were approximately 60 officers sitting on backless benches, tiered in three semicircular rows.

On the ground in front of us there was a large scale model of the small sector of the Continent which this particular Beach Group was to occupy. It was on a very large scale and had taken the Beach Group Intelligence Section a while to build. We were told that the information on it had been accurate up to 48 hours ago. Every tree was in its proper place.

Certainly the picture was detailed. The country it showed was fairly featureless - open stretches of cultivated land with few hedges and ditches. Good tank country.

On a diagonal across the model there were three villages. The orchards and copses were nearly all centred around these.

The wall at the back of the model was taken up by a large map of the same area, on the same scale. On this map the place names were shown, but not the right names. The villages were referred to as Alberta, Derna and Regina.

The Colonel commanding the Beach Group stood up, grasped his pointer and started his story.

Three beaches had been allotted to this Beach Group and two of them would be used during the first 48 hours of the assault. The job was to establish and maintain dumps for all stores landed and to land troops, vehicles and stores for the assaulting formations and follow up troops. The Group would land with an infantry brigade whose job would be to mop up any enemy not disposed of by the preliminary assault flights and the air and sea bombardment.

Forward battalions of the brigade would fan out; one to the left in a sweep enclosing Alberta; the other to the right. On the existing information it wasn't likely that the battalions would have to cope with more than a platoon each of low category enemy infantry, not more than half of whom were likely to be Germans. We felt rather sorry for this miserable enemy.

We seemed to know so much about him. For instance, consider the position of one enemy platoon.

Of this we were told that the four pillboxes faced north, were built on a level with the sea wall; weren't considered large enough to hold a gun over 50 mm calibre. There was neither wire nor mines on the seaward side of the position. On the landward side there was a wire fence 8-10 ft thick, then a six-row mine-field bounded by a cattle fence.

The whole area was covered in similar detail.

Just as we were settling down to confident anticipation of a triumphant entry, the enemy's arrangements, which had so far seemed to be sympathetically superficial, began to be described in more detail.

Not nearly far enough behind the local defence crust of military martyrs (second class) there was a counter-attack force of distressing strength and renown.

During the last three months the enemy had shown considerable activity in laying minefields behind the-actual beach defences, building additional machine-gun positions and laying under-water obstacles; Hedgehogs had been laid in staggered rows along the whole length of the beaches, at about two-thirds tide, The distance between each hedgehog in the row was about 8ft and the rows were 30 yards apart.

Seaward of these some ramp-type obstacles had been laid opposite the main exit at Alberta. A double row had been laid, 75ft. apart, with 50-75ft spacing between each obstacle.

An anti-tank ditch had been started. Where completed, it was 15ft wide and 10 ft deep. The minefields were described in detail.

Besides these tactical obstacles there were natural ones. On the extreme right of the sector there, was a sea wall 4-10 ft in height but reduced in places to a pile of rubble and no obstacle for infantry.

But the sea wall at Alberta was a considerable obstacle to both wheeled vehicles and infantry, standing 8-10 ft and vertical.

Nor was the marsh, which ran from Alberta westwards along the entire sector, likely to be much help. It was 100 yards wide at the left extremity and 500 yards wide at the right boundary of the sector. A stream, which varied in width from 4-15 ft, ran through the middle of it.

It was problematical whether tracked or wheeled vehicles would be able to cross this' marsh unaided, except by the tracks.

The roads were not very brilliant. There were four. Two of them were not more than 10 ft wide and water-bound at that. In the centre there was a 9 ft road with a ditch both sides. The best road was at the Alberta exit and was 18-20ft wide.

In fact it was essential to keep traffic moving at all costs. There must be no waiting to form convoys, in fact, no halting on the roads at all.

The beaches themselves were flat and sandy, but with underlying patches of clay and peat, which in a number of places were exposed.

All types of vehicles could cross these patches reasonably well if they didn't follow in each other's tracks. There had been some doubt about whether the sand would stand it. But samples had been taken by a major put ashore by a submarine. Experiments had then been carried out on similar sand up on the East Coast, with satisfactory results.

The distance from the back of the beach to the water edge was 25 yards average at high water and 700 yards' average at low water.

There was a helpful "stand to" of the tide at high water, lasting for two hours 45 minutes, due, to the steepness of the beach at high water mark.

So much for topography and tides.

From these conditions provided by nature and the enemy, the Beach Group had to evolve an organised Beach Maintenance Area.

Every man in the Group must know his personal task for the first 12 hours' ashore at least. Every man must expect to work for 48 hours without pausing even to cook his 24-hour ration.

The Group's tasks were arranged in priority, the first job being to clear underwater obstacles and open a gap of at least 250 yards per beach. Then go on to clear certain specific entrances and exits, until a sound traffic system had been built up.

Military police would, of course, control the traffic, one of their first jobs being to control the English drivers into driving on the right-hand side of the road. Though, with roads as narrow as these, there wouldn't be much option.

One of the first jobs would be to establish transit areas, where men would remove their Mae Wests (has the good lady ever been photographed in one?) and vehicles would be de-waterproofed.

Briefing went on until late that night and continuously for the next three days. The various units and' sub-units were allotted different times in the main briefing hut and the subsidiary tents.

Each unit had plenty to talk about. To take an example, the RAMC had their own operation order nine pages long with five appendices, crammed with extraordinary information.

A reserve of pyjamas was being landed. Each heavy anti-aircraft gun of one particular regiment would land with 10 stretchers strapped to it. These would be cast off in the Vehicle Transit Areas and the Senior Medical Officer of the Beach Group must arrange to collect them as soon as transport was available. A hospital carrier would arrive on D plus I and thereafter daily.

From D-Day there would be a daily delivery of whole blood - approximately 100 pints - brought across the Channel by Naval Despatch Launch.

Each Field Dressing Station would land with enough hospital supplies for 200 patients for 14 days; also 2,000 tins of self-heating cocoa, 2,000 cigarettes, 2,000 tins of self-heating malted milk and 12 packs of playing cards.

Beach dressing stations, each of two doctors and 25 other ranks, would land 90 minutes after H-Hour and set up on the beach fringe. The main medical area would be a few thousand yards inland. (These arrangements were in addition to the assault units' own medical resources.) The medical job in the beach group was to establish a full-dress evacuation system as quickly as possible and also to do emergency surgery and transfusion.

Briefing had an exhilarating effect. In the officers' mess this exhilaration, together with the universal confinement to barracks, produced a more than usually crowded and excited atmosphere. Names were listed for the "D-Day plus 365 Reunion Dinner", provisionally at the Adlon in Berlin, alternatively at the Railway Hotel, Dunkirk.

There was a delightful atmosphere of burnt boats and happy-go-luckiness, though there was nothing to drink but stout. But the radio played old dance tunes and even the puddle of spilled beet and the cigarette ends all over the stone floor didn't seem unpleasant. They were so much in keeping with the barrack-room benches, the rusty stove, the biscuit tins on the elementary bar, the gym-shoed mess waiters, the not very good light.

Next day there was a pay parade in French, each man getting an issue of francs. We were issued with pocket guides to France.

"Any errors of conduct committed by individual soldiers will remain in French minds not simply as a slur on a single man or a single unit but as 'the way the British behave'... If you should be offered wine or spirits, remember that this will be stronger drink than you are used to. The same sort of girl with whom you can take liberties in England can be found in France; and the same sort of girl whom you would grossly offend in this country would be greatly offended if you were 'trying anything on' in France...

Some British peacetime visitors to France were shocked to find that the French had licensed brothels. Well, French visitors to Britain have sometimes been equally shocked by couples love-making publicly in our parks. The men may relieve nature rather openly in public and see little harm in frankness on various matters. But French people are rather startled when they hear a music-hall comedian in, this country joking about 'nancy-boys' or see some of us with drink taken, badly out of control.

"We are not the only nation to feel more virtuous than our neighbours, or to criticise their morals."

Everyone having pointed out these and other realistic passages to his neighbour, there was a considerable drive to learn the words and phrases which formed the second half of the book. Those who had been misled into a holiday mood by the French pay parade were brought sharply back to earth by such ominous phrases as "Poovon noo dorrneer dong votrer gronge? "(Can we sleep in your barn?).

Things were moving. But I stood in a queue for cigarette rations for 20 minutes without hearing any mention of the Second Front. They were talking mostly about the night's film, "Hellzapoppin."

I spent the following morning at the briefing of the senior officers of an Armoured

Brigade by' its brigadier. Operationally, it was unpublishably far ahead. Mostly it was a maze of timetables and arrangements for mutual support.

The brigadier was a tall, youngish man with red hair and a subdued voice which was extremely effective in urging the audience to hit the enemy hard with every weapon at every opportunity. There was no prefabricated belligerence in his voice, no overt appeal to animal emotions. He made cool, calm blood-thirstiness sound like a sensible idea.

During the day the troops changed old socks, shirts and drawers woollen for new ones, and were issued with their "bags vomit". Each man had two of these brown, waxed-paper shopping bags, with instructions not to throw one away until it had been fully used. But right now one of the two bags contained 12 ounces of mixed sweets bought with unit funds to maintain the men's energy in the early food-scarcity days.

One man had his head shaved bald in anticipation of unhygienic conditions in the field. "What's it matter now" we aren't on show," he defended himself and presently others followed suit.

Next day was much the same. Briefing and looking at air photographs of the beach area. One photograph showed under-water obstacles being maintained by a man working from a horse and cart. This was regarded as encouragingly primitive equipment. Once they had been briefed people were much more optimistic.

The most appealing event of the day was the issue of a most humanly generous rum ration. Afterwards I went to the briefing of one of the sub-units of the Armoured Brigade. It was impressively detailed and intelligent in handling.

Last phase. I found myself in a unit craft serial with four doctors and two medical orderlies. We had been issued with rations for the first two days overseas. Each man had two 24-hour rations, a tommy cooker with two re-fills, a tin of corned beef, a packet of biscuits and of chewing gum; two packets of chocolate and a waterproofed tin of 20 cigarettes, a water-sterilising outfit and an emergency ration. It made an awful lot more to carry.

And next day we started to carry it. The holiday was over. We formed up after breakfast and travelled the last few miles to the docks.

No one looked very excited. It wasn't much like the Charge of the Light Brigade. But everyone was mighty glad to get started.'

Sitting On The Fence by Major Anthony J. Cotterell, an Army Bureau of Current Affairs Staff Writer, which issued fortnightly 'WAR' bulletins to soldiers. Major Cotterell was taken prisoner at Arnhem in September 1944 after reporting the battle at first hand as usual, for the Army Bureau of Current Affairs. On Saturday 23rd he was in an open German lorry taking captured officers towards Munich when two of the men jumped from the vehicle in an escape attempt. One of the German guards panicked and turned his Schmeisser on the other men in the lorry. A German soldier and four airborne men were killed outright, while a further two were mortally wounded. Amongst the dead was Major Tony Cotterell.

A Division of infantry soldiers, of an average weight of 11 stones each, will weigh a total of something in the neighbourhood of 1,200 tons. Their clothes and personal equipment will add half as much again to the load. They are the lightest single component of the Division: Take their vehicles, of an approximate total of 2,400. Allowing an average of six tons each for these, the weight jumps up by another 14,400 tons. Even if every vehicle is not taken on the first flight, they must all be shipped as soon as possible.

And, of course, there are their weapons, from the mortars to the gunners' pieces of artillery, field, Anti-Tank and AA (which total 252).

It takes seven ships to move a division on an administrative move. Spread the men and equipment out in assault order; add in the assault craft that are carried in the ships and the Naval and. Royal Marine crews that man them, and the specialists that go with them, the beach parties, the signal contingents and all their stores, not forgetting the three RAF men for each barrage balloon flown from a ship in the convoy and you have an impressive total to organise.

And you must supply them once they land. Each soldier will eat (or expect to eat) 41b of food a day. He will also be using quite a lot of ammunition and petrol (it needs about 400 gallons of P.O.L. to move a division a mile).

Then multiply your total by the number of divisions you are using and add in the right amount for Corps and Army troops and HQ. In the end you should have some inkling of the problem that SHAEF and its subsidiary formations arc tackling.

But let us confine ourselves to the problem of mounting the invasion preparing the springboard from which this colossal body has jumped.

The responsibility has been divided into two. Operations are the job of SHAEF. The preparation and the administration of the bases in England and the marshalling area of the force is the concern of the static commands in Britain and the Districts under them. The US Army calls its Command a Base Section and its Districts· are numbered and not given territorial names. Otherwise the organisations correspond.

It is no secret that part of the area used for the invasion base lies within Southern Command (D.S. Southern Base Section). Part of this area was made into a D.S. Army Area, part into a British Army area and part into a joint area. Each army worked out its own problems, with mutual aid, save that we took responsibility for all liaison with the civil authorities, so that each US Army HQs has a British Liaison Officer through whom contact with the Regional Authorities, the Ministry of War Transport and such other Ministries as are involved is made.

The plan called for concentration areas, marshalling areas and embarkation points. Once embarked, the Navy takes charge. A concentration area is the area in which units assemble prior to the start of their journey to embarkation. A marshalling area embraces camps serving a group of embarkation points.

In this area the units as they move into the camps are broken down into unit parties formed into craft and ship leads. These unit parties are then re-organised within this series of camps and are called forward in that new order for embarkation. The embarkation area is the area between the marshalling area and the yards. It is a transit area only. No accommodation is made there for overnight stay, but tea is served at the water's edge.

So far as the static Commands were concerned, preparation was in two phases. Phase II, the planning and construction of camps and installations throughout all areas, road improvements and signal installations. That was started early in 1943 and was reasonably complete in 12 months. Phase II involved the staffing of the camps and installations and the final arrangements preparatory to and during the operation. That began early in 1944 in order that all the staffing and control personnel coming in could be trained and exercised in the work they had to do. That phase is in progress now.

It is impossible yet to give any totals, but here are some details concerning one camp in a marshalling area designed for 2,500 men.

Because of dispersal and the maximum use of natural cover, its perimeter is three miles. That was wired. 500 tents and 24 huts were needed, total area 143,000 square feet, 8,000 ft of water piping (½ inch to 4 inches) and 1,000 ft of main drainage piping were laid. The camp absorbed 18,000 ft of electrical cable and 1,250 ft of steel conduit, 350 lamps, 250 water taps and 150 latrines were installed. 4,000 square yards of path and 8,000 square yards of road were laid inside the perimeter and 20,000 square yards of hard standings for vehicles outside.

In the cookhouses (two, one alternate) 22 72 inch ranges, 18 40-gallon farm boilers and six vegetable paring machines were set up. It needed a store of 7,500 blankets and 2,500 each of bolsters and palliasses to fit up the sleeping tents. Finally, the camp was stocked with a completely representative reserve of all personal kit and equipment so that any soldier coming in deficient (or being made deficient from any cause afterwards) could be kitted up within the camp.

It was given a communications system (branch telephone exchange, about 'two miles of wire in the camp and three miles of cable to connect with the civil system) and a public address system (to call craft and ship loads forward as necessary). It needs for daily maintenance 4½ tons of food, 28½ tons of fuel and 37,500 gallons of water.

Each camp also needs a staff. The troops occupying it have packed all their equipment. They are on FSUK rations, they need three hot meals a day, they come in and go out in small parties and it was worthwhile making some effort to keep their morale up to concert pitch in planning the scale of service they were to be given.

The camp staff number 13 officers and 402 ORs in all. First, the administrative staff for the camp, 6 officers (including 1 MO) and 33 ORs, Movement, Controlling officers and 13 ORs, Housekeeping Staff, 288 ORs (which includes 60 cooks, 30 guides and 12 regimental police), REME, 2 officers and 33 ORs, CMP (Traffic Control), 33 ORs and 14 NAAFI staff. The majority of these men (excluding the specialists, like cooks) were men drawn from reserve divisions and other units within the Command, put through a short training in their duties and taking on the jobs of scullery maids and bottle-washers with every willingness. The camp, in effect, supplies a combination of a hotel service and tourist agency.

But it would be giving a false impression of the operation if you were to think of it in static terms. It is much more a problem of controlled movement.

The rate of flow of men and materials is determined by the operations themselves. What the static commands have had to do is to provide an apparatus, a series of conduit pipes, along which any selected men or selected material can flow from the depots to the ships without interruption or congestion. On board ship, the Navy take control, over the other side the field force itself.

For, one thing, the plan demanded that the roads should be made capable of taking the traffic. In one District alone, 13 miles of new road were made and 157 miles widened or straightened. Three new bridges were constructed and 35 re-made, 155 concrete aprons and 317 passing places laid out. And in one Command, 150 miles of new railway line were built and approximately 90 new sidings or unloading bays erected.

To cope with traffic each Command has its road traffic control room. There is a daily staff conference to plan the moves for the following day and to provide, the means of: transport and everyone, including M/C, MP and civil police, are present.

The movement tables made out in consequence go direct to the units affected the same day and the progress of each convoy is plotted visually on an illuminated map, kept up to the minute by the reports passed back from each traffic control point on the road it travels on the line of movement. That means that an immediate diversion can be arranged by telephone if, for instance, the enemy did bomb a bridge or crater a road.

Movement Control is in control all the way, from the MP on point duty to the staff working with the Navy and deciding, from what shipping is from hour to hour at the hards or alongside the quays, what units and what stores can be shipped next.

Fluid movement is very dependent on Signals. Each marshalling area has been equipped with its own 100-line telephone exchange, with smaller exchanges in each sub-area and camp. All the telephonists are men, British and American.

In one group of camps 175 telephone exchanges were installed and 700 private wire circuits set up. 172 additional DRs in that area do 300 additional DRLS runs each day. And besides the adaptation of existing civil lines, 1,500 miles of field cable were laid. That was mainly done by the GPO, assisted by British and US Army signal sections.

A separate Signal Office was opened for each area controlling a group of camps. It serves all sub-areas and camps within its group and requires a staff of five officers and 30 ORs for its manning. The Signal Station, of course, manned day and night.

In one District 79 static sets of public address equipments were installed and a further 50 mobile sets, mounted in trucks were made available for broadcasting information and orders through the camps.

Signals also undertook the provision of sufficient plant to provide a full maintenance and battery charging service for all signal equipment coming into the area.

The total line network involved in the operation used 3,000,000 miles of wire of various types. The pre-war annual rental payable to the GPO for the facilities they provided would have been about £500,000.

In conjunction with the Navy and the RAF Signals have organised an Air Letter Service (official mail only) and a Naval Despatch Boat Service across the Channel.

Finally, the whole system of cross-Channel wireless communications had to be laid on and perfected without a single test. Wireless silence was essential until the operation started. Then it had to work properly from the movement of landing. The links came through one by one and it did work.

To cover breakdowns and replacements generally, arrangements were made to establish reserve dumps of everything, so that whatever became US in a concentration or marshalling area could be replaced within a few hours.

These parks range from heavy REME tank recovery units (to pull broken-down tanks out of the way), through reserve stocks of every type of vehicle to stores of new socks and underclothes. In the concentration area every man of the assault force was issued free with two new sets of underclothing and a new shirt, as well as normal replacements.

Here are some figures of the stores handled in one Command, not the largest; 200,000 bolsters, 30,000 tables, 15,000 chairs, 25,000 hurricane lamps, and 10,000 scrubbing brushes. Their only increase in strength was five additional DIDs. The rest of the load fell on their normal personnel (of which 20 per cent are ATS). Their petrol depots have issued as much as 500,000 gallons of petrol to the Army, the RAF, AA Command and the NFS in a month.

Incidentally, they have 700 NAAFI Institutes in. their Command area, plus 88 mobile canteens, employing a total of 8,400 personnel.

All this has taken a long time to prepare. If you could work it out in man-hours the total would be astronomical. And it isn't a bad thing to think of it that way, if only to emphasise that if your manpower is limited, as ours is, it is the hours that run into the big figures, stretching out into weeks and months of work.

The manpower was limited. For instance, on the road works listed above, only 2,365 civilians, five Road Construction Company's, RE and five Company's, Pioneer Corps were, at a maximum, employed. And all for the camp construction work in the British area of one Command no civilian labour at all was used. The whole job was done by company's of the Pioneer Corps and the average number of company's employed throughout was only five (2,400 officers and men).

What it Takes by Captain Ernest Watkins RA. WAR Staff Writer.

'I'd feel a lot happier if the Australian 9th Division was going ashore with us.'

Major General Francis de Guingand, chief of staff, 21st Army Group, shortly before D-Day, in a conversation with General Montgomery. The Australian government had withdrawn the last of its divisions, the 9th, from the Mediterranean early in 1943 in order to reinforce their armies in the Pacific.

'Neptune' Fact File

May   D-Day is set for 5 June, a time of favourable moon and tides, conditions which would still prevail on 6 and 7 June but not thereafter. Naval units are required to be in their designated assembly positions by 29 May, a directive which involves shipping movements at almost every southern British port from the Mersey to Harwich as well as at Belfast and a number of Scottish locations. Majority of 300+ large cargo vessels are of the American-built Liberty type, many of them carrying vehicles (mechanised transport) and their attendant troops.

Over 1,500 craft and barges are required as ferries between the anchorage position of the larger ships and the shore. After completing their initial task, the LSIs are to head back to the UK to reload.

23 May Because of their slow speed, being old or damaged ships, the section of the 'Corncob' (block ship) fleet which had assembled in the estuary of the Forth set out to be scuttled or 'planted' off the French coast.

30 May First of a fleet of coasters which have been waiting in the 20-mile stretch of the Thames, sail to take their places amongst over 500 ships in a vast anchorage, extending from Hurst Castle in the west to Bembridge in the east. 362 coasters are to help maintain a continuous flow of supplies to the beaches.

2-3 June From their anchorages in the Clyde or Belfast Lough, the battleships of the bombarding fleet sail.

5 June Landing craft with the longest crossings set out. HMS *Scylla*, a Dido-class cruiser, flagship of the Eastern Task Force, leaves Portsmouth Harbour at 1340 as the first assault forces pass through Spithead Gate. The US HQ ship *Ancon* leaves Plymouth so as to reach her assigned anchorage at 'Omaha'. Troops joining their 'Utah'-bound LSIs at Tor Bay anchorage are ferried to their ships in landing craft from Torquay. Troops embarking in Weymouth Bay, where over 80 ships are anchored and Portland, are similarly transported from Weymouth Quay.

2130   During the night the biggest invasion force the world has ever seen sails from

British ports across the English Channel to France. The two Naval Task Forces (Western - and Eastern off the three British and Canadian beaches - 'Sword', 'Juno' and 'Gold') total 672 warships for assault convoy escort, minesweeping, shore bombardment, local defence, etc and 4,126 major and minor landing ships and craft for initial assault and ferry purposes: a total of 4,798. They carry the force of 39 army divisions - 20 American, 14 British, three Canadian, one Free French and one Polish. To this ship total can be added (A) Home Command for follow-up escort and Channel patrols, plus reserves: 1 RN battleship; 118 destroyers and escorts (108 RN, 4 US, 1 French, 5 Allied); 364 other warships including coastal forces (340 RN, 8 French, 16 Allied). (B) Western Channel Approaches A/S Escort Groups and reserves: 3 RN escort carriers, 55 RN destroyers and escort vessels. (C) 864 Merchant ships (mainly British liners, tankers, tugs, etc) to supply and support the invasion and naval forces. Grand Total, 6,203 vessels.

The Armada converges on an area south of the IoW code-named Area Z but known unofficially as 'Piccadilly Circus'.

0500 6 June First of the bombarding ships open fire. The heaviest bombardment takes place during the first 50 minutes after the sun rises at 05:58. Task is to silence, with saturating fire, not only the 13 main coastal artillery batteries but also the beach defence forces and then, after the assault has gone in, to engage other targets assisted by ground and air spotters. Destroyers assist the larger warships in these tasks.

0530 Naval action occurs early at the eastern extremity at when three German torpedo boats on patrol, finding themselves unexpectedly confronted by an enemy fleet, fire and narrowly miss *Warspite, Ramillies* and the 'Sword' HQ ship *Largs* but sink the Norwegian destroyer *Svenner,* 12 miles west of Le Havre. A delayed action mine sinks US destroyer *Corry* in the western sector while, just inside the northern limit of the eastern assault area, HMS *Wrestler* suffers a mine strike and has to be taken in tow.

0900 German 84th Corps informed of seaborne landings

0930 announcement of Overlord released to the press. British troops one mile inland on 'Gold'. British capture Hermanville.

Tactical surprise is total. Ship casualties are less than anticipated. Casualties to landing and small craft prove higher than allowed for, although 75% of these are attributed to the weather. All told, 59,900 personnel, 8,900 vehicles and 1,900 tons of stores are landed. By D+50 631,000 personnel, 153,000 vehicles and 689,000 tons of stores, plus 68,000 tons of fuel and oil are delivered to the bridgehead.

'30 May. Everyone excited. Got up at midnight, had briefing at 0400 for our first combat mission over Europe. The target was a Luftwaffe field at Oldenburg, Germany, 40km west of Bremen. We had P-51s, P-38s and P-47s as escort.

'We had 42 aircraft on takeoff, 40 bombed the target. Lieutenant Clark's aircraft went missing. They were the only crew that went down from flak - no fighter opposition. The flak was very heavy; *Rebel Gal* was hit several times, knocking out the boost to #2 engine. One piece of shrapnel came up through the plexiglass bomb aiming panel and missed me by inches, continuing back up through the floor of the flight deck - almost hitting Buck's left foot before it exited through the top of the cockpit. When the flak first started I didn't have enough sense to be scared, I just watched the puffs of black smoke as if they were mere firecrackers. When the second barrage hit at our altitude, I just crawled into my flak suit and helmet, and prayed. We found out later that on the return leg Lt Ed Clark's *No Nookie Now* ditched in the North Sea when they ran out of fuel due to hits in the tanks. Their tail gunner was killed in the ditching, but the other eight got out and drifted in two life rafts for three days in the freezing water until they were picked up by a Dutch fishing boat. The Dutch crew turned them over to the Germans. After returning to base, we discovered 25 holes in *Rebel Gal* and this was just our first mission!'

Diary entry, 2nd Lieutenant Paul Valachovic, bombardier on 2nd Lieutenant Wendell Robert Buck's B-24 Liberator crew, 845th Bomb Squadron, 489th Bomb Group, 8th Air Force at Halesworth, Suffolk.

'We lived in a rented house in Derby Road, Southampton, a very neighbourly area. I was one of five sisters who had moved back to Southampton from Bournemouth with our mother after being evacuated in 1939. US convoys were parked all along the streets, waiting for the 'off'. One was composed of black men - they didn't mix races. My 14-year-old sister and I were besotted with one of them. He was charming. But after a couple of days they moved on. They were replaced by a convoy of white soldiers who included Julius Kupke, a German who had become a naturalised American and hated what the Germans were doing. He was short and squat - no oil painting, but my, could he sing. Whenever I hear 'Rose Marie' my mind goes back to D-Day.

'My mother took pity on the men who were desperately tired and had been forced to sleep in their lorries. She invited several into our home where they crashed out on beds and chairs. My mother didn't have much to offer because of rationing but she made gallons of tea and cut up piles of bread for cucumber sandwiches, which they thought so English. In return, they gave us their rations. They made our eyes pop out - tins of meat, fruit, sweets and chocolate.

'When the convoy moved off we said farewell with promises to write. My mother was upset, knowing where they were heading. Julius returned early the following morning to say thank you again with another parcel of goodies. They had been held up at the docks, waiting for a boat. My mother kept her promise and wrote to him and his fiancée in America for quite a while but we lost touch when he moved around after my father was de-mobbed.'

15-year old schoolgirl Jan Caesar.

'I queued with the Americans for breakfasts, which included a pint of tomato or fruit juice, a large plate of sweet pancakes with eggs and bacon and a pint of coffee with sugar and carnation milk. We also had the US Women's Voluntary Service calling at the camp. They'd walk around with trays loaded with free cigarettes, glucose tablets, chewing gum and ring doughnuts, chewing and pipe tobacco. In the Big Tent there were also live shows with US artistes.'

Bill Goodwin, bricklayer on the maintenance staff sealed into the US Camps D2 and D4 in Dorset two weeks before D-Day.

'After a few weeks on Bren Gun Carrier driving at Bowness on Windermere, mechanics at Fords of Dagenham and range firing at Harlech in Wales, I finally arrived at a wooded camp just outside Fawley, Southampton, posted to 1st Battalion Dorsetshire Regiment. Time was spent studying maps and a sand tray model of our next exercise, Overlord.

We were issued with waterproofing kit (side extensions, gunge for dill and brakes, breathers, etc.). During the week American MPs were posted outside the camp to prevent us from leaving but vehicles and drivers were sent onto the road outside to line up on painted white squares. We outsiders had heard that the lads inside had been paid 200 francs apiece, so thought the next manoeuvre must be the real thing.'

Private Ken McFarlane, Anti-Tank Platoon, 1st Battalion Dorset Regiment, 50th Northumbrian Division.

'Inevitably all good things come to an end and we received our 'Marching Orders' to proceed in convoy to the London Docks. The weather was worsening putting all the best-laid plans 'on hold'. Although restrictions as regards personnel movements were pretty tight some local leave was allowed. It would have been possible for me to see my folks just once more before heading into the unknown but having said my farewells earlier felt I Just couldn't go through that again.

'With the enormous numbers of vehicles and military equipment arriving in the marshalling area and a continuous downpour of rain it wasn't long before we were living in a sea of mud and getting a foretaste of things to come. To idle away the hours whilst waiting to hear the shout 'WE GO', time was spent playing cards (for the last remaining bits of English currency), much idle gossip and I would suspect thinking about those we were leaving behind. God knows when, or if, we would be seeing them again. By now this island we were about to leave, with its incessant Luftwaffe bombing raids and the arrival of the 'Flying Bomb', had by now become a 'front line' and was good to be thinking that we were now going to do something about it!

'All preparations were made for the 'off'. Pay Parade and an issue of 200 French francs (invasion style) and then to 'Fall In' again for an issue of the 24 hour ration pack (army style), bags vomit and a Mae West (American style). Time to write a quick farewell letter home before boarding a troopship. Very soon it was 'anchors away'. I must have dozed off for I awoke to find we were hugging the English coast and were about to change course off the Isle of Wight where we joined the great armada of ships of all shapes and sizes. It wasn't too long before the coastline of the French coast became visible, although I did keep looking over my shoulder for the last glimpse of my homeland. The whole seascape by now being filled with an endless procession of vessels carrying their cargoes of fighting men, the artillery, tanks, plus all the other essentials to feed the hungry war machine.

'That first night at sea was spent laying just off the coast at Arromanches ('Gold' Beach) where some enemy air activity was experienced and a ship moored alongside unfortunately got a HE bomb in its hold. Orders came through to disembark and unloading continued until darkness fell. An exercise that had no doubt been overlooked and therefore not covered during previous years of intensive training was actually climbing down the side of a high-sided troopship in order to get aboard, in my case, an American LCT. This accomplished safely, with every possible chance of falling between both vessels tossing in a heaving sea, there followed a warm 'Welcome Aboard' from a young cheerful fresh faced, gum chewing, cigar smoking Yank. I believe I sensed the smell of coffee and do'nuts'!'

24-year old Lance bombardier Frank Scott, 165 HAA Regimental HQ Royal Artillery, Three Batteries, each of two Troops of four 3.7-inch guns; some 24 guns in all, were tasked for Ack-Ack protection of airfields once a foothold had been

The Allied High Command Team for North-West Europe. Front row (left to right): Air Chief Marshal Sir Arthur Tedder (Deputy Supreme Commander), General Dwight D. Eisenhower (Supreme Commander), General Sir Bernard Montgomery (Commander 21 st Army Group and initial overall land commander). Back row (from left to right): Lieutenant-General Omar N. Bradley (Commander US 1st Army for the invasion and subsequently 12th Army Group) Admiral Sir Bertram Ramsay (C.-in-C. Allied Naval Forces), Air Chief Marshal Sir Trafford Leigh-Mallory (C-in-C Allied Expeditionary Air Forces), Lieutenant-General Walter Bedell Smith (Chief of Staff Supreme Headquarters)

Senior Meteorological Officer Group Captain John Stagg.

General Dwight D. Eisenhower's tour of airfields on 11 April included a visit to Great Dunmow. Here, strike photos are shown to General Eisenhower in the operations building. L-R: General Lewis H. Brereton, Commander 9th Air Force; Lieutenant General Sherman Beaty, 386th Bomb Group Executive Officer; Eisenhower; Colonel Herbert B. Thatcher CO, 99th Bomb Wing, which was also based at Great Dunmow; General Carl A. 'Tooey' Spaatz USSAFE (US Strategic Air Forces Europe). (USAF)

Right: US soldiers on board LCI (L) 326, a Landing Craft, Infantry (Large) on their way to Utah Beach. 'Elsie' 326 was one of many craft manned by the US Coast Guard on D-Day. (US Coast Guard)

Above: One of the Mulberry Harbour 'blocks' is moved out of Southampton ready for the invasion.

Right: PLUTO - Pipeline Under The Ocean - was designed to supply petrol from storage tanks in southern England to the advancing Allied armies in France in the months following D-Day. The pipelines were pulled across the Channel by tugs in 30 foot diameter drums called 'Conundrums'

Below: Every harbour in the south of England was filled with Landing Craft, such as these LCTs at Southampton.

Air Chief Marshal Sir Trafford Leigh-Mallory, C-in-C Allied Expeditionary Air Forces, talks to a mechanic working on B-26C Marauder *The Yankee Guerrilla* during a visit to the 386th Bomb Group at Boreham. (USAF)

A Commando in training holds a Fairburn-Sykes Fighting Knife in his teeth which left the soldier's hands free when climbing or crawling towards an objective.

An A-20 Havoc of 9th Bomber Command wearing D-Day invasion stripes

British Commandoes practice their rope-work ready for the invasion.

GIs assembling a
Waco glider.

Many railway
targets were
bombed in
preparation.

Ed Murrow of CBS under the fuselage of a B-26 Marauder of the 386th Bomb Group (Medium) at Great Dunmow, Essex with Colonel Joe W. Kelly the CO (right) who piloted ten of the more than twenty combat missions that Murrow flew. On D-Day Murrow was in London and his broadcast to the USA included the transcription of General Eisenhower's message to the troops.

Admiral Sir Bertram Ramsay and General Dwight D. Eisenhower outside Southwick House, *HMS Dryad*, Southwick, Portsmouth.

British MTBs.

The damaged stern of LST 289 in the aftermath of exercise 'Tiger' at Slapton Sands on the night of 27/28 April when two German E-boats in the English Channel sank two American LSTs and damaged others. A total of 946 US personnel were killed.

Last orders are given to men of the 3rd Canadian Infantry Division on an LST.

Above: A number of C-47s pass low over the invasion fleet.

Opposite page: Formation of Martin B-26Bs from the 555th Bomb Squadron, 386th Bomb Group 9th Air Force overfly the invasion fleet. Closest aircraft is B-26B-15-MA 41-31612 'Mr. Five by Five'

Below: HMS *Beagle* off the beachhead with tank landing ships in the distance. The destroyer, part of Assault Convoy J8 escort, left the Solent at 1400 on 5 June, arriving off 'Juno' on 6 June. This vessel participated in several campaigns - Norway 1940, Battle of the Atlantic 1940-45, North Africa 1942, Artic 1942-44, English Channel 1943 and Normandy 1944 - HMS *Beagle* became most famous for liberating the Channel Islands in May 1945. (IWM)

A woman hangs out her washing in her garden in Southampton. Vehicles are parked in the road prior to loading.

Left: a British Despatch Rider grabs a quick drink on his way to the invasion ports.

Colonel (later General) Harold L. Mace leading the 416th Bomb Group in A-20G 43-9701 5H-H
in the 668th Bomb Squadron.

The US 4th Division en route to Utah Beach.

The naval bombardment begins.

Captain Robert Kirkwood, smoking a cigar and Lieutenant Pat Ward, Battalion intelligence officer, with twenty men in the stick from 505th Infantry, 82nd Airborne wait to board their C-47 on the evening of 5 June at Cottesmore. At least three 'sticks' from the Third battalion were dropped off target at Montebourg, about 6 miles north of Ste-Mère-Église and Kirkwood, Ward and Lieutenant Jack Issacs of Company 'G' managed to gather and assemble 33 men in the subsequent fighting the group were dispersed and many casualties sustained. Kirkwood said later that 'it took me three days to get back to our lines and in those three days I saw more Germans than I ever wanted to see again'. *(US Army via Deryk Wills)*

Among the first of the airborne troops to land in France were four lieutenants; Bobby de La Tour and Don Wells, both from London (pictured), John Vischer, Newport Pagnell and Bob Midwood, Scarborough, here setting their watches before taking off. Captain de La Tour was KIA on 20 June.

Some of 'Hobarts Funnies' - in this case a number of DD Tanks - the DD standing for Duplex Drive, but nicknamed Donald Duck tanks, were a type of amphibious swimming tank which had a 'floatation screen' around it which enabled it to float.

A number of US 4 x 4 half-ton amphibians in a storage park in the UK prior to being used on D-Day. These, and other amphibious designs became commonly known as DUKWs or 'Ducks'

successfully gained and a position firmly held in Normandy. As it turned out, the Regiment not only fought in an AA role but 275 Battery came under command of Guards Armoured Division for ground shooting; 198 Battery deployed in the AA role defensive conc. Area and 317 Battery deployed in the Anti-tank role.'

'We knew D-Day was coming because we were inundated with young midshipmen. Shoreham harbour became so full of ships you could walk across it on the landing craft. For at least a month before 6 June I couldn't get home from Hove to Worthing without a pass. On the night of D-Day I was on fire duty but when I came off at midnight I was told not to bother to go to quarters. They wanted me to help cook 2,000 bacon, powdered egg and tomato breakfasts at 2 am. So we knew this was it. We had a hot plate ten feet long. It was a very sustaining breakfast but I learned later many of the sailors who left from Shoreham were awfully seasick.'
   WREN Doris Hayball, 23.

'We knew there was something different happening. Dozens of planes were flying over us. One girl called Lynn said, 'Oh my Colin, he's a commando'. Just two weeks later, they heard he'd died. In 1945 I met a marine on his way to Burma. He told me he'd lost his friend that day. Yes, the friend he had lost was Colin.'
   Mrs. E. Stewart.

'We had been told just before we landed that there was a whisper something was afoot. I was therefore hoping that there wasn't anything going on that would stop me from getting back. We freshened ourselves up and then we went into this little tent where there was just a handful of officers. We said, 'Right, let's turn the radio on.' There was this little wireless in the corner. And that's when the news came over that the boys had started and the operation had begun. We all gave a little toast in that tent. And we said we hoped that this was the beginning of the end.'
   Forces Sweetheart, Vera Lynn who in June 1944 was homeward bound and exhausted after a gruelling tour of Burma and the Middle East when her plane touched down in Jerba, Tunisia for a night stop over.

'Along with hundreds of other children I was at the Odeon Cinema at Bury Park, Luton. We were practicing for a concert when a man walked on the stage and told us that the Allied Forces had landed in Normandy and it was the beginning of the end of Nazi Germany. We all cheered and clapped even when most of us did not know where Normandy was. I ran home to tell my mother. She said, 'Well it looks like your brother did not die in vain'.
   11-year old George Jackson

'I was living with my parents in an old pub in Gosport. A lot of noise and commotion woke me early and I went down and opened the door. There were soldiers and army trucks, all making for the harbour. I put my six-month-old daughter in her pram and walked the short distance to the seafront. Little boats were bobbing waiting for the troops to climb aboard. One American boy said he was so afraid. I said to him. 'You will be all right, I know it'.
   Mrs. J. Charlesworth.

'It seemed to me that it took at least a week for all the ships to gather just outside our hospital in Southampton Water. The Royal Victoria Hospital at Netley was a very cold and damp monstrosity and certainly not conducive to treating patients. The Seabees [US Navy construction battalion personnel] remodelled the whole thing to make it usable. We could go outside and sit on the waterfront and watch. One day it seemed like the whole area was full of ships and the next it morning there was not a single one. We were on duty 24 hours a day but we didn't know what we were waiting for.'

Nurse Helen Pavlovsky USN, The Royal Victoria Hospital, Netley.

'I was 12 and old enough to understand what was going on. At breakfast the radio announcer gave out a carefully worded message to the nation saying our troops had made a landing on the beaches of Normandy and were fighting for them inch by inch. I sensed that I was witnessing history being made. I lived in Portsmouth and the streets were filled with equipment. I will always remember a young soldier stopping me and putting his hand in his pockets. He pulled out all his money and cigarettes, pushed it all into my hands and said, 'Here kid, take this. I won't be coming back from where I'm going.' I still wonder if he ever did.'

P. McElhinney.

'On arriving home from work I noticed an envelope on the mantelpiece marked OHMS. It said that if I signed the form enclosed, I would be deferred from the services until the end of hostilities, but I would have to go and work down the pit at Elsecar Colliery. My father worked at Elsecar Colliery as a miner. Those were the days of getting bathed in front of the fire in a tin bath, no such thing as pit baths. In the early 1930s my father had an accident which caused complications. He died at the age of 38. When my father passed away I made a promise to my mother that I would never go to work in the mines, so the decision was easy. I burnt the letter; hence the following letter to report to Cooper Art Gallery, Barnsley for a medical examination for the army, which I passed A1. I got my calling-up papers and had to report to Fulwood Barracks, Preston where we had eight weeks training on the double all day. After three weeks I was made a lance corporal and had the experience of drilling my mates on the square. My earlier training in the Home Guard was paying off. After the eight weeks I was posted to Caterham to the Coldstream Guards which was the Brigade of Guards which meant square bashing for twelve weeks prior to moving to Pirbright Battle School. The first two weeks we were not allowed out of camp until we could salute properly. It was while I was there I met RSM Britton with his pacing stick. I was on my way to the camp barber crossing the parade ground when he yelled out. He asked me how long I had been at the camp. I told him two days. He said that while I was there I was to conduct myself as a Guardsman at all times. Then he marched me down to the barbers at the correct pace. What an experience.

'After three weeks it was found that I was half an inch too short, so I was posted to Berwick on Tweed to join the King's Own Yeomanry Light Infantry at Magdalene Field for 18 weeks infantry training. At Berwick I met up with comrades with whom I was later to land in France. My mate, number 2 on the Bren, was Frank Williams from Birmingham. Later he was best man at my wedding and I was best man at his. Sergeant Rawson was in charge of our platoon. For eighteen weeks he was just like a father to us. We came out on top in drilling and won the one mile obstacle battle course. I was chosen as the battalion two mile runner and relay team. We finished our training at Berwick and were posted to the Hamilton Racecourse to join the 1/4th KOYLI 'B' Company. We were ordered to pack our kit and get ready to move off. When we arrived at our destination we were told to board the ship which was the Ben a Machrie and we sailed to Rothesay, Isle of Bute, which was a submarine base during the war. Every morning we went down to the beach to board landing craft which then took us to the Ben a Machrie ready to take us to the practice landing area at Blackpool Bay further up the Isle of Bute. Every day the Navy would stand off the beach about twenty yards so we were wet to start with. The training there was rough. It was landing craft exercises ready for D-Day. Two weeks we were out there, wet through every day and the final week we had to do it at night with live ammo and live shells. Returning from the Isle of Bute to Hamilton we had a week's rest and then we were off again, this time to Lowestoft for more training; river crossing, fast route marches, digging in and sleeping in slit trenches, advancing under fire and on top of that, PT every day, so that everybody was fighting fit. It was now May and things were buzzing.'

Lance Corporal Geoff Steer, born in St. Helens, Elsecar in 1923.

'At the end of 1942 the government lowered the age of recruitment for the services to 18, I was just coming up to that age, so I registered for service at the start of 1943, I told them I wanted to be in the RAF, but they were short of infantry so that's where I ended up, I was sent to an infantry reception area at Brecon, where my training started, After six weeks I was sent to another infantry training centre where I did ten more weeks. At the end of that I joined the 2nd Battalion King's Shropshire Light Infantry, which at the time was stationed at Lockerbie in Scotland. In the autumn of that year the colonel told us that our battalion had been selected for the D-Day landings, We realised that this would be dangerous and that we would have to do the job properly if we were going to survive, so we all knuckled down and trained extremely hard, Of course we didn't know at the time when D-Day would happen. As far as we were concerned it could have been any day. As part of our training we practiced getting onto landing craft and landing on a beach that had been covered in barbed wire, while being 'under fire' all the time. It was utter chaos. I was always very glad when it was over, because I wasn't much of a swimmer and didn't fancy my luck in the middle of a freezing loch. We also learned how to do river crossings, mountain warfare and other weird and wonderful things. We learned about the different kinds of coastal defences the Germans had built and how we would have to get across them. Most of us were just 18 at the time and it was all new to us!

'In all the time we were training we had no idea where we would eventually land. I remember once a lieutenant commander from the Royal Navy came to talk to us. He had been on the beach where we would land and had even taken samples of sand - but of course we were not told where the beach was.

'One day we were told to put on our small packs, which were filled with stones and to swim a certain distance into a loch and back again. It was November and it was snowing, but we did it! Back on shore we were dried off immediately and were all given a good tot of rum. Soon after that we all got leave. I went to visit my parents and went down with pneumonia almost the moment I arrived there. I stayed at home for about ten days and when I got back I found out that someone had died from exposure after the loch exercises.

'When we finished training in Scotland our regiment was moved to Chailey in Sussex. We did a lot of training in night fighting down there and also took part in street fighting exercises in London.

'In the spring of 1944 we had a visit from General Eisenhower. We were all put on parade on a landing strip somewhere in Sussex for the visit. He walked along the lines inspecting us. He then got onto the bonnet of a jeep and gave a little talk, saying, 'If anybody can do it, you chaps can.' It was very good for morale. We were all expecting the invasion to happen in the summer of 1944, because of the weather conditions. By the late spring of that year we were getting leave quite often and I was going home almost every weekend. On one occasion my dad, who had fought in World War One, took me to the top of a hill in Herefordshire, where the view was absolutely brilliant. He said, 'This is what it's all about, this is why we are fighting this war and if you see a view like this you know it's worth it.' I couldn't have agreed more. That's what you want in life - a beautiful view like that, not a jackboot stomping on your neck.

'Towards the end of May we were taken to a sealed camp, so we knew that the invasion had to be imminent, although of course on my level we didn't know the exact timetable. At this stage of our training they showed us sand models, maps and photographs of where we would land. We knew how wide the roads were, how deep the ditches and where there would be obstacles in our way - but we still had no idea where exactly it would be because code names were used rather than real names. By late May we knew that the assault would happen within ten days or so, depending on the weather conditions, although no one still knew the exact date. We were told that another brigade had been selected for the initial assault and that we would go in second as the penetration brigade, to get inland.'

Bob Littlar, 2nd Battalion King's Shropshire Light Infantry.

Daniel Frank Lyons was born on 4 May 1925 at Wood Green, North London. His father, also Daniel and a Scot, twice wounded in the trenches of Ypres, was a buyer for Barratt's Confectionery, his mother Doris, a Londoner and housewife, kept a warm, secure and loving home for her young family. Every summer the family packed their suitcases, clambered aboard a Royal Blue coach and journeyed across the South of England to Paulton in Somerset, for a week with Uncle Charlie and his family. Paulton was a coal mining village and Danny and his cousins spent many a grubby hour scrabbling amongst the coal heaps and doing all those things that keep young boys amused on long summer days. In 1938 the Emergency Powers Act was passed prompting over 500,000 people to join the ARP and swell the ranks of the 200,000 who'd volunteered a year earlier. Many others joined the Territorials or the RAF Volunteer Reserve. Danny was in the Scouts and they bravely took on the role of messengers for the ARP. Danny left school at 16, taking a job as an electrical instrument assembler and when he was old enough joined the Home Guard. In March 1943 Danny volunteered for the regular army and signed on for seven years.

Danny spent the first six weeks of army life in a converted holiday camp, No.1 Primary Training Centre (PTC) in Prestatyn, where there was a new intake of would be soldiers every two weeks. After basic training he was sent to the Royal Signals Regiment in Catterick to train as a wireless operator and to learn Morse code. Whilst he was there two officers from the 6th Airborne Division, the sinister sounding Lieutenant Colonel Pine-Coffin and another officer by the name of Dust, came looking for men to train as Airborne Signallers. Danny put up his hand, 'Well it was an extra two bob a day and it sounded like fun'. His name was taken, then duly forgotten and was posted to Egham where he trained as a Signal Interceptor. Eventually though, the call came and Danny went to Claycross for basic jump training. Then he was transferred to the Central Landing School at Ringway airfield for his eight qualifying jumps. The first two jumps were from 800 feet, from the basket of a tethered balloon. Then they jumped from aircraft - Whitleys, Stirlings or Halifaxes. To qualify for airborne wings they had to make eight jumps. Up to and including the seventh jump a trainee could back out and say, 'No, this isn't for me.' But if they went on to the eighth jump, there was no going back. Danny made his eight jumps and proudly took possession of his parachute wings and red beret in the autumn of 1943. Training now intensified they had to get used to going out as a group, as a 'stick', getting 20 men out of the aircraft as rapidly as possible, 20 men in 20 seconds was their target. From Ringway he moved to Bulford and was assigned to the Divisional HQ Signals Section and of course the training continued. Jumping, landing and re-grouping had to be as natural as breathing.

At the end of April maps started to appear, training became less physical and more technical as they studied plans and relief models. They were given their destination, Normandy, but kept in the dark as to the size and nature of the operation. They just concentrated on their own little bit of the action; they had no idea that 156,000 other men of all nationalities and services were learning their little bits too. Armed soldiers now patrolled the perimeter and no-one was allowed in or out. This was as much a safeguard to keep intruders out as it was to keep the soldiers in. At this late stage High Command couldn't afford someone inadvertently speaking out of turn.

The 6th Airborne Division was mobilized on 25 May and Divisional HQ dispersed in its specialist units to transit camps somewhere in Southern England. It was a big division so quite a few bases had been prepared to receive them, Tarrant Rushton, Keevil, Blakehill Farm, Down Ampney, Fairford, Broadwell, Brize Norton and Harwell. And of course wherever the 6th went, the armed guards went too. To this day Dan still isn't certain which airfield his unit was taken to. It was possibly Fairford or Keevil; they were the only bases with serviceable Stirlings in late May, early June.

On Sunday June 4th Lieutenant Colonel 'Pygmy' Smallman-Tew (he was well over six foot!) sat his Signalmen down and said, 'We go tonight.' But later that night as storms gathered over the English Channel, Pygmy came back to his eager young men to tell them the mission had been postponed. Twenty four hours later, with improving weather Pygmy was able to give his men the thumbs up. It was on! He wished them well and then read an order from Major General Gale, Officer Commanding 6th Airborne Division. 'All reports I have had from civil and military sources reflect greatest credit to all ranks for their loyal and rigid security. My final words to you are to see to it that what you gain by stealth you hold with guts. In the words of a great Captain, 'Pray to God and keep your powder dry. God bless you. Go to it.'

At 22:30 Monday June 5th, Danny and his mates struggled aboard their Stirling aircraft and waited for the off.

***Into the Night* by Snoltz.**

'On the night when D-Day was postponed a fellow officer and I had spread out our maps of the little section of Normandy which was going to be our world and played soldier. Solemnly, we decided which routes we would take and marked our march route knowing all the time and very well that after the beach we'd take whatever road or field lay in the direction we wanted to go.

'The next night as we sailed towards France again we had all night to ourselves to go over it again and... that was what let fear in. You could count on your fingers the things that could happen to you and nothing could be done about any of them. There were the E-boats that had sunk our landing craft on manoeuvres the month before, no further from the English shore than we lay at anchor. There were the submarines that we knew the Hun might risk in the Channel if he knew this was the real thing. There were the mines. Most of all, on a crossing like ours, there was the air. No cover could wholly seal the air over the Channel and the long lines of landing craft would be bobbing ducks in a shooting gallery... On the far shore, there were underwater obstacles and the shore batteries... but most of all, for us, there was that damn strip of beach with the flooded area just beyond. This was the assault beach called 'Utah'.'

Ralph Ingersoll.

'Once I arrived at Southwick House in May, I was sealed inside the gates until after D-Day. I was working in a Nissen hut adjoining the house and my job was to file and type and organise secret documents. We were under terrible pressure. We worked 80 hours a week for more than four months. It was so exciting to know everything that was about to happen. On 5 June we played cricket, but on the night of the invasion itself I stayed up all night. On the morning of D-Day I fell asleep at my desk - there was such a relief of tension.

Jean Irvine, a Wren in her twenties serving on the planning staff of Admiral Sir Bertram Ramsay at his HQ at Southwick House, ten miles north-west of Portsmouth. Throughout the spring of 1944 General Eisenhower worked at SHAEF HQ in Bushy Park, southwest London. But the site was too far from the action to serve as his HQ on D-Day. It was decided that in the days before the launch of Operation Overlord the supreme commander would move nearer to Admiral Ramsay's naval HQ at Southwick House. Requisitioned from the Thistlethwayte family in 1941, the building initially housed the Royal Naval School of Navigation, but was taken over by the Allied naval commander-in-chief in 1944. Plotting rooms and training facilities were created and temporary accommodation huts, workshops and other buildings were constructed in the extensive grounds. By 1 June General Montgomery parked his famous caravan in the grounds.[17] Monty's staff ran the 21st Army Group from tents hidden among trees to the north of the house. Early on 2 June, Eisenhower moved into a trailer which he dubbed 'my circus wagon' hidden under camouflage nets in woods to the south. Ike's camp, code-named 'Sharpener', lay a mile from the main building and included the general's armoured caravans and office tents. When not in conference or visiting troops, Ike would try to relax by reading westerns on his bunk and smoking. Although outwardly relaxed for most of the time and 'a ready smile for everyone whatever their rank' Ike was in a nervous state, smoking up to four packs of 'Camels' a day. His nerves were not helped by 'constant pots of coffee'. British born Kay Summersby, Eisenhower's personal driver, drove

---

17 Montgomery used three caravans. A 'map caravan' was ordered from the British Trailer Company, Manchester and was delivered to St. Paul's School on 17 April. The BTC map lorry and two Italian caravans captured from Maresciallo Giovanni Messe, commander of the First Italian Army in Tunisia and the vehicle liberated near Benghazi from Generale di Corpo d'Armata Annibale Bergonzoli, commander of XXIII Corps during the North Africa campaign. Monty was allowed to keep the vehicles during his lifetime and they were stored in a barn at his home at Isington Mill in Hampshire until four months after his death in March 1976. Today all three caravans are on display in the Land Warfare Hall at the IWM Duxford.

Eisenhower up to the house in his Cadillac and it was in the library that he made the historic decision to launch D-Day. The library was near the map-room, which was the hub of Southwick.

'The operation has begun and it is too late to stop it now... There is wireless silence and we can expect no signals. I am going to bed.'
Bertram Ramsay's response when asked by General Montgomery what the admiral was going to do now that the decision had been made.

'There was a complete hush in the room - a cool, calm atmosphere that one of quiet confidence. Everything had been thought out but we all remembered the old adage that the finest of plans comes to an end when the shooting starts. The weather was blowing a gale. The wind was howling and the rain was lashing down but inside there was almost complete silence. There were only a handful of people in the map room itself. There were no raised voices and no raised tempers. And there was none of the normal backslapping or laughing. In our hearts we all knew this was it.'
27-year old Major Tom Normanton, intelligence staff, Southwick House. One wall was devoted to a plywood map of the whole of southern Britain, the Channel and Normandy on which the progress of the Invasion was to be charted. In May the Midlands toy company, Chad Valley, had been ordered to make a map covering the entire European coastline from Norway to Spain. The two workmen who delivered it were told to erect only the Normandy section and were then held at Southwick until the invasion was under way. The 40 or 50 people who worked in the room included WRENs who plotted the positions of convoys on a huge table. The ships' progress was mapped using chinagraph pencils on Perspex and the plots were frequently updated based on information constantly supplied by radar stations along the coasts. The map and the room fell into disuse after D-Day and it was not until after the war that the operations room was restored.

'At about four o'clock in the afternoon we were told to stand down - the invasion was off. We were given the reasons, we were told the weather had broken and it was unlikely that we would be landing for the next twenty-four hours. We were told that a decision would be made by midday on Sunday. After that, every man Jack - whatever your religion - went to church. It didn't matter what denomination you were - agnostic, atheist, Church of England, Roman Catholic, Presbyterian or Jewish - you stood in some church and someone blessed you.'
Private Peter Fussell, 1 Commando.

'On our return from Italy, we were not earmarked for the assault. But that changed and from then on the whole of our training was geared to the actual landing in Normandy. Perhaps this was a mistake, because after the landing we had to fight the war ashore like everybody else. Also we had carried out landings in Sicily and Italy, so we knew about landing craft. We felt confident that having done it before, we could do it again. But there was also a feeling that as this was the third time, something might go wrong. At the same time everyone was one hundred per cent sure that the operation would work, whatever happened personally or to one's unit. What we all felt - and this was the most astonishing thing about the Normandy landings - was that everyone was 100 per cent confident that whatever happened to you or to anyone else, the operation would be successful. There was no question that it might not be. And everyone was glad to get on with it because it felt like the green light for the end of the war, or so we thought.

Lieutenant Colonel David Warren 1st Battalion, Hampshire Regiment. 'Security was very tight. Brigadier Nelson Smith my brigade commander told me after the war, that after attending a briefing in London for all brigadiers, he went to the flat his wife had up there. When he arrived, she said she would like him to tell her where the landing would be, because she might be able to help with information. She said that her family had always spent their holidays near Arromanches. He had to keep a straight face and say nothing. Our beach was nearby.'

'When we were reconnoitring, they used to take us within three miles of low-water mark and we used to leave her submerged... and go ashore, reconnoitring up the beaches and taking the samples of sand in little canvas bags and fetching them back and then being towed back by a trawler in the early hours of the morning. We only spent an hour on the beach.'

Lieutenant (later Lieutenant-Commander) Ron Howard RNVR originally was a trawler engineer, who was chosen by Admiral Ramsay for the key role of beachmaster at one of the landing zones because of his stentorian voice but he was also a trained frogman and canoeist and had been on secret reconnaissance missions by X-craft (midget submarine) to beaches from Norway to Normandy. Late on June 4 Howard squeezed himself into X20, commanded by Lieutenant Ken Hudspeth, an Australian, for passage to 'Gold' Beach and there to take up station offshore (with X23) to act as navigational markers off the coast at Ouistreham and Le Hamel, pinpointing the landing positions of Force 'S' (for 'Sword') and Force 'J' (for 'Juno') with automatic radio beacons and telescopic masts fitted with powerful lights. '...the craft was rolling and pitching considerably... The sea and swirl made exit and entry difficult and considerable water was shipped, necessitating continual pumping. Diet consisted mainly of nutty, bread and jam, chocolate biscuits, orange juice, hyocine and oxygen and this proved adequate. Only two hot meals were prepared; smell and oxygen used when heating made more undesirable.'

'Our particular operation for D-Day was called 'Gambit'. We were to leave Gosport in X23 on the night of Friday the 2nd June, to cross the 90 miles to France unobserved and land at a fixed position and set up a telescopic mast some 18 feet high with the beam pointing out to sea, which would act as a navigational beacon for the DD tanks which would be launched all around us. We spent all Saturday and the following night crossing the Channel. On Sunday morning we reached the French coast and to our joy found that we were very close to our marking position. We observed the coast through our periscope and found it easy to fix our position as we had RAF photographs showing the churches and other landmarks on shore. There was even a light at the mouth of the River Orne. Having fixed our position, we bottomed and waited until nightfall. On the Sunday night, we surfaced and dropped our anchor so we would stay right on our marking position. We could see a lorry load of Germans playing volleyball and swimming. Little did they know that we were there and what was waiting for them. We hoisted our radio mast and got a signal that the invasion had been postponed. We didn't know for how long. So then we had to retreat to the bottom again and wait until Monday night.

'That night we resurfaced and received a message that the invasion was on. This surprised us as the weather was as bad as the previous night. But anyway, we were very relieved as we had no idea how much oxygen we had left and were afraid it might run out before the invasion came. So we went back to sit on the bottom and at about 4.30 am on Tuesday, 6th June, we surfaced again. As we came up through the hatch and looked seaward, there was nothing but ships - a great fleet from tiny landing craft to great battleships - stretching as far as the eye could see. By then the Allied bombardment had started and the shells were flying overhead, trying to winkle out the batteries on the shore. We put up all our navigational aids - 18-foot telescopic mast with a light shining seaward, a radio beacon and an echo-sounder tapping out a message below the surface. This was for the navigational ML's [motor launches] to pick up as they brought the invasion in. We knew that the DD tanks would be launched all around us from tank landing craft and they would form up and swim ashore under their own power. They were in flotation bags, great big canvas bags and carried two propellers. And sure enough they were launched all around us and as soon as the DD tanks had been launched we'd completed our task. We cut the anchor rope, we were too exhausted to pull up the anchor and then we had to rendezvous with our escorting trawler.

'We were especially relieved to get back to England safely, as, on looking up the word Gambit in a dictionary, much to our horror we saw it was defined as 'the pawn you throw away before a big move in chess - which didn't encourage us too much.'

Lieutenant George Honour (later Lieutenant Commander George Honour DSC RNVR), Midget Submarine X23. The X-craft, which had a crew of five, were battery powered with a diesel engine for re-charging, which took about two to three hours. A tiny galley had an electric cooker known jokingly as a 'gluepot' and the crew took it in turns to cook rations. 'The boats had their own oxygen supply' said Honour 'but after 48 hours 'it was almost as good as a strong Bass (beer), so you start to get a bit ga-ga. It's like being half canned, half-tight, being shut up like that on oxygen. We played poker dice; we all lost a fortune but that was about all you could do.'

'I was Duty Petty Officer on the night of 5 June. It was remarkably quiet and after the previous night's cancellation because of adverse weather conditions, the operation was under way. For once the operators had time to chat amongst themselves, wondering if their boyfriends had sailed off to France too? Would we get any leave beforehand? Would the invasion succeed? How bad would the casualties be? All of these thoughts were bandied about, helping to pass the time - it was a very long night. Because of the use of scramblers we could only anticipate what was happening, but a call from General Omar Bradley at about 0200 gave us cause to hope that everything was going to plan. The RAF had bombed the coastal batteries between Le Havre and Cherbourg and gliders had landed Airborne Divisions behind the coastline of Normandy. By the end of the Middle Watch we received news that everything was going well and at 0630 the first seaborne troops were landing on the beaches. I finally went off duty at 0800 and then came the BBC announcement of the landings. The Mess echoed to an almighty cheer. After all the planning the beginning of the end was in sight. Our lads were in France and we had been part of it! I walked down the tree-lined drive at Southwick House very tired but very happy.'

Ena Howes.

Under the command of General Eisenhower. Allied naval forces, supported by strong air forces, began landing Allied armies this morning on the coast of France.'
New York 3.32 am, Tuesday, 6 June

'This is London. Early this morning we heard the bombers going out. It was the sound of a giant factory in the sky. It seemed to shake the old grey stone buildings in this bruised and battered city beside the Thames.'

Ed Murrow of CBS who at 3.37 on 6 June was heard reading General Dwight D. Eisenhower's Order of the Day. Just after midnight in the United States, CBS interrupted its network dance music programme to tell listeners 'A bulletin has just been received from the London Office of the Associated Press which quotes the German Transocean News Agency as asserting that the invasion of Europe has begun.' Ed Murrow's 'boys' were deployed with the Allied troops in the air and at sea. Murrow himself was selected as one of the American 'pool' reporters locked in a guarded basement studio at the British Ministry of Information to report on the events as they were cleared by the military censors.

'The Allied forces landed in France this morning. I watched the first landing on the beach exactly on the minute of H-Hour. I was in a 9th Air Force Marauder flying at 4500 feet along 20 miles of the invasion coast. From what I could see during those first minutes, there was nothing stopping the assault parties from getting ashore. We spent about half an hour over enemy territory. We flew over and bombed some of the coastal fortifications but except for some light flak, from inland positions and some tanks firing at us we saw no enemy gunfire. The only other sign of life in enemy territory was some white and yellow parachutes dotting the ground where our paratroopers had hit the ground.'

Deeply air sick from the rough return to Great Dunmow in one of the 386th Bomb Group's B-26 Marauders, Richard C. Hottelet, a CBS newsman who was a young reporter in Berlin before the Americans entered the war, made it back to London with a slop bucket at the ready to describe the pre-dawn raid. On his return Hottelet told a colleague: 'If I had to parachute out of the plane, I could have walked across the Channel on the ships.' Cornelius Ryan, a *Daily Telegraph* correspondent who in 1962 wrote *The Longest Day* and A Bridge Too Far flew in on D-Day.

Other correspondents included Drew Middleton, Alan Moorehead and Ross Munro. Those correspondents chosen at the end of May in great secrecy at Wentworth Golf Club west of London to go ashore with the troops on D-Day were few. Doon Campbell (24) of Reuters, who was born without a left arm, had filed well-received stories from the bitter fighting at Monte Cassino in February 1944. The youngest of the British correspondents, he was 'overjoyed' to be selected and he would go across on D-Day with Lord Lovat's Commando Brigade. When Lovat looked at him and his baggage he said to Campbell: 'You don't need that 'stuff'. It was the 'stuff' Campbell had made do at Cassino but the Scottish brigadier said, 'You'll get everything you need in a pack on your back'. Campbell responded, 'Including a typewriter?' To which Lovat said, 'yes, including a typewriter.'

Some correspondents would not be going to France for a week. When one complained at missing 'the biggest story since the crucifixion' an officer replied: 'Yes, but they managed very well with just four correspondents!'

'Supreme Allied Headquarters have issued an urgent warning to inhabitants of the enemy-occupied countries living near the coast. The warning said that a new phase in the Allied air offensive had begun. Shortly before this warning the Germans reported that Havre, Calais and Dunkirk were being heavily bombarded and that German naval units were engaged with Allied landing craft.'

BBC 8 am bulletin on the morning of 6 June read by Frederick Allen.

As our nurses' home next to the Royal South Hampshire Hospital had been bombed, we had been billeted out in a large house in Highfield, Southampton. For weeks before we had become used to the movement of troops and the droning of aircraft which had disturbed our sleep. On 6 June someone dashed into our room and gave us the shock news. A reliable source on the wireless had broadcast that we had made a landing on the Normandy coast. We dressed hurriedly and in small groups made our way to catch our tram. The streets were filled with people as we tried to get to work and the tram services were in chaos. Breakfast roll call at the hospital was at 7.30 am. We could not be late so we decided to walk, or, as it happened, run! But to no avail. We were 20 minutes late. Home Sister was already doling out the porridge. She said, 'What time do you call this? We tried to explain we had walked because the landings had disrupted public transport. She just said 'You should have made allowances for that' as if we young nurses should have known one of the biggest secrets of the war! Then she sent us on duty without any breakfast! That evening, we walked up The Avenue instead of getting our hospital bus and saw the convoys going down to the docks. Southampton had almost become an American town!

Mary Hoskins, 21, student nurse.

'We won't just shoot the sonsabitches; we are going to cut out their living guts and use them to grease the treads of our tanks.'

Lieutenant General George S. Patton, commander, Third United States Army. The creation of the 1st Army Group commanded by Patton was part of the deception plan ('Fortitude South') used to try to convince the Germans that on D-Day the landings would take place around Calais.

'Do you realize that by the time you wake up in the morning 20,000 men may have been killed?'

Winston Churchill to his wife Clementine before retiring, on the eve of D-Day.
'He was much on edge. Once again, he could hear the tramping of Housman's ghostly legions.
Far and near, low and louder
On the roads of earth go by
Dear to friends and food for powder
Soldiers marching, all to die.
Commander Walter Thompson, Mr. Winston Churchill's personal bodyguard.

'We'll have only one chance to stop the enemy and that's while he's in the water. Everything we have must be on the coast... the first 24 hours of the invasion will be decisive. For the Allies as well as Germany, it will be the longest day.'

Feldmarschall Erwin Rommel who took command Army Group B in northern France in January 1944.

A Bodyguard of Lies – Deception, Double-Cross and Decryption

'In order to deceive and baffle the enemy as well as to exercise our forces, there will be many false alarms, many feints and many dress rehearsals.'
Winston Churchill, from an address to the nation, 26 March 1944.

Operation 'Bodyguard', an overall plan to mislead the enemy about the intentions of the Allies, was agreed at the Anglo-American summit in Cairo in December 1943. A month earlier, COSSAC's security plans for Overlord required that all personnel granted access to top secret documents should be given an ID card stamped with the word 'Bigot'. Secret documents were also stamped 'Bigot'. In March 1944 the FBI reported that papers marked 'Bigot' had been discovered in an army mail-sorting office in the USA. The package had been addressed to the US Army's Ordnance Division, but was delivered to a woman who lived in a German suburb of Chicago. A huge security operation eventually found that a clerk had mistakenly sent the documents to his sister. On 22 April 1944 (by which time COSSAC had given way to SHAEF (Supreme Headquarters Allied Expeditionary Forces and coordination of the deception effort was assigned to a London Controlling Section[18]). General Eisenhower was greatly upset to hear that security had been compromised by Major-General Henry Miller, chief supply officer of the Ninth Air Force, who on 18 April during a cocktail party at Claridge's hotel in London had talked freely about the difficulties he was having in obtaining supplies but that things would improve after D-Day, which he said would be before 15 June. Miller had been a former West Point classmate of Eisenhower's. He was demoted and sent home in disgrace.

On 2 May a British staff officer doing the *Daily Telegraph* crossword worked out that across - 'A US state'; was 'Utah', incidentally the codename for one of the invasion beaches. On 22 May 'Omaha' appeared and then came 'Overlord' on 27 May, 'Mulberry' on 30 May and 'Neptune' on 1 June! That same day MI5 investigated the compiler, Leatherhead schoolmaster Leonard Dawe and cleared him of any wrongdoing. It was put down to a coincidence but 40 years later it was revealed that the schoolmaster would get his pupils to fill out blank crosswords and then concocted clues to fit. These pupils spent some of their afternoons at American and Canadian camps nearby where they heard the soldiers using the code words. These came swiftly to mind when they were filling out the crossword blanks in the classroom!

The British security service had captured all German agents in Britain; most of who had been 'turned' to transmit misleading information back to their controllers. This 'Double Cross' system under the direction of the XX Committee was designed to confuse the Germans as a key part of 'Fortitude', the most ambitious deception in the history of warfare. Two Norwegians sent to Scotland in 1943 to spy for the Germans defected on landing and 'Mutt and Jeff' as they were christened by their British handlers, were recruited to help 'Fortitude North', a deception plan carried out almost entirely by fake wireless messages. A fictitious British 'Fourth Army' of eight divisions was established in Scotland for a planned invasion of Norway to keep German divisions there. Dummy aircraft were constructed and some of the ships that would take part in the invasion of Normandy were anchored in Scottish harbours as a decoy to suggest an attack on Norway. Soviet officers were seen in Edinburgh and their presence reported to the enemy by former

---

18   The LCS liaised with all manner of Allied intelligence agencies gathering information about the German military operations from photo- reconnaissance, captured documents, wireless intercepts, code breaking and counter-espionage by agents and Resistance groups.

German agents who had been turned.

On 22 April 1944 'Station X'; the Top-Secret Bletchley Park Manor, home of the British Government Code and Cypher School in Buckinghamshire, about fifty miles north-west of London, decoded a German 'Enigma' signal which identified the 'Fourth Army', with its headquarters near Edinburgh and two component corps at Stirling and Dundee. Other messages showed that the Germans believed that the Lowland Division was being equipped for an attack on Narvik and Stavanger in northern and southern Norway.

'Enigma' was a highly sophisticated mechanical encryption system that superficially looked like a typewriter. The German engineer, Arthur Scherbius, developed it in 1923 from a design by a Dutchman. The German Army and Navy bought it in 1929, believing that it would make the transmission of radio messages faster and completely secure. In its simplest form, for every letter it sent there were hundreds of millions of possible solutions. However, the Polish Army had begun decrypting some signals in 1932, the French intelligence services in 1938 and the British in February 1940. The encryption of enemy codes was at such a high level that it was classified as 'Ultra Secret' so it became known as 'Ultra'. Bletchley could also decrypt Japanese diplomatic cyphers so that reports sent from Berlin to Tokyo were made available to British Intelligence services.

'Fortitude North' proved a complete success and Hitler kept a sizeable army there. 'Fortitude South', the main deception effort, set out to convince the Germans that any landings in Normandy were a large-scale diversion to draw German reserves away from the Pas-de-Calais. The actual invasion was supposedly to take place between Boulogne and the Somme estuary during the second half of July. A notional '1st US Army Group' or FUSAG under General George S. Patton Jr, with eleven divisions in four corps (150,000 troops) and located on the east coast between the Thames and The Wash was established. An entire dummy oil-tank farm with mock containers designed by the architect Sir Basil Spence and made to look as realistic as possible by magical illusionist, Jasper Maskelyne was erected near Dover[19]. Fake and real landing craft, vehicles and inflatable tanks, together with 250 fake landing ships were constructed in Kent and Sussex were positioned to look like an invasion force and false radio signals were broadcast from Kent by mobile transmitters to simulate large military formations. The sending of 21st Army Group's communications to London along a landline from Portsmouth to Kent and then by wireless to London contributed to the illusion. Y Service dutifully marked General Montgomery's HQ next to Patton's. [20]

19   The War Office had at first been highly sceptical of Maskelyne's ideas but they were won over by his usefulness in employing mirrors and a scale model to create the illusion that a German battleship was sailing up the Thames. Maskelyne's first assignment was in North Africa where Maskelyne and his small group of hand-picked assistants created a series of ruses that helped confound the Germans. They built a replica of the city of Alexandria to divert Luftwaffe bombers; hid the Suez Canal with a system of dazzling spotlights; and created a dummy army to confuse Rommel about the true location of the British forces. Maskelyne's unit was disbanded after the battle of El Alamein in late 1942 but the master illusionist carried on his work with Operation 'Fortitude' and other deceptions.

20   That the Luftwaffe did not carry out even minimal reconnaissance of the east coast must rank as a miracle of the same dimensions as the destruction of the Armada in 1588. German records of April, May and June 1944 show how the assessment of the threat from England gradually changed. On 29 April the intelligence section of Foreign Armies West decided that the Allied invasion forces must already be assembled and ready to embark...A fortnight later - on 15 May the Germans decided that new formations, including US forces, were appearing in south-east England. Deception In World War II by Charles Cruickshank (Oxford University Press 1979).

From the 'Ultra' intercepts code-breakers were also able to monitor the success of 'Fortitude' disinformation provided by 'Double Cross' agents such as Dusko Popov ('Tricycle' - so named because he liked three in a bed sex) and Roman Garby-Czerniawski. Juan Pujol Garcia, a Catalan; code-name, 'Garbo', was the top double agent to work for British intelligence and his contribution to 'Fortitude South' was crucial. Known to his German paymasters as 'Arabel', he had in fact been working for the Allies since 1942. With his security service handler 'Garbo' constructed a network of twenty-seven completely fabricated sub-agents across the length and breadth of Britain and fed the German intelligence station in Madrid a rich diet of misinformation carefully prepared in London. About 500 wireless messages were sent to German intelligence officers in the months leading up to D-Day. 'Garbo' was finally allowed to send an apparently harmless message at 2020 hours on 5 June suggesting that from this point onwards the Germans should be monitoring their radio all night to hear the latest reports instead of just listening in at prearranged times. Not until 0608 hours on 6 June did 'Garbo' make contact to ultimately complete la Grande illusion.

To prevent the Germans moving troops to Normandy from other parts of France 'Fortitude South II' took place after the Normandy landings and again used false communications to help convince the enemy that FUSAG would soon be crossing the English Channel and land in the area near Calais. 'Ironside' conveyed the impression that two weeks after the first landings a second invasion would be launched on the west coast of France directly from the United States and the Azores. To prevent them moving the 11th Panzer-Division near Bordeaux north into Normandy, a controlled agent in Britain, known as 'Bronx', sent a coded message to her German controller in the Banco Espirito Santo in Lisbon: 'Envoyez tnte cinquante livres. J'ai besoin pour mon dentiste.' This indicated 'that a landing would be made in the Bay of Biscay on about the 15th June'. The Luftwaffe ordered the immediate destruction of four airfields close to the coast. Another diversion, Operation 'Copperhead', was mounted on 26 May when Lieutenant Meyrick Clifton-James of the Royal Pay Corps a Montgomery look-alike, who for years had toured the provinces as a bit-part actor, visited Gibraltar and Algiers to suggest an attack on the Mediterranean coast.

From 22 May 1944 a new watch system for Overlord was adopted at Bletchley. Ultra decrypts revealed in May that the Germans had carried out an anti-invasion exercise, based on the assumption that the landings would take place between Ostend and Boulogne. Two weeks before D-Day an 'Enigma' decrypt revealed that Rommel had moved a fresh division into the very area of the 82nd Division's dropping-zones around Ste-Sauveur-le-Vicomte. On 1 June the Anglo-American team began to use 'Colossus', the world's first computer to break German codes, developed at the Post Office Research Laboratory at Dollis Hill. Finally, on 2 June, Bletchley felt able to report: 'Latest evidence suggests enemy appreciates all Allied preparations completed. Expects initial landing Normandy or Brittany followed by main effort in Pas-de-Calais.'

A report submitted to Hitler at midday on D-Day made clear the extent of the Germans' miscalculations. 'Not a single unit of the 1st US Army Group located north and south of the Thames has so far been committed. The same is true of the ten to twelve formations stationed in central England and in Scotland.' The report concluded that this could only suggest a further large-scale operation in the Channel, which one must expect to be made against the Pas de Calais.

Chapter 2

'The Days Are Really Long Now'

'The Atlantic Wall was a myth...any resolute assault was bound to make a breakthrough anywhere along it in a day at most.'

Feldmarschall Gerd von Rundstedt. Born in 1875 the son of a Prussian family, he had resigned in 1938 in protest at Hitler's sacking of the army's commander, but commanded army groups in 1940 and 1941. He was forcibly retired twice during the war due to clashes with Hitler but he was recalled and became Commander in Chief West in 1942. To von Rundstedt Hitler was always 'that Bohemian corporal' (the Führer's rank in WWI) and Rommel, the 'Marschall Bubi' (the boy Marshall). von Rundstedt rarely left his HQ at Ste-Germain-en-Laye where he enjoyed dining early on eintopf, a meat and vegetable stew before reading paperback whodunnits, especially those of Agatha Christie. He complained that the only troops under his direct command were the guards outside his HQ. Von Rundstedt was captured in 1945 and taken to Britain where he was accused of war crimes but were not proceeded with because of his poor health. He was held in captivity until 1949 and after his releases he lived in Hanover until his death in 1953 aged 78.

'If we do not stop the invasion and drive the enemy back into the sea, the war will be lost.'
Adolf Hitler.

'Our landings in the Cherbourg-Havre area have failed to gain a satisfactory foothold and I have withdrawn the troops. My decision to attack at this time and place was based on the best information available. The troops, the air force and the navy did all that bravery and devotion to duty could do. If any blame or fault attaches to this attempt, it is mine alone.'

General Dwight D. Eisenhower's prepared speech which he drafted, without telling anyone, some time on 5 June, in the event D-Day did not succeed. (Perhaps because of the pressure he was under, he dated it July 5). When he had written this, he put it in his pocket in case it was needed. Six weeks later, he found it again, still in his pocket.

When the war broke out Jim Tuff was in the cruiser HMS *Kent*, as personal servant to the C-in-C China Station, Admiral Sir Percy Noble. Then, after the Kent was torpedoed in the Mediterranean and came home for repairs, they sent him on a coxswains' course and then to the River Medway on landing craft. Then he went to Dover to the Royal Marine Siege Regiment, to help crew one of their cross-Channel 13.5 inch rail guns and then, on 30 November 1943, he was sent to Devizes to join the 2nd Royal Marine Armoured Support Regiment, where he was introduced to the Centaur tank fitted with a 95mm howitzer. The Centaur was a variant of the British Army's new 27-ton Cromwell, but with a less successful engine because of shortages of the Meteor, the tank version of the legendary Rolls Royce Merlin used in the Spitfire and Lancaster.

'That's the thing about Marines - we're such a versatile lot. As we used to say about the difference between us and the Guards, 'Not so big, but twice as smart!'

'We drove down to Southampton and parked our Centaur in the streets and then you were put into an encampment. It was a sealed area - the civilians and everybody were sealed in. We were in with some French Canadians from the 3rd Canadian Division, because we were going to be landing with them. There were landing craft everywhere. Six deep. You'd go down the hard [prepared ramp, usually concrete, leading down to the water's edge], load up and the landing craft'd be off, to let another one in.

'There was a mate of mine on another one about two quays along and so I said to my officer could I go and visit this bloke. He came from Norfolk, same as me. I was born in a little village there - beautiful country, away in the wilds, with pheasants running everywhere. My father worked on the land as a teamster - two horses, ploughing with a single-furrow plough. All agricultural work round about was done with horses. Anyway, my officer said he'd have to come with me, so I never did go. The security was so tight. We were all writing letters, though none of them were posted. They just held them, for security. So the families got them all in one batch.

'...Eventually off we went. It was still very choppy. One of our LCT(A)s capsized before we even got past the Isle of Wight. A lot of them didn't make it. If you wanted to get out of the weather you had to get in your tank - there was no troop accommodation. We had a South African officer in our troop, a lieutenant. He was in the Sherman and we had a sergeant in charge of each Centaur. My South African officer went below and I remember him coming back on deck, absolutely green with seasickness. 'I'm coming up on deck Colours', he said. 'It's terrible down there'. Stuffy and claustrophobic. He looked absolutely awful.'

Colour Sergeant Jim Tuff, who would go ashore on the Canadian beach on 6 June. [21]

'On the morning of 6 June we heard on the radio that a large force of both our troops and the Americans had successfully landed on the beaches near Caen and Bayeux and also further down the coast towards Cherbourg. This was very good news and we felt that it would make up for the defeat in 1940 in which I had taken part. Immediately our own Battalion was mobilized and we departed for Southampton. In hindsight, Hitler was our greatest ally. He made the mistake of thinking our attack was a diversionary one and that the main attack was to come in the Pas de Calais area. It was a mistake he repeated many times in the war and, perhaps, had he left it to his generals, we may have lost, instead of won.'

Ron Mailey, 4th AGRA Signals, in a holding battalion in Kent.

'We were on guns at dawn on 6 June watching huge fleets of planes and gliders bound for France. We were warned to expect dive-bombers, rockets and God knows what. We prayed for the boys going over. Overlord had begun.'

Gunner Alfred Sewell, 124 Light AA Regiment Royal Artillery, Lewes, Sussex.

---

21   Adapted from *Invaders: British and American Experience of Seaborne landings 1939-1945* by Colin John Bruce (Chatham Publishing 1999).

'I was catching a bus to work when I noticed things were different. Usually the town was full of commandos and as I stood there, wondering what was different it came to me... silence. There were no boots, no troops, not even the usual singing. We were planting tomato plants on the farm, so we didn't miss anything in the air over the Isle of Wight. We saw the planes returning, some on fire and some with smoke pouring from them and many spaces in their formations.
June Telford.

'When I joined the 5/7th Gordons they were training for the invasion of Normandy. I was quite proud to be joining, as my father served in the 7th Battalion Gordons in World War One. Plus we had heard so much about the famous 51st Highland Division and their exploits against Rommel in the desert campaign. All we did was train and you could feel the tension in the air. We knew that the invasion was coming and the old hands knew what was in front of them. I was going to win the war single-handed. Dream on Bruce. What an idiot! Us young lads did not know what it was like to really be under enemy fire and still thought that war was a great adventure. That thought would soon be shattered and quite a few of us did not survive. One day all leave was cancelled and we were moved nearer the coast and put in a huge compound under canvas. The Battalion was on the move and heading for the embarkation port and the invasion.'
Stan Bruce, 5th/7th Battalion, The Gordon Highlanders.

'We didn't know, of course, when D-Day was going to be - in fact we knew very little about anything. We were given training directives and facilities in Norfolk at that time were quite good. But there were things other than training to be dealt with. Everyone had been abroad for a very long time. Leave was the first thing. I remember we got as many people as we possibly could away on leave. I forget how long they had now, but this was the first time they had seen their families for a long time.

'One other aspect is that we were back in England again for the first time after a considerable number of years and this meant being at home as opposed to being in the desert where there were virtually no inhabitants, so all needed reminding of the importance of local public relations, which in our case included the people of Kings Lynn and the villages around it which we would be passing through for training. We were trying to weld ourselves into the community and become part of it, although we knew we weren't going to be there for very long. The people of that part of England were open-hearted and kindness itself and they gave us a marvellous welcome - they could not have made us more at home.

'There was also a memorable day which General Erskine, our divisional commander, arranged specially for the division and that was an investiture at the Palace, when every member of the Division who was due to receive a medal, won during the previous months and years abroad, was included, so it was very much a family affair at Buckingham Palace. All these things, including the visits, tended to raise our spirits and morale and made us feel we were in for something very important.

'Training directives indicated that we were going to be fighting in fairly close country and in the event, when we got to Normandy, we found the so-called bocage country there even more restricting and close than even we had anticipated. It was, because of its nature, almost as great a change from Italy as the desert had been to Italy, because the fields were so very, very small, with high banks with hedges on top of them dividing up the fields, making fields of view and tank movement very, very difficult indeed. Of course, the Germans had the advantage over us there - they were familiar with it.

'Of course we were aware from the start that we were going to take part in the invasion of Europe, but we didn't know where we were going. Very late on, all the officers had to assemble at some cinema somewhere and the Army Commander, General Miles Dempsey, was to address us. I had served under him for a short time when he was commanding XIII Corps with his headquarters in Syria. He very kindly spotted me in the audience and had a few words with me and something I said must have caused him to say, 'But surely you know you're going to...' and he got 'Nor' out and then he checked himself. He said, 'Didn't you know?' He had stopped at 'Nor', so I thought Norway. Then he realised we didn't know - weren't supposed to know - so he deftly changed the subject. I went round in a haze for the next day or so, wondering if we were going to Norway or Normandy!

' So it was as closely kept a secret as that, right up to the end and when our time came to get ready finally, we moved out of our areas in Norfolk down to camps, very sparse, primitive tented camps - but perfectly adequate for the purpose, in Essex. It was there that our camps were sealed, or we were sealed into them and we were briefed properly and allowed to brief right down to soldier level - but up 'till then, no-one had known. 'It's very relevant to talk about fear. The unknown that we were going into meant uncertainty. You don't know and uncertainty very naturally leads to apprehension and so the adrenalin is flowing, quite rightly. I don't think fear actually comes into one's thoughts until one is confronted with something dangerous, but the apprehension is there all the time. I would say I felt really frightened on several occasions. I think too, that the definition of war (which is anonymous, though someone may lay claim to it) that 'War consists of long periods of intense boredom, punctuated by short periods of intense fright', is a good one. I think it was coined for the First War and it was very relevant for the Second War too.

'Once confronted with a situation, there are certain sorts of fear. I think the predominant sort of fear, in the case of some, is 'Am I going to be up to this myself?' I think it's awfully important to recognise that - it takes a certain amount of personal drive to overcome it and to say, 'Yes, I am'.

'Certainly, while people were very frightened, they went on because they felt they couldn't possibly not go on. Esprit de corps is very important for morale because you drive yourself to meet the challenge and you know other people are meeting it too and you are going to be in it with them.'

Lieutenant Colonel Michael Forrester DSO MC (later Major-General CB CBE DSO MC) - CO of I/16th Queens, was serving with his Regiment in Palestine when war broke out. Joining the 7th Armoured Division, he fought through Greece, Crete, the Western Desert and the Italian invasion before returning with the 'Desert Rats' to train for the European invasion.

'Father had arrived from France on 4 June and we were planning a simple family lunch for my mother's birthday. Speidel kept saying he was not sure the landings had taken place and father should continue with his intention of speaking to Hitler about the strategy of repelling the invasion. My father disagreed with the other generals over this. He favoured a confrontation on the landing beaches while von Rundstedt wanted the

Panzer divisions to be kept back to the north of Paris. Father was very calm and cautious, as always. He agreed Speidel should call back in an hour but he began packing immediately. When the call came, Speidel told him the landing had happened. The Navy had told my father before he left France that no landing would be possible because the seas were too stormy. It had not been an easy decision for my father to return to Germany but he had believed the Navy. Now he was getting reports of Allied landings from all parts of the coast. He was calm but he was not happy that he had been at home when it all happened. He left immediately for the 500-mile journey back to Normandy to lead the men who had long expected the invasion, yet had been caught by surprise just the same. Mother took it completely in her stride. I talked to my father a lot about how the invasion happened. For a long time, everyone thought the Allies would land in the Pas de Calais because it was the nearest point to the English coast, only 25 miles away. On the other hand, the German fortifications were strongest there, so Normandy began to be considered the likeliest.

'One thing everyone believed was that the Allies would first have to capture and hold a harbour. But, of course, they brought over their own mobile 'Mulberry' harbour - a masterstroke by Churchill, which no one could ever have imagined.

'My father was tremendously impressed with the organisation and the imagination Involved. It was a glorious battle for the Allies and, as a soldier, he admired them greatly. Father knew from North Africa that the British were good soldiers. But, as he said, Normandy showed him they were even better than he had presumed. He knew by then that Germany could not win the war. He had often discussed it with me. He said anyone with common sense could see that the only solution on the Western Front was to achieve a position in which to make peace. He would say: 'Even if you have to give in, as long as you are strong, you can achieve peace'

Fifteen-year-old Manfred Rommel, about to celebrate his mother's 50th birthday on 6 June. On 5 June, because the weather in northern France was so bad that he did not think an Allied invasion would take place at this time, Field Marshal Erwin Rommel travelled from the Normandy front to Herrlingen near Ülm in Swabia, southern Germany to be with his family and to give his wife Lucie-Maria a pair of grey shoes before seeing Hitler at Berchtesgaden to ask him for two more Panzer divisions. At 7 am Generalmajor Hans Speidel, Chief of Staff of the 7th Army in Normandy told them the long-feared invasion had started. Rommel rang the Berghof to cancel his visit with Hitler and he set out for France immediately and was back at his HQ at the Château de la Roche-Guyon at 16:00 hours on 6 June. That evening Rommel was angered when he found that the Panzer Lehr and 12th Waffen-SS Panzer Division were not under his command. Had they been, he would have ordered them closer to the coast and in position to deliver an immediate counter-attack. Rommel said, 'If I was commander of the Allied forces right now I could finish the war off in fourteen days... If Montgomery only knew the mess we are in, he'd have no worries tonight.' Ironically, this was the second time that Rommel had the misfortune to be away from his HQ at a turning point of the war; in November 1942 he had missed the start of El Alamein.

'I was asleep when the invasion began. The first bombardment started at about lam and it was so loud and shocking that all of us knew instantly it was something out of the ordinary. I shot out of bed and went straight to the battalion staff quarters to organize

my men. Then we hung around until 0700, waiting for orders. Feldmarschall Rommel was away and so was our divisional commander so there was no one to give orders. We were told to push on to the coast in our armoured personnel carriers and we had almost got there when we fell upon English troops. I've no idea to this day who they were but they were on foot. During that night, my battalion lost three-quarters of the men. I've no doubt that if we had not wasted those valuable first hours waiting for orders, we could have pushed the Allies back right away. Those hours from 0100 to 0700 were critical and our tanks were left idle for too long.'
Panzer Leutnant Günter Halm.

'So it's started then!'
Adolf Hitler's seemingly unconcerned response after lunch on D-Day when the Führer finally appeared and was told of the 'invasion'. Hitler held his first meeting about the landings at 1400.

'About midday the usual assemblage collected for the briefing conference, but on this particular day there was a Hungarian state visit in honour of which the conference took place in Kiessheim castle, at least an hour by road from the offices of those involved. As usual when visitors were involved, it was a showpiece, but in view of the events in the west a preliminary conference took place in a room next to the entrance hall. I and many of the others were keyed up as a result of the portentous events which were taking place and as we stood about in front of the maps and charts we awaited with some excitement Hitler's arrival and the decisions he would make. Any great expectations were destined to be bitterly disappointed. As often happened, Hitler decided to put on an act. As he came up to the maps he chuckled in a carefree manner and behaved as if this was the opportunity he had been waiting so long to settle accounts with his enemy. In unusually broad Austrian he merely said, 'So, we're off.' '…the usual overestimates of German forces and confidence in 'ultimate victory' were more than normally repellent.'
General Walter Warlimont, the Oberkommando der Wehrmacht (OKW) Deputy Chief of Operations. It was not until nearly 1700 that Hitler finally gave permission to move just two armoured divisions and the counter-attack could not be mounted until the morning of 7 June, by which time the bridgehead was 30 hours old and it was too late. Hitler and many of his generals, believed that Normandy was simply a diversion for a larger attack on Calais, a view he clung to until August 1944.

'*Jane* was much more than a cartoon character. She became Britain's unofficial weapon in the war. The troops avidly followed the daily cartoon strip showing how she constantly lost her clothes but never her virtue and it was a great help in boosting their morale. The popularity of the cartoon meant I had a very busy war, making frequent public appearances for the Armed Forces. I also had a stage show called *Jane In The Mirror*, which toured the country in 1944. By the time we arrived in Bournemouth in June, it was clear that a big push was about to get under way. There were troops everywhere and there were even tanks in the cul-de-sac where our theatrical boarding house was situated, with soldiers busily waterproofing their vehicles.
'One day the manager of the theatre in Bournemouth called me into his office. When I got there, I was told the army wanted me to go and entertain some troops in the New Forest. They had been due to land in France as part of a major military operation, but

had been unable to leave because of bad weather and were getting very restless. I was put into a car, with curtains all around the passenger windows so I could not see where I was going and driven off to an unknown destination. I found myself in the middle of an American army camp. There were marquees and tents and soldiers sitting around looking absolutely bored. When the soldiers saw me, I was given a marvellous welcome. I gave a little speech wishing them luck, sung them some songs and got one of the boys up on stage.

'The next day I was asked to entertain more troops and was again driven off with curtains over the passenger windows. We arrived at what I now know was Hurn airport in Bournemouth, which had been turned into an RAF base. This time I was entertaining British Typhoon pilots from 182 Squadron and I did a similar impromptu performance for them which also got a great reception. Amid all the excitement, though, could not help wondering how many of them would come back.

The next day we were all backstage at the theatre and we heard the invasion had taken place. There was great excitement, but a lot of people were also very worried. I don't think I had realised at that stage that this was the big thing, as there had been so much talk about a threatened invasion and so many small battles.

'The day after D-Day Jane did her bit for the war effort by appearing nude in the Daily Mirror for the first time - very tastefully, of course, because although Jane oozed sex appeal, part of her charm was that she was also very innocent. They dropped a consignment of the papers to the troops near Caen at the Pegasus Bridge and they made huge advances into France after that. The joke during the war was that the British Army always attacked when Jane stripped to her scanties. I don't know if there was any truth in it, but she certainly had an active role in the D-Day landings.

'I read in the newspapers that the first tank to land in Normandy had a Jane cartoon painted on its side and I also have letters from soldiers who took part, telling me how they had Jane painted on their lorries and tanks. One platoon even went over with a series of Jane cartoons - depicting her undressing for a bath - painted on their four half-track vehicles. The one on the fourth vehicle showed Jane her in her bra and knickers! Sadly, they had to scrub them off shortly after the landing, because they were about to be inspected by Monty. It was amazing how the cartoon strip caught people's imaginations at that time. The boys just adopted me and they always made a tremendous fuss of me.

'The funny thing was that I became Jane purely by accident. I was the youngest of eleven children from Eastleigh, Hampshire and came up to London to see my sister, who was on her own because her husband had been taken ill. I had only just left school and had never had a job, so I decided to earn some money by modelling for art students. When I first posed nude, I felt rather strange, but soon I realised that as far as the artists were concerned I might as well be a flower vase, so I did not feel as if I was being ogled. I was modelling for a class one day in 1940, when Norman Pett, the cartoonist who had recently created Jane, came in. He had been using his wife as a model, but she was a golf fanatic and wanted to be out on the course, so he was looking for a new model. He saw me and said 'That's Jane' and asked me to work for him - and it all snowballed from there.

'It was a dog's life trying to get nice clothes and shoes in the war, but I had to because it was my job to look nice to boost the boys' morale. They certainly boosted mine in return - I was showered with attention and received endless proposals of marriage, including 62 in one week! One of the worst things was the lack of heating in the theatres, as they were trying to conserve energy because of the war. I had to cover myself with brown body make-up for every show and afterwards - standing on newspapers in a freezing room - wash it off with cold water. I hated the awful food and the dreadful digs in which we often ended up and I loathed the way the lights were blacked out. When my show was on in London I used to stay with my sister and her husband in Wimbledon and he would ride to the theatre with my bike to escort me home. Often with bombs going off all around us, we would ride back with Fritz - the dachshund from my cartoon who also appeared in the stage show - sitting in my wicker basket on the front of my bike. When I went back to the theatre the next day I would see big craters in the road I had cycled over the night before, but, maybe because I was just young and stupid, it never scared me.

'After D-Day I kept in touch with the Typhoon pilots of 182 Squadron. It was through the squadron that I met my husband, Arthur, who was one of its flying officers and we got married just before the end of the war. It had to be very secretive as *Jane* was supposed to be available to be adored by everyone.'

Christabel Leighton-Porter, the model for Jane, the popular saucy wartime cartoon strip which appeared in the *Daily Mirror*. Christabel continued modelling for the *Jane* cartoon until 1959 when it ended and she concentrated on bringing up her son Simon, who also joined the RAF and became a squadron leader.

Lance Corporal Wingfield, an infantryman of the Queen's Royal Regiment and his platoon stood by their kits, ready for inspection. Their platoon sergeant stepped forward and announced: 'The Company Commander will now inspect you and your kit for the last time before you go overseas. He is a man of vast experience. He will ask each of you a question of vital importance to see if you are ready for battle. You must know the answer to that question. It may save your life one day.'

When the Company Commander came to Wingfield, he walked all around him then halted. The Lance Corporal stared 'frozen-faced at his Adam's apple' waiting for that 'question of vital importance'. It was: 'How many needles in that housewife of yours?'

Lance Corporal Wingfield was killed in action eight months' later.

'We were on our way. Little did we all know that we were to go through parts of London where we lived. One of my mates who joined up with me and who was our piano player, saw his mum in Leytonstone. We all looked a sorry sight by now because the fumes of the engines were coming through into our vehicles and it was making, us all look as if we were crying. We came down the A 12 through Wanstead, Gants Hill, Whalebone Lane and then there I was passing the fields that, as kids, I used to play on. I could see the ponds that we used to go fishing for newts and tadpoles. Next came Mawney Road roundabout, only a few yards from home. I could see the barber shop where my brother George and I used to have our hair cut and then there was the 'Marlborough Arms' with the fish and chip shop next door. Then, to my surprise I saw my sister Kath standing by the Post Box only a few yards away. I am sorry to say that she didn't see me; maybe it was for the best though. We then passed North Street, Pettit's Lane, Gallows Corner and then all of a sudden it was gone. I remember thinking to

22 *British Liberation Army 1944-45* by the late Charles Whiting. Spellmount Ltd, 2008.

myself 'will I ever see this again'? Maybe I would or maybe I wouldn't. One thing we all knew was that a lot of us would not be coming home.

'Tilbury was our port and we stayed in a transit camp for the night while our vehicles were loaded onto the ships. One thing that really annoyed us was that the dockers were on strike and they refused to load our transport. Our own engineers and the ships cranes had to do the job. The names we called those dockers; well they are unrepeatable. As we went to board the ships the people of Tilbury lined the streets to bid us farewell. They did all right because we all threw all our spare change to the children. The ship we were on was really dirty. It was an old Yankee ship, called *Samsit*. We didn't know what it was used for before but the holds stunk of everything. We had hammocks to sleep in and it was also the start of many months of not removing our clothes.

'We set sail from Tilbury, what time of day or night it was I hadn't a clue. We moored off Southend to wait for the other ships coming out of Tilbury and London. We woke next morning to find we were on the move. We were not allowed on deck but by standing on ladders we were able to look out and we could then see the huge convoy of ships being escorted by the Royal Navy destroyers. We sailed through the Straits of Dover and lay off the Isle of Wight to wait for the arrival of more ships from the south coast. We were told these ships held the rest of our Division. We were soon on our way again.'

Rifleman Eric Patience, who joined the 8th Battalion Rifle Brigade, part of the 11th Armoured Division, in May 1942. After over a year's training he was expecting to be sent to the Middle East to support Monty's 8th Army. Instead, the 11th Armoured Division was kept back for the invasion of Normandy.

'I lived with American troops in the barracks where they passed their enforced 'purdah' (confinement). And all day long the huge concrete squares rang with the sound of their energy. They played interminable games of volleyball and football and baseball. Then suddenly one morning the squares, instead of being full of racing figures, were dotted with heaps of equipment in long lines. The men stood by their individual piles with their helmets and rifles and life belts around their waists. They piled into lorries and saw the leafy English countryside rush away. And they waved and whistled at the girls. They came by main roads and by lanes, by night and by day and all their journeys led to one or other of the many points by the sea. The men stood in their lines by the shore, waiting for the boats that were to take them out to the bigger ships. And they saw for the first time something of the size of the operation - although everyone saw only one little bit. At our point of embarkation before the assault, they counted the Tank Landing Ships here and the Infantry Landing Craft there and watched dozens of Infantry Assault Craft dashing about among the bigger ships carrying the troops from the shore. They were quiet in the main, although there were always one or two to wave and whistle to the seagoing British WRENS on some of the little ferry boats.'

Robert Dunnet of the BBC with American troops at an embarkation port, broadcast on 6 June 1944.

'You went inside and the gate closed behind you; and that, without any ceremony, was the act of renunciation. Once the gate was closed you could no longer return to the normal world outside, not even to buy a packet of cigarettes at the shop on the corner of the street, nor have a hair-cut, nor telephone your friends. You were committed irrevocably to the landing...

'On board the US transport swing music blasted out eight or ten hours through the day and a black GI sat in the stern peeling potatoes endlessly. It was a time when one had no desire to think or write letters or engage on any distraction from inevitable thing ahead.'

Alan Moorehead, an Australian War Correspondent a veteran of war in ten countries. The captain, who had already made three assault landings in North Africa, Sicily and Salerno, told Moorehead, 'this will be a bad one.'

'Some of them shout farewells, some of them sing. Some are silent. Some of them laugh, some smile, some look thoughtful, some look grim. One thing is common to all of them - an unmistakable air of purpose and resolve. You will now hear some of them calling out: ... 'Hallo, Betty darling - how're you getting on? Back soon when it's all over - don't get worried. George.' 'Cheerio, mother - keep smiling. Up John Smith.' 'Hello, some public house. Save us a pint!' 'We're off on a little trip. Love to you all. Frank.' 'Hallo, Mum and Dad. This is Derek speaking. All the best. We're going to give Jerry all he gave us at Dunkirk and, boy, we're going to give it to him strong.'

BBC reporter, Colin Wills, watching the embarkation.

'I was working in Plessey's underground tunnel at Redbridge, Wanstead, making Spitfire vacuum pumps. I was walking to the top of the road towards East Ham High Street to get my 101 bus from Woolwich when I heard such a noise and thundering. I reached the High Street and thousands of lorries and tanks loaded with soldiers were making their way to Woolwich. They were laughing and waving their hands and Mrs Larkin from Larkin's sweet shop was throwing them packets of cigarettes and chocolates and peanuts. They were catching them and saying, 'Thank you, darling'. The older people were standing by the kerb crying and saying, 'Good Luck, boys', 'God Bless You'... When I walked across the road to get my bus, they all gave me the wolf whistle. I smiled and waved my hand... needless to say, I was crying too.'

Mrs. Nellie Nowlan of Basildon, Essex.

'Getting light now and a few people coming out of doorways, on their way to work I suppose, so are we in a different sort of way... turn down a narrow road, must be near docks - wonder which. A few more people about now - suppose it's around half six... not the kind of send off we would have liked... their faces half awake - wonder - a few waves and one silver-haired old lady coming to our side of the truck and saying, 'Have a fag, boy and Good Luck!'... we're through the dock gates and there are the LCTs which are to be our life on the ocean wave... I wonder what my wife and daughter are doing... I had a sinking feeling at that moment... my father already dead, my brother shot down in Southern France, my father-in-law blinded at Hill 60 in the '14-'18 war... was it going to be my turn next?'

H. L. Barclay, 33rd Armoured Brigade Company, RASC.

'On 2 June, the Friday before D-Day, they told us to be ready to go the following day. Next day they shipped us down to Newhaven harbour, where the LCAs (Landing Craft, Assault) were waiting for us to get on board. I think the idea was that we would sail out of Newhaven at about 21:00, but then the departure was postponed because of bad weather. So we were still in the harbour on Sunday morning and they took us off the LCAs and fed us a fantastic lunch. We got back onto the boats at about teatime, feeling very happy because we had been so well fed! At about 9pm that night the four LCAs carrying our battalion quietly slipped out of the harbour and into the English Channel. We spent the entire Monday at sea and we could see ships from horizon to horizon, all along the Channel. We'd all been issued with French francs and to pass the time at sea the lads were playing cards and gambling with the foreign currency. We'd also been issued with a terrible kind of soap, it was just about impossible to wash with the stuff. At 4am on 6 June, I was trying to shave using this stuff and it was just impossible, so I decided I would just have to invade France wearing a moustache!

Bob Littlar, 2nd Battalion King's Shropshire Light Infantry.

'Concentrated air attacks on the coastal defences between Dunkirk and Dieppe and on the ports strengthen the supposition that the main invasion effort will be made in that area... Since 1 June an increasing number of warning messages has been broadcast to the French Resistance... Air reconnaissance has not observed a great increase in the number of invasion craft in the Dover sector. No flights have been made over the other ports along the south coast of England. It is essential to send reconnaissance planes over all the harbours of the south coast.'

Report by Feldmarschal Erwin Rommel, 3 June.

'A group of Royal Engineers heard that they would be landing on a piece of the French coast called 'Cape Town'. Practice boarding drills were held on the small assault landing craft that the troop-ships carried on the lifeboat davits. On board *Clan Lamont*, Sergeant Smith of the Royal Engineers acquired an unwilling addition to their company. 'We practised jumping into the canvas chutes and sliding down into the landing craft. Unfortunately, one of the soldiers ripped up the chute with the foresight of his rifle. They had to send ashore for a naval sail maker. And having got this chap on board to sew it up, they then discovered that he was a security risk. So this poor chap, who was about sixty-five, had to come with us. He's the only man I ever saw panic in the whole operation.'

D-Day by Warren Tute, John Costello and Terry Hughes (Pan 1974).

'Tonight I have seen the assault force move out from Spithead from the bridge of HMS *Southern Prince* in order to break open the defences of the northern coast of France. Nothing as great, nothing as world changing and gigantic has been undertaken in these waters since 1066. This night we invade the continent of Europe from the west, the awaited hour has poured itself through the hour-glass and tomorrow morning we strike. The sky's grey overhead but the wind is veering northwards and the glass shows signs of rising. The moment is one of great suspense and tomorrow will bring us news of the battle as we await our orders to go forth.'

Lieutenant Michael Chodzko RNVR 5 June.

'My girlfriend knows two other women with men in England. They have put their heads together and have come up with - invasion very near. Looks to me as if the top brass might as well have taken full page ads in all the papers and announced the news.

Women aren't fools. Stop their mail and they begin to add two and two and come up with four. I think such close security is its own biggest gossip.

'... when it's going to take place, where it's going to take place, how rough it's going to be and of course, are we going to hit the beaches?. .'

'God, yes! Bound to be. What the hell do you think we've had all this training for?'

'They've got us pinpointed,' was the common opinion.

'Sure. We'll be the suckers who hit the beaches... they say Engineers will take ninety per cent casualties... Goddamn! Do you have to talk about it? Ain't it bad enough without bringing it up all the time?'

'This is the way I see it. Must be a hundred or two engineer outfits on the damn island. Say our chances of being picked are 150 to one. That's pretty good odds, I'd say.'

'One of the soldiers shuffled a pack of playing cards: 'If they was 1,000 to one, I'd still have the shakes.'

'The whole outfit now has a very bad case of the invasion shakes. Very little talk about anything but assault landings, what it will be like, what the casualties will be etc. Any way you look at it, it's not going to be any piece of cake. After the alert this morning, I caught myself several times looking around and wondering for the hundredth time how the hell 1 got here and what the hell I'm doing here - me, Henry Giles, an old farm boy from Caldwell Ridge, Knifley, Kentucky! For the first time in years a uniform doesn't seem to fit me. A little too tight.'

Staff Sergeant Henry Giles of the 291st Combat Engineer Battalion. He and his platoon had arrived in Britain in October 1943. Since March 1944 they had been intensively training for combat in the Gloucestershire countryside and by the middle of May there was talk of little else but the coming invasion. While waiting Giles complained: 'No work, just a hell of a lot of recreation - baseball, volleyball, basketball, etc.' And double British summer time meant that 'the days are really long now. Doesn't get dark until ten o'clock.'

D-Day Fact File

More than 130,000 men were landed from the sea and over 20,000 men from the air in the first 24 hours. Americans suffered over 6,000 casualties. Casualties in British 2nd Armoured amounted to 4,000 from a force of 82,000.

The end of D-Day established almost 155.000 Allied troops across nearly 80 square miles of France: 55,000 Americans were ashore, plus 15,500 who parachuted or glided across the Channel. Anglo-American co-operation had secured a bridgehead in Normandy.

One out of every eleven Americans who took part in the cross-Channel invasion was dead, missing or wounded. There were 6,000 American casualties (of whom 700 were airborne troops): more than half the total Allied casualties on the day. By the end of July the Americans were the majority Allied force in France with 980,000 troops compared with 660,000 British. By VE-Day 3 million US troops are fighting on the continent.

As night fell on D-Day all five beachheads had been established and 150,000 Allied troops were on French soil along a 50-mile front. 55,000 American and 75,215 British and Canadian troops came ashore during D-Day. In the first six days over 300,000 men, 54,000 vehicles and 104,000 tons of stores were unloaded.

'I was born aboard a houseboat on the Neches River. The water was my second home. I made a promise that I would never be a dogface and have to sleep in the mud and eat cold food. When I read in the paper where the Sutherland brothers had gotten killed, I just couldn't hold myself back. I felt like I was just obligated to go and the wife, went right along with me. She knew how I felt, I suppose. My brother, J. D. Esclavon went in the same time I did because he said if I was going, he was going. So my wife had to sign for me to get in and mother and dad had to sign for J. D. Esclavon to get in. My brother and I were two of the closest people in the world. I was a first class mechanic, diesel engineer on a tow boat hauling oil into Texas City to use to make fuel and all kind of bunkers for our ships and our airplanes. Fortunately I did keep that promise by not being a dog face. I made diesel school, went to the GM plant in Cleveland, Ohio and trained on the engines on the assembly lines and after training at Solomon's Island, Maryland, was shipped us up to New York to a Navy Pier. One night they come into the barracks and they said, 'Pack your gear; we're moving!' And we did. We went to Pier 19 where that old Normandy cruise ship was sunk. We loaded onto a big LST. Our LCT was already down on deck and tied down and we were ready to hit the wild blue Atlantic Ocean and it was wild; 29 days travelling, zigzagging before we could get to Africa.

'We made four invasions, two from Africa. We didn't have the least idea that we would be making history. All through Africa, we didn't have an ice box. Then we started leaving for England and then they put us a doggone ice box in. It was certainly convenient. The cook cooked up as much as he could and we stored it in this big ice box.

'We arrived in Plymouth on 23 December 1943. We thought we were going to have a terrible time in England because all we were used to were seeing these Arab women with their faces covered up. We were really startled when we found out that the people were just like those at home. That really helped make it a great day. Then we met some people and they invited us to their home for Christmas. Two Americans, two Scots and two English servicemen and we really had a swell first Christmas in England. The people were just beautiful and some people don't seem to know what a terrible time the English people had during the Blitz. You could go uptown to Plymouth; that's where all the dry docks were and that's why the Germans tried to knock it out. So their ships couldn't be repaired. But they failed because those little Spitfires were pretty deadly fighters and they kept their porch pretty clear there. They were still using the dry docks when I left.

'About February they called us all into a big room and they swore us to strict secrecy that we would be shot if any of this was divulged to the public. They would come up and grill us but I guess we convinced them because there was no way that we would give out anything on this DD drive tank; a 30 ton Sherman with a big canopy around it. It had a periscope built into it, a bilge pump and a periscope to guide them to the beach. We trained with those on Slapton Sands all summer long and one of them broke down. They had a rope that we could hook onto it and tow it in. My boat would make about 8 or 10 knots and when we hooked on to that 30-ton tank with this big 9 foot high canopy around it, we found to our surprise that running with three 225 horsepower supercharged diesel engines that it wouldn't hardly move that tank. So we just had to wrestle with it and just keep pulling on it till we got it to the beach. Then a big bulldozer come out and hooked on it and pulled it on the beach. But we trained there until we were real efficient in putting them out. They had to have special ramps so you wouldn't drag the canopies off of it or anything.

'The Army had gunnery practice off our LCT shooting targets. It looked like it was impossible because you barely could see with a pair of binoculars. But they would shoot at them and we would wait, it seemed like ten minutes. Finally the big projectiles from those cannons would hit. They knocked this target out with the first shot. Then they went to the second target and one of them missed so they made him do it again. At that time we were, gee, thousands of yards from the beach. It was clear and they hit that darned thing and knocked it out. I just couldn't believe that people could do something like that - knock something out that you couldn't see.

'So I gained great respect from the men in the Army training with our DDs. Our dress of the day was just plain denim blue jeans that the USN issued and a little sock cap that we would wear and that was just great. Even the officers would wear those jeans like that so they wouldn't stand out from the crew showing that they were officers. We trained all summer with these DD tanks. We went into some port and dropped our ramp on the beach and all the boats was just loading up and getting out just as fast as they could. Right then we knew that something was in the air. No one said so but we knew we were getting ready for something because we'd been through it three times before. It gave you a terrible feeling knowing that you were fixing to make a landing somewhere because we had met so much opposition in the other landings we had made. 'The first five days in June, at Weymouth harbour, we were awfully uptight, because the way the traffic was in England and tanks running, big trucks all loaded, we knew that something was coming up. We knew what to get prepared for and we filled up all our fuel tanks and all our water tanks, got a good supply of food and ammo because we didn't know where we were going or how long we would be there. The sailors that were loading up talked in a hushed tone, like it was something anonymous that was coming up and they didn't understand what it was. You could tell from the way they talked that they were fearful because ordinarily the old GI, he's a boastful dog and he would just be popping off all the time as the Navy would. We loaded up the tanks and everything on the LCTs in my flotilla and also the LSTs - they'd hold about 60 or 70 tanks. Silence kind of fell around the harbour. It seemed like you could penetrate it with a knife. People knew that we were getting ready for something, but we didn't know what. We had to get prepared and just wonder where we were going.

'Frankie Powell our signalman was a regular Navy man. He was flags and he had come off of a big cruiser, the USS *Milwaukee* and they let the Russians have it right out in mid-Atlantic and he ended up amphibious force. But that was our gain and their loss. We were the three of the oldest amphibious force men in the European Theater of War. We got all our gear aboard and everything and on deck it was very hushed. No one was making any noises, no one was talking loud. It was like we knew something real dangerous was coming up but we didn't voice it to each other. We kept it to our own selves.

'On June 4 we left Weymouth where we were anchored and we put out to sea. They had a little patrol boat to lead us and they pulled a paravane in the water and it would throw a phosphorous glow into the water and that was the way we would keep up where our lead guide was and we kept pretty much in a tight pack. Then after we got into the open waters, it was so ungodly rough, you couldn't stand on deck. You had to hold on. I don't see how the tanks kept from sliding. I guess the weight of them. They told us to go back into Weymouth and our guides turned around and we went back. We got there the morning of June 5 because we just wallowed around out there in the Channel all night it was just about to roughest voyage I had ever made on one of those LCTs. But, they were made up of just dozens of steel boxes welded together and they had a hatchway in each one of them. We had fresh water in one, diesel fuel in the other one and that was how we carried our supplies.

'After we ventured out into the Channel the night of June the 4th it was so rough, so we went back and tied up in Weymouth. Then we had a terrible air raid. The big Heinkel bombers plastered us and sunk some of our landing barges and stuff. We rode that out and the next afternoon, kind of late, well, this picket boat come around and tell us to get ready and get underway. They weren't hollering it; they didn't call it on the radio or nothing. They just went to each individual landing barge, LCT, LCI and LST and they were telling them to get ready to get underway. Then the armada moved out from Weymouth.'
Joseph Henry Esclavon.

'An Indianapolis boy going to Butler University when the war broke out, I volunteered to join the Navy. I was ordered to attend the Notre Dame Midshipman School and was commissioned an Ensign. We were called '90 Day wonders' because they crammed us through a four year training programme in 90 days and then on to Little Creek on the Chesapeake Bay for more training. I was assigned to be a skipper on a landing craft for tanks. I felt a prodigious pride in commanding one of these. They were 112 feet long, 32 feet wide, three engines, two generators, two 20mm anti-aircraft guns. The hull was constructed with 32 separate watertight compartments so the craft was virtually unsinkable. They had a range of only 700 miles so we were carried on larger ships across the Atlantic. It took us 19 days to cross the Atlantic taking a northern route. The sea was so rough that sometime the ship next to us in the convoy would disappear from sight. I was seasick every one of the 19 days.

'We were launched in Plymouth. One day a British destroyer came into port and gave me a verbal order to meet at the breakwater early the next morning. The escort vessel sailed among the several LCTs and with a loudspeaker instructed us to keep our radios turned off and to follow in single line the ship ahead of us. No sooner had we gotten underway than a heavy fog enveloped us. It was so thick that I had to station a man on the bow to keep a sharp lookout to help us follow. We were underway just a few minutes when the ship ahead of me sent a message that it lost the ship ahead of it. I wasn't too concerned. I was sure the British escort ship would miss our presence and return to look for us. I continued going east but after about an hour I realized we were lost. I had no idea where we were or where we were going. I asked the quartermaster to break out the charts and we assumed a position. We were a few miles east of Plymouth, our starting point. I saw on the map that a naval base was at the south end of the Portland Peninsula so we made that our destination. We approached land just before nightfall and we were challenged by the shore battery and a heavy cruiser. Fortunately we knew the answer to the challenge and we continued. We did notice some debris in the water but gave it little thought. We were more concerned with the mines that the charts said were ahead of us. We gave them a wide berth and about 01:00 entered the harbour.

'There were many ships and crafts and the place was so crowded I had to look for a place to tie up to. No craft would grant me permission. Later I learned that many of these boats had on them the top secret floating tanks and no one was allowed near them. We finally found a place to tie up and settled in for the night. I was fast asleep when the Bosun opened my hatch and yelled, 'Air raid and God I'm not kidding'. I got out of bed to chew him out because I thought he was still hung over from the night before. Suddenly a bomb exploded near us that knocked me off my feet. This was everybody's first encounter with the enemy. We manned our battle stations and when the searchlights got the airplane in its sights every ship opened fire. It was like a hundred 'Fourth of Julys' in one night. The tracers from our shells lit up the sky. Our shells had to come back down and it was a wonder we didn't kill ourselves. The irony was that our 20-millimeter guns were not powerful enough to reach the airplane. It was too high. The big guns shot it down and we all got a feeling of satisfaction.

'The next morning I went ashore. I reported at headquarters that I didn't know where I was supposed to be. I was talking to a yeoman when a commander overheard our conversation. He stepped out of his office and asked me where the other ships of the convoy were. I explained what had happened. He replied, 'You mean to tell me that you crossed E-Boat Alley unescorted?' It was then that I realized that that was Lyme Bay, the area where just days before German E boats sank two LSTs with the loss of 551 American lives. The convoy that I left Plymouth with was his charge and he was the flotilla commander. This convoy was to take two days and make a stop at a port for the night. It was too dangerous for ships to be out there at dusk where they are vulnerable to the E-Boat attacks. This conversation with the commander of our flotilla had a bearing on my assignment for the invasion.

'June 3rd I attended a top-secret meeting where I saw pictures and a model of the beach that we were to assault. I was told that the beach would be bombed from the air, that the air force bombers were to make 5,000 sorties and devastate the enemy positions. The army engineers were to blow up a path 50 yards wide to clear out the underwater obstacles. My mission was to enter 'Fox Red' at H plus 220. I was to be in the lead of a column of 10 other LCTs. My instructions were to memorize my point of entry to the beach. I was to memorize only by the contour of the land. I was told that all man-made objects would be destroyed. I went to my group commander and facetiously told him I was not qualified to be the lead ship and the honour should go to someone else. He told me that the order came from the commander himself. He put me up front because he thought I was 'all right'. So the fact that I got lost and crossed Lyme Bay qualified me for the lead position.

'We all went back to our ships and were restricted aboard. Because of this briefing, we now had top secret information and no one was permitted to go ashore. I had a complete crew of 16 men but I was short one officer. A full complement called for two so an officer was assigned to me from the staff. He had just recently gotten his commission, married and shipped overseas in a matter of days. He was in England just one week when he was given temporary orders to be my executive.'

Ensign Joseph Alexander, Officer in Charge, LCT 856.

'This morning the anchorage has suddenly come to life, not as in the last few days with sporadic movement here and there, but this is a large-scale business with columns of smaller ships and craft threading their way down the Channel between the larger ships that still lie moored. These are the preliminary moves that, weather and weather alone, permitting, will develop into the greatest assault on the European shore. We've

watched in the last hour or so a flotilla of fleet sweepers moving down in line ahead down to - down to the west. And among the many hundreds of the larger vessels that still crowd the anchorage as far as the eye can see - the smoke is beginning to pour from their funnels. So the long months of preparation - the weeks of waiting - are within hours of perhaps being over. The first move has been made and under the providence of God the mammoth fleet is now ready to sail.'
Michael Standing of the BBC on board HMS *Hilary.*

'On the decks, in the holds... the soldiers were waiting, for the most part standing about looking out to sea, talking now and then and thinking. In the wardroom: dinner. From the menu, soup, roast beef and green peas and apples and cream. It might have been a crossing to Cherbourg in peacetime. And then you realised that your hand was moving just a little sluggishly to your mouth. Your tummy wasn't just where it usually was. The men around you were rather silent and when they spoke they were self-conscious. It was a roomful of men on the way. Wondering, waiting and listening. On deck, signals were flashing between ships. Enterprise had run up a flag signal. Boat crews were making their final preparations. There was a tenseness and a sense of good humour and good fellowship that were impossible of translation into words.'
Robin Duff, BBC.

'On the whole, everyone is glad. We have known for the past three weeks now that once more *Orion* would have a place in the front line and knowing this, the feeling has been - it's got to come, the sooner the better. Many people will be killed. It certainly will be many, many times worse than Anzio. He's ready for us, knows it must be soon - let's hope that no one has told him where. This afternoon will be one of tension and nervousness - I feel it now, it's only natural. But when the dirt begins to fly tomorrow, I don't think we'll have time to worry about things. If it's our turn, it'll come too quick for us to think about it.'
Ian A. Michie, Leading Radio Mechanic in HMS *Orion.*

'We were located in one of the inside columns and spent our entire time trying to keep station. We had the misfortune to have a British 'lettered craft' behind us which had the ability to go ahead twice as fast as the Americans, but lacked the backing power that we had. We would pound along, the whole boat bending and buckling; then the one ahead would slow down. We would go into full reverse to keep from riding up its stern and then the Britisher would start to climb ours. To avoid collision, we would go full speed ahead with full right rudder and sheer off towards the other column. The vessels of different columns would close to about five feet or less, usually crashing together then separating with one going full speed at right angles to the course of the convoy. All day there was always someone heading off by himself having a wonderful time. Sleep was almost impossible, as you couldn't stay in your sack.'
US Navy Lieutenant, Stanley C. Bodell aboard an American LCT.

'They sealed us all off in the dockyard area around Southampton. We weren't allowed out or to make contact with anyone outside for at least three days before the loadings, but there was a telephone box on the quay and they'd forgotten to disconnect it. You could ring anywhere in England... I used to ring up my girlfriend [who was a nurse] at the nurse's home and ask for her and I always got through.'

Lieutenant Roderick Braybrook, who was in the first LCT to leave Southampton for 'Gold' beach.

'We spearheaded the invasion; we were to go in even before the minesweepers. We were in Southampton Water and I remember the Skipper calling everyone together and saying, 'Right, from such and such an hour the ship is sealed off.' That meant nobody could go ashore or nobody could come aboard and then he said, 'There's one post going out now and there'll be one collection of mail.' Words to the effect that you'd better write your last letters. It wasn't quite as dramatic as that, but that's what it meant... I wrote to my mother and father and of course, my wife, Lisa... and I remember the difficulty that I had in writing those letters because you couldn't write home, 'Well, I'm going into battle. I'm going into the unknown. I might not come back.' You couldn't say any of those things. All you could say was, 'Well, we're off on an adventure and I'm sure we'll be back and when I get back we'll look forward to doing this and that. And you know what a wonderful mother and father you've been' and that sort of thing without making it too sloppy or sentimental. At the same time you could imagine them receiving the letter and reading it. So I didn't want them to say, 'My God, you know this is the last letter we're going to receive from our boy,' so they were very difficult letters to write, there's no doubt about that. However they were written and sent and that was that.'

Joseph Martin, a sick bay attendant on a naval landing craft that was to bombard the beaches in advance of the landings. He found it very difficult to look at his wedding photograph at this time. 'I kept it on board in my sick bay and when times were really 'dodgy' I had to put it away. It was a constant reminder that perhaps I would never see her again... so I used to have to put it out of sight then.'

'I had almost daily reviews of the men's equipment and told them to get rid of anything that was non-essential. But one of our medics had this huge Bible, it was his family bible and I told him, 'Can't you substitute a smaller book?' But he wouldn't budge and so in the end I let it go. Ironically that boy was killed in Normandy...'

Larry McLaughlin.

'To liven matters up, they shaved their heads leaving tufts of hair as diamonds or squares, or sometimes they'd give themselves a Mohican cut or shave it in a line from ear to ear, or from forehead to nape. Next activity was to swap their cigarettes for 'Tommy Cooker' heating tubs - which were pure meths. It wasn't long before the craft was full of drunks, but within twenty-four hours, they were in the thick of the fighting all cool and calm.'

A member of No.7 Beach Group attached to the 4th Canadian Division.

'On 15 May, after nine months of intensive beach battalion training and dry runs at Camp Bradford, Fort Pierce, Solomon's Island and several practice invasions on the English coast, under realistic conditions of live mines on the beach and naval gunfire from supporting ships of the British and American navies, 7th Naval Beach battalion left our training bases for the marshalling area for the invasion of France. As the trucks loaded down with the battle clad men and tons of medical communications, boat repair and hydrographic gear rumbled noisily out of the strangely quiet and vacant camp the feeling of 'this is it' was evident on the grim faces of the veterans of previous invasions and all of the inexperienced men. We could all sense that this was not just another dry run but would be the test for all of the training and individual initiative that we possessed in a battle to obtain a foothold on a European continent.

'As we careened crazily down the narrow country lanes of Devonshire towards our unknown destination some of us started to sing some old songs to break the tension. Since most of our battalion consisted of young men averaging about 19 or 20 years old, it wasn't long before our entire company of trucks and jeeps were yelling away lusty on such refrains as *'Marching Along Together'* and a beach battalion song some of the boys had composed a few months before. It was a relief to get rid of the pent up energy caused by the weeks of waiting. At Paignton we disembarked from our trucks and boarded an awaiting troop train. Everywhere the British people gave us the 'V' for victory sign and they too saw that something was up. They had been waiting for a long time for this occasion since 1939.

'In Dorchester we detrained and an awaiting convoy of trucks transported us to the marshalling area which was located on a large estate outside of the city. Those of us who were assigned to this area were forced in being put on side of a hill in five adjacent buildings. In all of our operations we worked very closely with the army; thus the major portion of the area was composed of army engineers, MPs, infantry and medical units of the 1st Division.

'During the next two weeks our time was spent in writing letters, calisthenics and sports to relieve the minds and bodies of the men. Toward the end of the second week, officers began briefing the leading petty officers as to their definite assignments on the 'manoeuvre'. We were taken under guard into a big room which contained air photographs taken as recently as May 25 by low flying P-38s. And a huge rubber map approximately 20 feet x 10 feet, which showed us in minute detail the exact beaches we were to hit and the types of obstacles and their positions in the water with respect to our particular beaches; the two rows leading back from our beaches to Le Moulin and Vierville-sur-Mer; the sea wall along a portion of the beaches a ridge we could expect to sight on approaching a beach from the water; the gun emplacements; rise and fall tides, the proposed locations for army and navy evacuation centres, ammunition dumps, water and supply depots and the areas to be taken by the Rangers, Airborne troops and more details. In addition we were given several first aid demonstrations, gas mask drills, lectures and demonstrations on German uniforms, markings, weapons and equipment. It may seem incredible that so many men could keep so vital a secret but each and every man was fully informed not only to his particular job but as to the full import of this tremendous undertaking. It can be openly seen that the American fighting man is the best informed in the world.

'On June 1st we were broken into specially formed groups called boat teams, composed of both army and naval personnel and loaded onto trucks. Once more it was evident to all of us that this manoeuvre was soon to begin. Our boat team consisted of 220 men, 41 of whom were from the 7th Naval Beach Battalion and the balance composed of infantry, engineers, MPs and medical men of the assault wave. In an overcrowded port, we the navy clambered aboard the LCI 92 designated by the army as LCI L531. And were assigned to hold #3; 1, 2 and 4 being occupied by army personnel. Once aboard no one was permitted ashore for security reasons. We had been informed that we would not be in the harbour more than three days. Our quarters consisted simply of bunks stacked four high and rows so close together that it was impossible to go between them clad in battle togs. As we scrambled down the ladder we shrugged out of our packs, gas masks and ammunition carriers and carried them in our hands along with our weapons in order to squeeze back to our assigned bunk. We felt reasonably that we would be here for a couple of days anyway so everyone set his mind to that fact.

'From June 1st until the afternoon of June 4th we spent our times playing cards, reading, passing rumours, eating our K, D and C-rations in shifts up on the open deck and waiting our turn to use the limited supply of water in the two wash basins on the ship. Considering the fact that so many men were crowded with equipment into this small space there was little or no bickering or arguing.

'On the morning of June 4, a Sunday, services were held on the open decks and few if any failed to whisper the prayers regarding some protection in the great undertaking we were about to experience. Shortly after noon I went up on the bridge with a pair of binoculars. I could see that already many of the ships had left the harbour and others were getting up steam including our own. The scuttlebutt passed as we were all sure that June 5 would be D-Day and we were going to shove off soon.

'However, around 4 o'clock the ships shut off their motors and by morning of June 5 the harbour seemed full again with ships of all descriptions, LSTs, APAs, LCTs, etc. High winds and stormy weather caused a 24-hour postponement. A good part of the slower vessels such as APAs and LCTs had started out earlier on the 4th were considerably on their way towards France before turning back because of the rough seas. In any event, by noon of June 5 the harbour was again pretty devoid of large and stronger vessels and at 5 o'clock our flotilla of LCIs got under way. We were permitted to remain above deck until blackout time. Fore and aft on both sides of the ship as far as you could see, were ships, ships and more ships. Despite all that lay ahead we somehow were able to drop off to sleep after our boat commander read us Eisenhower's speech. Some of the ship's crew passed down to the less sleepy occasional reports describing huge armadas of airplanes passing overhead towards the French coast for the apparent purpose of softening up the Jerries.'

Chief Yeoman William Garwood Bacon, USNR, naval engineer, 7th Naval Beach Battalion. He was born on 26 June 1920 in Camden, New Jersey and had enlisted in the Navy on Navy Day, 11 November 1941. He had left for England in March on the Mauritania which is sister ship to the Felicitania and was quartered in the fourth deck below. It was only his guitar that saved him from being seasick the whole trip. In England his unit did some combined exercises with the army at Slapton Sands which had similar surface and tides that they would be landing in Normandy. 'Actually it was shell and rocks anywhere from two inches to four inches in diameter and it was impossible to dig a normal foxhole. On one of the live ammunition practice landings we saw what was to be one of the surprise weapons of the war. There were some tanks which would float but when they got in the water they actually did look like a small boat.'

'After the African and Sicilian campaigns, including the Alamein line where I served as Mortar Platoon second in command and became Battalion Transport Officer (BTO), we returned to the United Kingdom in November 1943 [23] . We were told that the brigade would be augmented for the invasion of Europe by numerous other supporting arms and to include medium artillery, certain 'funny' tanks from 79th Armoured Division, barrage balloons and an anti-aircraft artillery regiment. There were to be about 3,000 vehicles under brigade command for the invasion itself, compared to maybe 900 or 1,000 in the normal strength brigade. We immediately began combined operations training in Essex and Suffolk. At the same time, we began acquiring new vehicles and gradually waterproofing them to enable them to drive through moderately deep water. All the while we continued to teach driving skills to our private soldiers and NCOs, most of whom had never driven at all. On the whole, drivers were self disciplined. After all, if they misbehaved, they would be returned to rifle companies in their infantry battalions and endure the much more rigorous infantry training and combat experience.

'Our training was interspersed with small exercises and then in April we moved to the New Forest area near Romsey, north of Southampton. Travelling by motorcycle on this two day move in showery weather, I developed malaria, presumably acquired in Tunisia, or Sicily. For several days doctors thought I had influenza and then an American navy doctor at the Netley Naval Hospital near Portsmouth found the malaria bug in blood samples.

'On a comic note, my Brigadier, Ronnie Senior, visited me in hospital and was put out a bit to receive a sharp reply when he addressed a senior American nurse as 'sister,' which is, of course, a very proper rank in British nursing. My wife had been sent for because of my high temperature and my mother accompanied her. I remember my wife's disgust when the Brigadier thought my mother was my wife, believing my wife to be much too young to be married. Fortunately I recovered in time to rejoin my unit a couple of weeks before D-Day.

'The move to Romsey placed us close to open spaces for manoeuvres and to the coast for combined operations exercises. All this culminated in a mock assault on the Isle of Wight. One of the lessons from that assault was that much of our vehicle waterproofing was quite inefficient. Many vehicles 'drowned,' causing us to reappraise our methods and to check on and improve the waterproofing of all our vehicles. We were, of course, a well blooded, experienced infantry brigade with several major campaigns behind us. But this extra training was vital to bring us up to the standard required for the biggest combined operation of all.

'About ten days before D-Day we moved nearer to Southampton. In fact, we were almost in the city in tented accommodation on Southampton Common and from that time on we were forbidden to leave camp, or to telephone, or to have any contact with anyone outside the camp. Our vehicles had been moving onto ships in small groups for

---

23 'Out of action, the prime purpose of the BTO's job was to coordinate the activities of the MTOs [Motor Transport Officers] of the subordinate units, to make sure they carried out all army orders concerning vehicles and driving. This meant ensuring that maintenance and training were properly carried out and that vehicles were correctly equipped and secure when they could not be parked in guarded compounds. In action, the BTO was in command of 'B' Echelon, comprising all non-fighting vehicles and having under his command the Brigade Electrical and Mechanical Engineer, and Brigade Royal Army Service Corps officer as well as battalion MTOs and quarter-masters. He was responsible for ensuring that officers under his command, or supervision, properly serviced forward units with food, water, ammunition and other essential supplies. When the brigade was on the move, in a non-combat situation, he had to send scouts ahead of the main body, to find suitable parking for all the numerous vehicles well before they arrived.'

some time. They were dispersed over a number of ships to minimize losses by a particular unit in the event of ship sinkings. This was a major lesson learned in the Sicily invasion when our field regiment, that is the 74th, suffered many truck losses when the ship carrying them was sunk. The direct result was that three battalions, 6th, 8th and 9th Durham Light Infantry had to yield their personnel carrying 3-ton trucks to the 74th Field Artillery Regiment - to tow its guns. And then of course, the infantry companies, deprived of their troop carriers, had to march rapidly over 100 miles in two days and a bit in intense July Mediterranean heat, so that they were exhausted on arrival at Primosole Bridge in front of Catania and were quite unable to deal with the German paratroops newly flown in from rest and recreation in southern France. Other infantry battalions suffered similarly.

'On 1 June we left camp and marched the few miles to Southampton docks. This was a strange experience because the road was lined at frequent intervals with military policemen wearing green arm bands. That was a rare sight indeed. I do not recall ever seeing policemen with green arm bands on any other occasion. There were few visible civilians as we marched through the streets. Clearly they were being held back from those streets. We marched straight on to LCI 502 of the US Navy. This brought back miserable memories of the invasion of Sicily when the British LCI I was on struck an offshore rock and we were stranded on it. Fortunately, the rock held us firmly and we could not sink. The Italians began to bombard us with heavy mortars and we were all very nervous because of our indefensible position. When the ramps were lowered it was clear that disembarkation would have to take place in more than six feet of water. This was something of a problem because although we might have got ashore, had we been unencumbered - every man coming off that ship had to carry something ashore. And then, whatever he took had to be serviceable, for use as soon as he got ashore. Fortunately, the Naval Officer in Command was already ashore and we borrowed his landing craft personnel (LCP - which we called the Admiral's Barge) and were soon carried ashore.

'Reverting to Southampton, the next day or so was spent in loading rations and other supplies, including radios, bicycles and several other items. For my part, I was to carry a mountaineering rucksack. This held a 24-hour or it might have been a 48-hour ration pack, clean underclothes and socks, shaving kit and a white towel wrapped around a bottle of Johnny Walker red label scotch whiskey together with 200 'Gold' Flake cigarettes; not in a carton, but in a yellow paper wrapper. The whiskey and cigarettes belonged to the brigade officer's mess. In addition, I was equipped with a 75cc James Airborne Motorcycle to use in the early days of the campaign until my jeep came ashore.[24] The little motorcycle was not heavy, but impossible for one person to carry down a landing craft ramp, so my batman, Private Blair, a canny wee Scot, had worked beforehand with one of our mechanics to produce two two-foot long steel tubes, each with a U-shape kink in the middle. The idea was for one of the tubes to go through each wheel from side-to-side, so that we could carry the bike ashore between us. We had some rehearsals and mutually agreed, because of our different heights, that he would take the tube through the front wheel and I, the rear.'

---

24 'Our brigade major, Lord Long of Wraxall, had agreed to take my jeep in exchange for his Humber four wheel drive staff car, an offer which no junior officer could refuse. The reason for his generosity was not altruism, but that the jeep was more suited to his visits to units in forward areas.'

Captain William John Arnold, 9th Battalion, Durham Light Infantry, born on 5 December 1921 at Henlow. He had enlisted as a rifleman in the King's Royal Rifle Corps, on 5 February 1941.

'Little did I know that I would take a wild ride into history in a Higgins Landing Craft, an LCVP. My crew and I picked up the landing barge at Little Creek, Virginia. There were no numbers, no nothing on it. The only thing that was stamped on the barge was a 'No Smoking' sign. Ed Meadows, my bowman was from up in the mountains of eastern Kentucky. John Lofton my Sternman was from somewhere about a hundred miles east of Houston, Texas and my Motor Machinist Mate was a boy by the name of Harry Anton. He had learned diesel motors well. He was very, very adept. I was the coxswain. At that time I was a Seaman First Class and everybody called me Larry. And I was very proud to be a part of this group. My crew and I then took off for destinations unknown. We were given a compass reading and told, 'Now way out there in the Atlantic on the horizon, you will see a ship and it's a quite sizable ship and it has big booms on it and derricks an davits and everything and you just go out there and you'll find it. It's got a great big '33' on the bow. And when you find that ship, that's your ship. They'll hoist you aboard and cradle your barge and then you will be assigned. So, that's what we did and we went aboard the *Bayfield*.

'After a few days aboard ship we were assigned to different boat divisions. There were three boat divisions and I was assigned to the first boat division. Then they told us to paint our number on our barge. Well my number ended up as PA 33-3. So we painted our barge and we painted it inside and out. We got a great big stencil that they had made for us I think in the carpenter's shop aboard ship and they brought it to us and with the paint brushes and the stencil and we put the numbers on our LCVP.

'We went on shake down cruises and on manoeuvres and we got to be pretty good at running this little boat and taking on troops. Then we were told that we were going to be in this big convoy, so we went back to New York and I swear I believed it was Pier 13. We picked up troops and then we embarked for Britain. We landed in Scotland arriving on the 22nd February 1944. At Weymouth, Falmouth and Plymouth we did a lot of manoeuvres. We went through several nights of bombings. It seemed to me that it was sometime around midnight on 5 June, like the rest of the guys, I couldn't sleep, so I ended up in the galley and so my crew came on up and we all were sitting around drinking coffee and they were telling us that the weather was pretty foul and they didn't know what they were going to do. We were told that the Bayfield was going full speed ahead and we were going over to start this invasion. A lieutenant laid maps out on the tables and we were shown what to do and what not to do and what to expect, what to see and what to look for. We took it in as well as we could...'

Larry Orr USS *Bayfield*, Coxswain of Boat Three. The *Bayfield* was an attack transport which could discharge over 1,500 troops via LCVPs. It was also the HQ ship for 'Utah' under Rear Admiral Don P. Moon.

'On 30 January 1944 our unit boarded the British ocean liner, the Mauritania, in New York harbour and after eight days of rough seas and constant seasickness, we arrived in Liverpool. My company was sent to Falmouth in Cornwall. The first night resulted in a rather humorous introduction into the war. Falmouth was a town about a mile square. Scattered throughout the town were large blimp-like balloons tethered by steel cables. Every night, in addition to a total blackout, these balloons were released several hundred feet into the air. There were also several large machine gun emplacements and search lights located throughout the town. Near the town was a long railroad bridge which every night would attract at least one German aircraft. We were quartered in some steel barracks called Butler buildings. Sometime after midnight a German plane came over, the searchlights went on and the machine guns started firing. If that racket weren't enough, we heard loud explosions on the top of the barracks. Sure that we had been bombed, we all scrambled out of the barracks like a bunch of rats in varying degrees of undress only to learn that some of the bullets from the machine guns had come down on the buildings. So much for our introduction to the war. At Falmouth I went to signal school and learned both semaphore and Morse code by light. Morse code by sound would have involved the use of radio, which would have enabled the enemy to hear our communications.

'Shortly after our arrival at Falmouth, the 111th Battalion was designated a pontoon battalion. We were to build the Rhino ferries and tugs, man them and then participate in the invasion of France. Our company built the barges in Plymouth. Each Rhino, which was built of large steel cubes, approximately 6 feet on a side, was accompanied by a tug, which was three pontoons wide and six long. It also had two large inboard motors to aid in the manoeuvring of the clumsy Rhinos. A Rhino could completely unload the military vehicles on one LST (Landing Ship Tank), an excellent ship for transporting military vehicles. It was very effective in unloading vehicles and supplies on the beaches of volcanic islands of the South Pacific but it would have been very ineffective at 'Omaha' because it would have had to wait to the next high tide, until the ship could pull off the beach. The Rhinos were bolted together in strings of six pontoons wide and thirty long. They were powered by two large outboard Chrysler marine motors with a top speed of two to three miles an hour. When fully loaded they drew only about two feet of water. Since the Rhino's draft was so shallow, they had no difficulty getting off a shallow beach and underway once they were unloaded. Each Rhino and its tug were assigned to an LST, which was to tow them across the English Channel. We departed from Portland on the morning of June 5. The weather was terrible, cold, cloudy, windy and raining. The tugs had a pontoon tube mounted on the front with a hole cut in the sides so the crews could get some protection from the weather, but it was still a miserable, sea-sicky trip.'

'During our training I attended demolition school and became a squad leader. Just before we were shipped overseas I had one week furlough to go home to Ruth, Nevada to visit the family. We were sent by train from Texas to Boston on October 9th. After a week or two there we were loaded on a British ship and sent to Liverpool. The ship we were on was fast enough to outrun German submarines so we didn't have to go by convoy. A lot of us were sea sick most of the time and even though we had a submarine scare one evening it didn't take away the sea sickness. Upon arriving in Liverpool we took a train south to Barnstable, south of the Bristol Channel, where we started our invasion training on an old golf course. The club house was turned into the headquarters building. We lived in tents with five men to a tent. For training we made obstacles just off the beach out of cement, ditches, iron, etc., to stop tanks. I was over the mine and booby trap squad on our boat crew and we practiced picking up mines and booby traps and also laying them. We used giant firecrackers instead of TNT and dynamite for practice and I'm glad we did because I would have blown myself up a few times had we not.

'We did have a few accidents and fatalities during training. As we were practicing making hand grenades with ¼lb blocks of TNT, one of the fellows was killed when the grenade blew up as he pulled the fuse lighter. I turned around just as he was being blown backwards. The Lieutenant and I rushed over to him. We made a stretcher out of our rifles and took him to the hospital in a truck. His arm and leg were blown off and he was burned with internal injuries. On the way to the hospital he kept asking me to put a blanket around his foot as it was cold. He died soon after we arrived at the hospital so we went back to our tents. I couldn't smoke or eat dinner as I kept smelling and tasting burned flesh from picking him up and putting him on the stretcher. I think I took about three showers that evening with GI soap before trying to eat again and I still couldn't overcome the smell of burned flesh for about three days.

'One day Lieutenant Wesley Ross came to us and said that we would be leaving for the south coast of England for final briefing and the invasion. After arriving in Portsmouth we were given briefing about every day and told of our assignments. After being shown photos of the obstacles and being briefed on where we were to land on the beach in France, we were no longer allowed outside the fenced are and there were guards about every 50 feet. We were assigned to boat crew #8 and were to land in the first wave on 'Omaha' Beach with the 1st Infantry Division. The Ranger Battalion was to land and climb the cliffs to our right. Our boat crew's job was to make gaps through the obstacles at low tide so that the second wave could make it through as the tide would be coming in. The 1st Division was to attack the German positions.

'My assignment, as Sergeant with three other men, was to clear the area of mines and booby traps in a gap about 50 yards from the obstacles inland, obstacles to the tide high water mark. We knew that it was getting close to invasion time as were loaded on an LCT (landing craft tank) about a week before the invasion. While on board and waiting, the fellows in my squad wanted to grow goatees and moustaches and I told them to go ahead. They said we all had to or none so I agreed. The day before we left port, June 4th, Captain Howard told me to have everyone shave their beards off. I told him that I had checked beards with the gas masks on and they did not interfere, in case we got gassed by the Germans. He said to shave them off anyway and I refused. He said that he would court martial me and I told him to go ahead as none of us might be alive tomorrow anyway.'

Sergeant Roy Arnn, 146th Combat Engineering Battalion. 'Before I was drafted I was living with my mother and working, at the open pit copper mine in Ruth to help support my younger sisters Vera, Darlene, Neva, Peggy and my brother Lue. My older brother Ray was married and living in Ely, Nevada. Mother was working in the Post Office. I wasn't that concerned about being drafted so I decided to buy a car because we had no way to get around. I went to a garage in Ruth to look at an old used Dodge sedan and was going to take it for a test drive when the news came over the radio that Pearl Harbor was bombed. I told Mr. Hall, the garage owner, that under the circumstances, I did not think I should take the car because I knew that I would be drafted pretty soon and would not be able to afford it on Army pay. He told me that if I wanted the car to take it and if I was drafted I could finish paying for it when I got home from the Army. While I was in the service Grandma learned how to drive it.'

'Before leaving the States we got to go home on a week or ten day furlough. I went with my girlfriend to a fortune teller to see what my future was going to be. I knew I was going to be shipped overseas. I wanted to know if I was going to come back. She told me I was going to have a close call but I was going to come back all right.

'I left the States the 9th of October en route to England. We rode in the Martina, fourth size to Queen Elizabeth. We had approximately 28,000 troops on board, one third more than supposed to be carried. We docked in Liverpool. It was raining and muddy where they stationed us. At that time England was in blackout at night. No one could go to town on pass. We had our flashlights blocked off so there was only a small hole in the glass to see through. When coming to a street intersection you could barely make out where you were. We finally settled down on the south coast of England by the town of Barnstaple. It was winter and we burned coal in our tents at night.

'It was at Slapton Sands where we started our demolition training. This is where we studied mines, hand grenades, TNT, C2 satchel charges and so forth. We practiced on what we called hedgehogs. They were like little girl's jacks in shape, but were about 4 feet high. Our demolitions really worked fine on these. One day we were practicing tying short fuses on blocks of TNT and throwing them like hand grenades. One of our men drew back to throw and it went off. He lived 'till he reached the hospital. He was our first casualty. His name was Melvin Vest.

'I kind of liked working with demolition but I saw it could be pretty dangerous also, if not carefully seen after. We finished our demolition mines and booby traps and moved forward to the coast where we stayed in some Nissen huts, waiting to cross the English Channel where we were furnished our OD clothes and gear we would need. About this time we were divided up into boat crews. I was in boat crew number 8 and our lieutenant was Wesley Ross. Our medic was Lieutenant Max S. Norris. I always thought I was in the service with some of the best guys there were. Strict, but good. And I saw where it really paid off in the long run for me. In the last camp of preparation we were shown films of how the battle was to be carried out, how we were to land and what we were supposed to do. We had it all down in films and in our minds.

'Finally it came time to get on our LST. It had a half-track, an armoured tank, besides boat crew 8. It sure was crowded. We barely had room to get around by day, at night it was something else. Those army blankets sure were fine quality. I would tie one side of my blanket to the side of the boat and the other side to the tank very tight like a hammock. Before morning it was nearly hitting the bottom of the boat. The blanket had stretched so much but would all shrink the next day and the same thing the next night. I think we were on the English Channel four or five days. I had one close buddy, Willie Brandt that always worried about the crossing. He thought we were going to be shot like sitting ducks. I told him they wouldn't do us that way. He was found on the beach on D-Day, no bullet holes in him. I don't know whether he died from shock or explosion.'

William D. Townsley who was born 8 August 1923, entered the armed service February 1943 at Abilene, Texas, was made sharpshooter and was assigned to the 146th Combat Engineers Battalion, Company 'B'.

'We put in a wooden stake and then, at a distance of four or five metres, another stake. On top of these we attached a third stake with clamps - all of it done by hand - and secured by more clamps. Teller mines were attached to the tips of the stakes or beams, so that, at high tide, the mines were just below the water's surface, so that even a flat-bottomed boat would touch them and be destroyed. We did all this at low tide when the sea retreated a few kilometres.'

Grenadier Robert Voght of the 1st/726th Regiment. Beyond the high-water mark there were three lines of obstacles. Each varied in height so that the lowest were closer to the shore where the water would be shallower. Furthest out were large, fence-like beach obstacles, called 'Element C', which were also known as 'Belgian gates' with Teller anti-tank mines fixed to them. The second line consisted of mine-tipped tree trunks or log ramps staked into the sand and pointing out to sea, while the third line close to the high water mark consisted of hedgehogs typically made of three sections of steel girder joined together at their centres. The work parties used high-pressure hoses to blast a hole in the wet sand before inserting the stakes.

'We didn't talk of dying, unless it was a joke. We used to kid a guy named Gino because he carried a big wad of money, $700 or $800 and he had a beautiful ring. He was little Italian boy out of Jersey City. I would say, 'Ferrari, when you hit that beach and you fall, man, I'm going to be getting your wallet out.' And another guy would say, 'Yep, I'm going to have that ring of yours.' And we sat around and thought about that, never thinking it would really happen. But what else did we have to talk about?

'We were near a little town called Weymouth which is not the shortest point across the Channel, about 85 to 90 miles from there to where we were going to land. We still didn't know the exact day we were going to land. We boarded our ship at and waited. We were cramped up with all of our equipment on. I was a demolition man. I had a 50 pound pole charge and a 50 pound satchel charge made of burlap and TNT. I had an M-1 rifle, 286 rounds of M.1 ammunition. I had ten hand grenades, a two-day supply of K-rations and three D Bars. Can you imagine lugging all that stuff? That was part of the training that we had been going through. It was hard, but I was solid and in good shape. We used to boast afterwards, 'I wish I was as good a man as I was on D-Day. You couldn't drive a ten penny nail in my leg or arm or body.'

'On Saturday morning we heard Rome had been entered. We loaded up our equipment on Sunday afternoon, put all in our prospective places. Each one of us knew exactly aboard the landing craft where we would sit. We had done it so many times, we could be blind folded. We put all our equipment in so we'd have it all ready. And all we had to do the next morning was have chow and whenever we were going to land, hop right into our position in the boat, APA 28, the USS *Charles Carroll*. As we were loading in, I was bitching up a storm. They say a good soldier bitches. If he doesn't bitch, he's not a good soldier. I must have been the best in the US Army, 'cause I sure did my part. 'Damn, I hope we don't have to swim to shore tomorrow,' I said.

'Then this guy walking around with a stiff collar with his trench coat on and his hands jammed down in his pockets up to his elbows said, 'Soldier, I put 50,000 men ashore and I haven't got one of them wet yet.'

'The orders came out that we had to postpone. The storm had moved into the channel and we couldn't land. Well, we bitched up a storm, because we wanted to go. This sounds crazy, but we had come this far and we'd been sitting in England so long we wanted to get this thing over with and get the hell home. Well, as it was, we had to settle for another day. We loaded again on Monday afternoon. The rain was letting up some and we started to move out about 10:30 or 11:00 that night. It was still light.'

Felix Branham, who joined the Virginia National Guard, Company 'K', 116th Infantry, 29th Division in November 1938.

'I arrived in the Firth of Forth on the Queen Elizabeth, January 1943. I was a graduate of the University of Pennsylvania Dental School, class of 1936. I volunteered for the first draft, November, 1940, was inducted 31 January 1941 and entered the service through Fort Dix, New Jersey. A private for seven months, in August 1941 I received a commission as a first lieutenant in the Dental Corps. You may wonder why I, a practicing dentist, volunteered to go in as a private. I would have liked to go in as an officer, of course, but the table of organization at that time had no use for more DDSs. As the Army expanded, the need for officers grew. Secondly, I was a very patriotic American and also a Jew who had no use whatsoever for that Nazi bastard Hitler and his overall plan of genocide for my people.

'We were picked out and given the distinct honour of making the invasion of France, on 'Omaha' Beach. We boarded the *Charles Carroll,* the communication ship for the invasion after spending about one week in isolation at a marshalling area in camp in Plymouth, going over and over the plans for the invasion. We were well-trained, well-prepared, having gone through two to three problems at Slapton Sands, simulating exactly the conditions, terrain and so forth that we were expected to find on 'Omaha' Beach.'

Captain Bernard S. Feinberg, regimental dental surgeon, 116th Infantry Regiment, 29th Division, who was born 17 July 1912 in West Hoboken, New Jersey.

'The Captain had told the crew: 'We have the honour and the privilege to lead the Invasion Fleet across the Channel.' A senior Petty Officer alongside me muttered, 'what did 'e say? The Honour or the 'orrer?'

'We steamed out with the halliards streaming the flags - 'Nelson in the Van'. It seemed no different from all our previous trips to sea as a flotilla, except that as far as one could see on each side, stretching back away from us, were minesweepers. Pelorus was the point of a very large arrow. We were now at action stations of course and at about midnight the Captain spliced the mainbrace.'

A. F. Wilby in the minesweeper, HMS *Pelorus,* which played a leading part in clearing the Channel. She left the Solent early on Monday.

'When HMS *Danae* was nominated as a member of the In-Shore Bombardment Squadron for Operation Overlord the commander addressed the ship's company on a freezing quarterdeck in Greenock. His comment that we had the honour to be expendable was smartly countered by, 'Fuck that for a lark,' from the ranks of the stokers' division.

Royal Marines' Captain J. H. B. Hughes aboard the cruiser HMS *Danae.*

'I had never seen so many ships together at one time... thousands and thousands of ships of all classes stretched from horizon to horizon.'

Captain Eric Bush, a 45-year old veteran of Gallipoli, commanding Assault Convoy S5, aboard HMS *Goathland,* which left Portsmouth harbour at 1320 on 5 June and arrived off 'Sword' on the 6th.

'The best way I can describe this vast armada and the frantic urgency of the traffic is to suggest that you visualise New York Harbour on its busiest day of the year and then just enlarge the scene until it takes in all of the ocean the human eye can reach;, clear around the horizon and over the horizon; there are dozens of times that many.'

Legendary American war correspondent Ernie Pyle.

'We were going on the early morning watch at Portland dockyard and all along the bus route we could see the activity of troops marching to the landing craft. That was the first we knew that this must be THE day, D-Day. As we waited in the bus to be searched before we were allowed through the dock gates, one of the Wrens, Eileen from Bridport who had recently married a GI saw her husband. Against all the regulations she dashed off the bus and scrambled across the pebbly beach to kiss her husband goodbye as he got on the boat. We all looked the other way... not many hours later we saw ships bringing the wounded back to Weymouth and the same ships reload with replenishment troops. I felt very humble. I still wonder whenever I look at a photograph I have of those troops boarding the Consul how many of them came home?

'It was only a couple of days before we heard that Eileen was a D-Day widow. And we all shared her sorrow.'

Margaret Whittlesea a WREN billeted in Weymouth.

'I joined the 1st Infantry Division a replacement in November 1943. My unit had returned from Sicily after taking part in the North African and Sicilian campaigns. The Division who was spread out along the southern English coast and our company was just within a few miles of the English Channel itself. As a young replacement, I was only twenty years old; being thrown into an outfit with veteran tested combat soldiers was quite an experience. We spent all winter and spring training for the invasion. We ran field exercises and on several occasions we loaded on board LCVPs and made the run into the beach in simulated landings. On one such occasion we were loaded on board ships in Portland harbour and went up to the British naval firing range in darkness. While making the run on to the beach, live ammunition was being fired overhead; we sustained several casualties on the beach. A man just immediately to my left was struck with shrapnel in the head and killed.

'We had been provided with blown up photographs of the section of the beach that we were to hit on D-Day. We ran the exercise over and over again until we had it letter perfect. The ramp of the landing craft would go down and we would pour out onto the beach taking whatever cover we could find. The lead men would throw themselves onto the barbed wire so that the rest of us could follow through the barbed wire and whatever obstacles there were. The Bangalore torpedo men then would place their Bangalore torpedoes where we felt the mine fields were and blow a path for us to approach the pill box. At that point, the man with the satchel charge, who we would give cover to, would place the satchel charge in the aperture and blow the pill box if possible. After the detonation of the satchel charge the flame thrower man would then spray the burning fuel into whatever openings he could find.

'In the area where photographs had been taken, our section of the beach had a tank trap. My job in the assault group was to carry in an aluminium ladder in two sections that we could put together to use to cross the tank trap. I was also a rifle-grenade man. Our training in the English countryside was intense and we got in gear in January and worked up until the time we boarded the ships on June 4th. The southern part of the British Isles was in quarantine. Our training included long forced marches with full field pack in order to condition ourselves, firing our weapons on the rifle range and the period of acquainting ourselves with the use of the satchel charge with the TNT and the flame throwers. This was necessary because we felt the casualties would be quite high and that back up men would be needed to take over the job for those who were wounded.

'A great deal of time was spent on board ships making assault landings near the Dartmouth naval firing range. In March or April our division had a visit from British General Montgomery. He told us that we hadn't come to England to spend a warm winter by the fireside and a pleasant spring on the Channel. He reminded us that we were there to train in order to crack the German defences and liberate Europe. A feeling of the veterans of the 1st infantry Division was 'Why us again?' They had made the landing in North Africa at Oran, had gotten soundly beaten by the Afrika Corps at the Kasserine Pass and invaded Sicily at Gela. Their feeling was there must be other infantry units in the US Army that could be utilized in the assault on Western Europe. The big talk about opening a second front affected us dramatically and we were hoping that the assault would take place in the Mediterranean in southern France. We were trucked from our camp to Weymouth and boarded the *Empire Anvil* on June the 4th expecting that the next morning we would be hitting the beach. However, the weather was such that the invasion was postponed for a day and we didn't go in until H hour on June the 6th.'

Steve Kellerman Company 'L', 3rd Battalion, 16th Infantry Regiment, 1st Infantry Division, stationed in 'a small village, really just a cluster of homes called Longbreddy perhaps 25 miles from Weymouth.'

'The harbour of Weymouth was having a grand time. Battleships, troopships, freighters and invasion barges all mingled together. Floating in the air above them was a balloon barrage made up of many hundreds of silver blimps. The prospective tourists to France were sunbathing on the decks of the boats and lazily watching the giant toys that were being hoisted aboard. For the optimists, everything looked like a new secret weapon, especially from a distance.'

The veteran war photographer, Robert Capa, born Endre Friedman in Budapest on 22 October 1913 and who by 6 June 1944 had gained an internationally recognised reputation, underlined by an 8-page spread in the prestigious British magazine, *Picture Post*, in December 1938. It was headlined, 'The Greatest Photographer in the World'.

'I was drafted in May 1943. I decided to join the Navy. I had my boot camp training at Bainbridge Naval Station in Bainbridge, Maryland. After a short leave, I went back to Bainbridge and attended Boatswain School. I received further training in New Orleans, Louisiana. From New Orleans, I boarded the ship *General George O'Squire*. We docked in the English Channel. Here we picked up Landing Craft Tank ships. We trained for amphibious landings. On June 1 our LCT was loaded with 180 tons of ammunition. Then on June 4,300 combat soldiers entered our LCT. The soldiers were given invasion money. One asked me, 'What kind of money is this?'

'I told them they'd find out the next morning.'

James Hollis Bearden, boatswain, *General George O'Squire*, born 3 October 1922 in Shelbyville, Tennessee. He moved to Cairo, Georgia in 1938 and lived with an uncle so that he could play football for Cairo High School.

'After being trained at Solomon's Maryland and Little Creek, Virginia, I received orders to proceed to Lido Beach, Long Island. We were organized into crews and we debarked Pier 90 New York City for England on the *Queen Mary* on 19 January 1944. We had excellent quarters. We were 21 officers in a cabin for two in an upper deck. Even the ensigns didn't get very good treatment. But it was certainly a beautiful ship and we did have an effortless, uneventful crossing. When we got to Greenock, Scotland all the Army personnel were greeted by a band and hooting and hollering and put onto trains and trucks and busses of various kinds and taken away. We were 120 naval personnel standing on the dock and no one was there to greet us. Finally, someone in the Army said 'Why don't you get on the next train going south?' So we did. The 300-mile trip to Plymouth took approximately nine days, stopping and letting everything else cross in front. Our only food came from the Red Cross.

'At Plymouth crews were organized and assigned to various landing craft that were brought over in pieces and assembled in Cardiff to be used to carry tanks into the beach when the invasion begun. We practiced how to launch these tanks while three or four thousand yards from the beach and after a month or two, we became quite proficient. Early in May my 12-man crew were divided up and distributed so that each of the final crews to an LCT consisted of two officers and 15 men including two motor mechs, two signalmen, six deck hands and two cooks; so that we could operate on a 24-hour period, four on, four off, with no diminution in the efficiency of the boat. Dick Abernathy, Dominick Capuano and Larry Sender and me went to Cardiff and picked up LCT 607 and joined another crew so that we could operate four on four off. We sailed the LCT around Land's End to Queen Anne's Battery at Plymouth.

'On or about June 1 all units were quarantined and then we knew that the invasion was beginning. We didn't know the name Overlord at that time. On or about June 4 we assembled and were in the unit which preceded the first wave. The only thing in front of us was a picket boat showing us the way in because they had navigational equipment. However, the weather was so bad, the seas were so rough, that we received a flag signal to put about and follow the picket boat back into Portsmouth harbour. Imagine the confusion, 4,000 or so landing craft jammed into that small harbour. You could almost walk across the harbour by going from boat to boat.

'After considerable speculation, at about two in the morning, we received orders to re-assemble and proceed to our assigned beach. We were due to hit 'Utah' Beach at H-Hour minus 20 minutes. My unit, which consisted of six LCTs, were first in line. We proceeded in column form, passing underneath the eight-inch guns of the heavy cruiser USS *Augusta.* Wave after wave of fighters and bombers sortied overhead. It was just fantastic. It was almost like a dream.'

Sam Grundfast, born 5 February 1921, in New York City, Captain of an LCT (Landing Craft Tank). 'It was approximately 110 feet long, 33 feet wide and was powered by three 225 hp diesel engines. Top speed of about seven knots when empty, probably four and a half to five knots when loaded.'

'I believe there were about 12 or 14,000 of us aboard the converted *Queen Mary;* my first trip to Europe. She was stacked up with bunks from bulkhead to bulkhead and from deck to deck, but reasonably comfortable, good food. Crossing took place in about four-ish days. We landed in Scotland at Firth of Clyde. We were put on a train to go south through the English countryside to Plymouth. It was most confusing. We went east for a while and then west in trucks for a while. It was almost an all-night ride until we finally arrived at our correct billet, which was the beautiful town of Salcombe in the county of Devonshire. I spent a most pleasant winter and spring there. I learned to love the people and the countryside; the scenery was gorgeous. My group of boats then operated out of Salcombe and their duty for the next six months was to practice landing the United States Marines and Army on the Slapton Sands just east of us where time after time our flotilla of landing craft landed troops in rehearsals. LCTs were 105 feet long and there were 12 to a group and 3 groups or 36 boats to a flotilla. LCTs would hold theoretically five tanks or about a dozen or so trucks or 30 or 40 autos. They were not designed for personnel because other than those running the boat would have to sleep on deck although before the war was over, we carried almost anything. At times I was a medical officer of a group and at times there was no other medical officer in the two other groups so my responsibility was for the health of 36 boats. There were 12 enlisted men and one ensign assigned to each boat. They were diesel operated. The older ones had the engine and conning tower in quarters all in the middle of the back of the boat and later on over to one side.

'Each time that we were assigned to a landing operation, we did not know that might be the invasion. I was of little value going out with the boats, but St. Elmo, a little hotel, was commandeered by the Navy as our hospital. I was somewhat of an outsider since my primary assignment was my flotilla but I lived most of my six months in the hospital and those doctors became my friends for life. I spent no time administering to the local population, except in emergency. We handled troops - navy, army or otherwise - but primarily the navy. In Salcombe was a Seabee unit repair and maintenance of boats and they could just about make anything.

'Each time we made an 'invasion' on Slapton Sands we didn't know that might be the real thing. Finally I got my orders to catch a train to Cardiff in Wales. I was a doctor but I didn't really know what they were planning to do with me. After about a week I was put in command of the medical division aboard the *SS Woodward*, a liberty ship that was outfitted as a medical station and a supply and repair ship. A wonderful repair supply was under the command of Lieutenant Commander Murray from Philadelphia. We had a great deal of supplies to give to the boats. There was a Lieutenant Commander in over all charge of Navy operations as well as a merchant marine captain, mates and seaman who ran the ship. I was given blood supplies instead of plasma as an adjunct to my medical kit, so I knew the invasion had to be imminent. Plasma will last for a very prolonged period where blood has to be kept at the proper temperature and does not last long at all. Sure enough, in the first day or so of June we sailed.'

Lieutenant (JG) Simon V. Ward, US Navy Medical Corps. Born on a tobacco and cotton plantation in South Carolina on 15 June 1916, he finished high school in 1933 in the midst of the depression and graduated from the LSU Medical School in New Orleans in 1941.

'I was approximately 30 years old at the time of the invasion. On June 4 we went to the Highden Dock to load up small ships for the invasion. We took on trucks called DUKWs; there were twenty on one of them. They could also swim. We also had twenty-one tanks filled with ammunition. There were also half tracks, jeeps and a hundred men from the 101st Airborne Division because the weather was bad. We left on the afternoon of the 5th at 16:00 hours. I was told to get up as I was resting on my bunk watching the war going by. I looked out to see ship after ship pass by, destroyers, cruisers, battleships and every type you could imagine. The captain took us out on the deck and showed us a map of where we were going in case we got lost. He also gave us a paper copy from Eisenhower as to how difficult the enemy would be and what we were up against. The chaplain offered prayers and to tell the truth, his knees were really shaking.'

Maro P. Flagg, Chief Pharmacist's Mate, US Navy; a graduate from Miami Military Academy in Florida. When he was drafted he was a funeral director and had his own funeral home, a family of five children and also he was an embalmer.

'Colonel Canham of the 116th Infantry of the 29th Division spoke to us at Crown Barracks and explained to us that we are going to be the first forces into the Second Front in Europe and that two out of three of us aren't expected to come back and if anybody's got butterflies in the belly, to ask for a transfer now, because it's going to be that kind of an operation. We trained on the famous Dartmoor and we did tremendous forty-mile marches across England. We received combat infantry training where we did thirty push-ups every day, ran with a man on our back for seventy-five yards and crawled under barbed wire. We also went on amphibious training missions. We boarded little assault boats of the British Navy and trained in landing. Our manoeuvres were made on the beaches of Slapton Sands where there were pillboxes on the beach. We had a certain system of taking these pillboxes. We went to special schools where each man was trained to be able to use his weapon - me, the Browning automatic rifle. We lived and slept and ate in boat teams. Each boat team consisted of thirty men trained to work as a team to assault enemy beaches and be able to establish a beachhead by neutralizing all obstacles and pillboxes. There was a lieutenant in command of each boat team, a man with a walkie-talkie radio set, two BAR teams (four men altogether), one flame thrower and his assistant, two bazooka teams (four men altogether), a wire-cutting team with four men, a demolition team with five men, a 60mm mortar team with four men, a sergeant and a second in command and five riflemen armed with M-l rifles and rifle grenades. On amphibious training, we used real ammunition at all times and actually went out on ships and boats and hit beaches near Slapton Sands. These rehearsals were very realistic.'

19-year old Private Harold Baumgarten of Company 'B', 116th Infantry Regiment. Colonel Charles D. Canham, a southerner, 'tall and thin with wire-rim glasses and a pencil thin moustache' was known by the men in the 116th as 'Old Hatchetface'.

'For weeks before D-Day, all outgoing communications were restricted. No outgoing mail, for example. I kept getting letters from my folks begging me to write. I rarely missed more than a few days and I couldn't understand the problem. As liberty was restricted, the enlisted men spent the last five days aboard the LCT 544. At the time our craft was in Weymouth, along with hundreds of other ships and landing craft. LCT 544 was slightly larger and faster than the LCT 276 I had been on in the Mediterranean and carried six versus five tanks. It had much better living conditions, such as a refrigerator, ample fresh water storage, a hot shower, lockers, more bunks and relatively spacious quarters. Their two 20mm guns were the same, but the engines were more powerful and there were two electrical generators rather than one. We had a radio and transmitter so that we could talk to other vessels. It had a civilian band so that could be picked up. Crew members of older LCTs were distributed among the newer to make use of their combat experiences. My good friends Harry Hulscher and Don Gray and I were sent to the LCT 544 for this purpose. There were two other veterans assigned from other LCTs: Curly, who was a motor machinist's mate and Bob Fusik, a boatswain's mate. Curly was a survivor of an LCT which had been destroyed by shell fire in Italy.

'Our LCT, as others did, picked some extra enlisted men and a relief skipper shortly before sailing. The new members were all green, literally jumping from boot camp to combat, but they were willing and we soon became a confident and compatible crew. Our new skipper, Ensign Phillips, only around 25 years old, a 90-day wonder, was great. He had an unassuming manner and was never unjustly critical. Later he proved to be a courageous and resourceful leader and it was a privilege to have served with him. The reserve skipper - his name was Rouse, an ensign from North Carolina - was recently out of OCS with some amphibious training. We trained everybody as best we could, but with some sympathy, because they remembered that we veterans were in the same position just a short year earlier. Our complement on D-Day was around 14 enlisted men and two officers. Four men were assigned to the two 20mm cannons, a gunner and a loader on each. Two more were assigned to lower and raise the ramp. Another was reserved for special assignment at the bow and one to drop or raise the rear anchor. There were two in the galley to tend to the wounded and two in the engine room. I was on the bridge to handle signals along with the two officers, with two men in the wheel house, one steering the LCT and the other one on a standby.

'We kept a camouflage net over the entire craft when empty of vehicles, so that we always looked loaded, hoping that Germans couldn't estimate readiness by observing the number of loaded ships. As D-Day approached, our participation in the practice runs at Slapton Sands died off. After the middle of April, we only made a few trips up that way. What we did, however, was to join convoys of other LCTs, other types of landing craft and warships and head north and then turned towards France, usually some place off Dover.

'Our skipper attended briefings each day. Recon photos showed the Normandy beaches to be heavily protected with steel hedgehogs, (these were three pieces of steel welded together and then sunk into the sand) and wooden poles, also sunk into the sand. These devices would be covered by the sea at night tide and exposed at low. Mines were attached to the face of the obstacles and cross-wired, so that if one were struck by a landing craft and detonated, a series of others would also go off. To thwart these devices, underwater demolition teams were to go in advance of the invasion and blast paths through the obstacles. The first wave consisted of tanks and infantry. They were landed from LCVPs (landing craft vehicle personnel), loaded with about 30 men. The infantry would also come in on LCIs (landing craft infantry) carrying around 250 men. The plan assumed a waiting period of one hour giving this initial group time to secure a firm foothold. After an hour, beach engineers would land to prepare specific areas for the landing of heavier equipment. More tanks would also be landed to support the infantry. Many of the first wave tanks were fitted with canvas sleeves so that they could float and be launched some distance off shore from LCTs.

'In between hours of waiting, we would go into shore to load up supplies, ammunition, fuel and other things and lastly, about two days before we left, our cargo of vehicles and beach engineers and a 1st Infantry Division scout team of about eight men. In one of those rare coincidences, the 1st Division men were part of the group we had landed at Brolo in Sicily, one of whom, Bill Lynn, lived close to my home in New York. He was a few years older but we had many common experiences and family friends.

' As we were part of the lead assault force and relatively slow, we sailed early on 4 June. Around noon, the convoy was called back to Weymouth. The soldiers, who had been loaded two days before, stayed on deck, cold and wrapped in ponchos to stay as dry as possible. We were in a high state of excitement and the return was a real letdown; it exhausted the crew. The soldiers were better off with more time to rest, except for the discomfort of yet another cold day in the open. Next day, we set out again, this time for real. The weather was far from ideal, still cold and rainy with a heavy sea. Our cook Chuck Henson, who owned a family butcher shop in Minneapolis had set up the galley as an aid station, which precluded any cooking of hot meals. The crew settled for K-rations the same as the troops, with coffee available for all. The crew was dressed in fatigues, dungarees, blue shirt and blue zipper jacket. We wore our helmets and kept gas masks handy, except when catching up from sleep, we wore our life jackets.

'One of the beach engineers developed what we believed was an inflamed appendix. We described his condition to a doctor aboard a British cruiser by signal flag, because there was strict radio silence. The sea was too rough for transfer and the risk for stopping to do so was too great, so on the advice of the doctor we packed the appropriate area with ice and sailed on. The trip over was really uneventful. I stayed on the bridge most of the time, where I would be joined by Bill Lynn and we'd reminisce about the old neighbourhood, with frequent trips below for cups of coffee. Our course was first northeast and after a time, we turned due east and headed for the Normandy coast. As we sailed along, many more ships and other landing craft appeared to join the growing armada.

'Overhead, you could see vast flights of bombers and fighters, with their contrails filling the sky through infrequent blue patches. There were some odd sights, like a rhino ferry, which was just steel boxes about 10 foot by 10, welded together to form a long pontoon, propelled by two large outboard motors, except being towed then by a tug. They were designed to serve as unloading causeways. They had a crew of two unprotected on the open deck, undoubtedly completely miserable, leaning into the wind and spray. Also seen were huge concrete caissons the size of a house called 'Mulberries', to be sunk offshore to form a temporary harbour, towed by sea-going tugs. The skipper had set the watch so that we could all get some sleep, with the idea of course that we'd be all on duty somewhere during the invasion. The deck house was about six foot by six foot with a ladder to the top on the outside. There was a railing so that it would be safe to stand on the top with a voice tube to communicate with the helmsman. There was a trap door to the top and by standing on a small bench, the skipper could stay in the wheel house and look out the top. He could not see too well to the side so the relief skipper stood outside of the hatch door to act as a lookout for the port side and I stood to the rear just behind the wheel house, looking out to the starboard side.

'I went to bed fully dressed, around 23:00. It was still daylight, summer days are long and nights short in northern latitudes. I had a deep sleep and was awakened around 04:00. I splashed some water on my face and got a cup of coffee on my way up to the bridge, where the reserve skipper gave me one of his supply of candy bars for breakfast. Bill Lynn came up to complain that the short night meant about 20 hours of fighting per day for the troops. He was very unhappy about that.'

William Thomas O'Neill, LCT 6-544, was born in New York City on 4 September 1920, first generation of Irish parentage. He enlisted in the Navy in 1942 and by the early spring of 1943 was assigned to the USS *Chateau Thierry*, a Navy troop transport sailing for the Arzew/Oran/Algeria area.

'As a young sailor just getting to England was a chore, with the U-boats and bad weather. We lost all life boats and rafts and had to return to St. John's Newfoundland for three weeks of repairs and replacement of lost rafts and life boats and repairing the damage to the gun tubs, hull and as one blade of a 5-bladed propeller had broken off the tip, divers cut the other four blades to same length. This gave us slower speed and no vibration. We were then sent to sea again and a new convoy landed at King George IV Dock, Millwall in London (we were 87 days out of New York) with LCT 546 in three pieces. While the LCT was being assembled I lived in a Seaman's hostel, with the Blitz going on nightly. As the German aircraft dropped bombs on the area, we were instructed to go to the bomb shelters where we met people that had been going through this for years but though London had been flattened, they still believed in the end that everything would turn out better. All ships and guns were firing back. When LCT(6) 546 was assembled and supplied two crew members and me moved aboard. Commanding Officer Ensign Jerome T. Landsberger USNR arrived with the rest of our crew and we were ordered to move our vessel to Dartmouth. This done, we did a few practice landings. Later we moved to Portland and Weymouth harbours loaded with Army vehicles and men. As the German aircraft flew over head dropping bombs and mines in to the harbour, we knew our time to leave was close.'

Ralph E. Gallant, Motor Machinist's Mate 2/c, LCT(6) 546.

'We set up our office in a very secure and not easily accessible Quonset hut near Lands End which gave a very low profile to the Top Secret planning going on in such an unpretentious building and location. Our unit was created specifically for planning the V Corps part in the invasion when our mission was to establish radio communications with Major-General Leonard T. Gerow aboard the USS *Ancon* (the Flagship). Two regimental combat teams from the 1st Infantry division and two from the 29th Infantry division were designated for the assault wave on the coast at 'Omaha' beach. At H+60 minutes we were to follow them from our LST to the beach in a 2½-ton amphibious DUKW, obtain information regarding operations ashore and advise General Gerow of the tactical and supply situation in the V Corps' zone of action. A duplicate DUKW of ours was on another LST in the convoy along with two ¼-ton Jeeps on DSMs. The units were all outfitted with the latest equipment which included two SCR-399s mounted in both DUKWs and 2 SRC-193s mounted in the two Jeeps. The men were all highly trained radio operators and cryptographers.'

I. J. Degnan, Security Control Officer, V Corps' Information Detachment commanded by Colonel Benjamin B. Talley who also was the CO of the HQ V Corps' planning group for 'Overlord'.

'In June 1943, in the grade of Colonel, I had gone to England from Alaska and was nominally Engineer of V Corps stationed at Bristol. In early 1944 I was made Deputy Chief of Staff, Plans, V Corps, in charge of the coordination of the plan for the amphibious assault on the continent of Europe. At HQ V Corps we constructed a scale model of the 'Omaha' Beach landing area where each stream, highway, road, trail, orchard, fence and building were shown at proper scale and contour. Models were made of all types of landing craft. Major combat commanders studied these to become familiar with the area which they would land their units and to recognize amphibious equipment they had not yet seen. When I landed on 'Omaha' Beach I felt I knew the area as though I had been there before. The plan was so complete that each unit knew the day, the hour and the minute as well as the speed it should travel on the ground to reach the embarkation point on time without causing traffic jams at road intersections. This involved the scheduled movement of nearly one-quarter million men and more than 100,000 vehicles.

'The staging area in Britain, 15 miles deep and extending from Portsmouth on the south coast of England west 150 miles to Lands End was cordoned off. For two weeks prior to D-Day milk and mail trucks were the only civilian traffic in and out of the area. No civilians could leave the area. Only essential military personnel could leave and then only with special permission. All telephone conversations were monitored and mail written in the area was not posted until two-weeks after D-Day. Such were the requirements for mounting a military force of 250,000 men for immediate combat on the other side of the English Channel, a distance of nearly 150 miles to 'Omaha' and 'Utah' beaches.

'Rehearsals for the landing were held at Slapton Sands in Cornwall on the west coast of England. All US tactical units scheduled for the assault were to rehearse their operations under assumed combat conditions. In these rehearsals, without exception, the command headquarters afloat lost contact with troops ashore. I had learned from Lord Louis Mountbatten that in every amphibious operation in which he had a part, there was a failure in communications. I therefore proposed to General Gerow that I be permitted to form an Information Team consisting of 23 officers and men.

'We would be equipped with four radio transmitters, two command sets with a range of 400 miles to be mounted in DUKWs (Duplex Drive Amphibious Trucks) and two smaller transmitters to be carried in Jeeps. We were to land immediately behind the assault forces, collect information on the progress of the landing and transmit it directly to the command headquarters afloat. The high command would act only on messages from my radio. My proposal was approved. My personnel were all volunteers and I trained them as an extracurricular activity. Our two DUKWs would be loaded on two LSTs (Landing Ship Tanks) and the two jeeps would go over on LCTs (Landing Craft Tanks). I boarded the LST carrying DUKW #1 on 4 June and we put to sea almost immediately. At midnight, I learned that we turned back to England because of high wind and rough seas. Shortly after daylight, we dropped anchor and at mid-day again put to sea to follow the schedule previously established. Shortly after midnight, I joined my men on our DUKW in the hold of the ship just inboard of the ramp.

'Sixteen other DUKWs were aboard the LST. Each carried a 105mm gun. We didn't know it, but within a few hours 14 of these DUKWs would be at the bottom of the sea, swamped by the high waves or sunk by enemy gunfire. Only two reached the beach.'
Colonel B. B. Talley.

'I was a radio operator assigned to the 56th Signal Battalion located at Norton Manor a few miles from Taunton, Somersetshire and was the headquarters for Fifth Corps (V Corps), 1st United States Army. Our Battalion was one of the many service troops assigned to V Corps and, in our case, had the responsibility of providing the various communication media for V Corps i.e.: radio, wire, etc. About three months, or so, before D-Day a number of the Battalion's radio operators were ordered to attend a meeting at the V-Corps headquarter complex on the base. This came as quite a surprise to all of us as this was not our usual stamping grounds. Needless to say, we were curious, puzzled and more than a little apprehensive. We assembled in a private room, with doors closed and were introduced to Colonel Benjamin B. Talley. He explained that he was looking for fifteen men to participate in a mission during the initial phases of the upcoming landings. The mission would be dangerous but was a necessary gear in the machinery and could contribute greatly to the success of the invasion. We had a day or so to think it over and those of us who chose to volunteer met with Colonel Talley again. There was no lack of volunteers and through some process of elimination; fifteen of us were selected to participate in the endeavour. T/5 Joseph M. Amato, the other radio operator who was from LeRoy, New York, a small town about 35 miles from my hometown of Rochester and I, had originally met on the train from Rochester to Fort Niagara after our enlistment in October 1942.

'We were also informed that this meeting was the last chance to change our minds about volunteering. Once our training commenced, any man that chose to drop out would be confined incommunicado until the invasion was over. On 26 May our training complete, we left Norton Manor in our respective vehicles and drove to the coastal marshalling area where troops were amassing to launch the invasion. At the marshalling area we were thoroughly briefed and learned that we would be landing on 'Omaha' Beach at H+60 on Easy Red sector with Regimental Combat Teams of the 1st and 29th Infantry Divisions. The tension and apprehension was rampant among all of us as we learned of our roles and risks in this massive operation. But there was a feeling of elation too. We had been training for this moment for months, in my case, 17 months. We all felt that we were as trained as we would ever be. Now, at last, it was on.'

Robert R. Chapman, Technician 4th grade - Information Team - 56th Signal Battalion.

'On June 5 about midnight we were under way. The sea was still very choppy; and all the men on the ships had been kept aboard and had experienced a full day and a half of waiting. Our headquarters ship came into position off 'Omaha' around 3.30 am. I received orders from Captain E. A. Mitchell [Rear-Admiral H. Kent Hewitt (Commanding the Amphibious Force, US Atlantic Fleet)'s Operations Officer] to go ashore and check to see what the Naval Beachmaster might need in the immediate future. I was to report back to Captain Mitchell and Rear-Admiral Kirk. From the bridge of our command ship, the Duty Officer signalled a passing LCVP to come alongside and take an officer ashore. This was accomplished and I was bound for the Normandy shore - a lone coxswain running the boat and myself.'

Jim Van Orsdel, an officer in the US Navy aboard the USS *Augusta*.[25]

'We were shipped from Cookson, Northern Ireland to Quorn, a small secret airbase in England to train for D-Day. We were in a barbed wire enclosure so no one could talk to us and we could not reveal what we were up to. While we didn't like that, we climbed up the barbed wire fence and went down the road to a little English pub. The MP's came after us with Tommy guns and trucks. They took us and locked us up. Then it was back to our Quonset huts because we were pathfinders, D-Day was very close and we were going to lead the parade.'

---

25 *Invaders: British and American Experience of Seaborne landings 1939-1945* by Colin John Bruce (Chatham Publishing 1999).

Technical Sergeant Howard Hicks, Platoon Sergeant, Company 'G', 505 Regiment, 82nd Airborne Division who was born 2 November 1918, Fed City, PA, 30 miles south of Pittsburgh. In April 1943 he volunteered for paratroopers and joined the 82nd Airborne when he was shipped to Africa. He made a parachute jump on Sicily and also jumped on Salerno Beach in Italy.

'Memorial Day in May 1944 was spent quietly, if over 500 paratroopers could be quiet, at the Cottesmore airdrome in England's Midlands. There was hardly any reason to compel us to recall that which was past history, particularly since we had been ordered to collect our combat gear several days before and were transported here by the local bus company and our GI trucks from Camp Quorn. We were here to make final preparations for the long anticipated combat jump into the continent of Europe. Yet the past was important to us, for many had tramped through similar battle strategies and we could profit by their failures as well as their successes. I could still remember when this day was called Decoration Day and Civil War veterans paraded in the Hunting Park area in Philadelphia when my Grandfather took us via the #52 and York Road trolley #6, from Germantown.

'There may have been a special reason for the British buses to assist in our transport problems, but I was not privy to that mystery. We had our own GI 12-ton trucks, but perhaps there weren't enough of them to handle these runs to the airbase, because they helped out every time we made a dry run practice jump with all our combat gear. Loading was quite a hassle. If there were any Germans spies around, they would certainly be confused by all our manoeuvring. We would pass through Loughborough and on to the east through Melton Mowbray then head for Cottesmore. Cottesmore here we come again! We never really knew whether this would be our last trip for the invasion jump, or just another dry run. We would have to wait for the briefing to determine that information. We made this trip many times before and each time we had returned even as we had come. Sometimes we made a practice jump if the English weather permitted. This time we felt it was different as we boarded the busses at our camp in Quorn and chugged our way through the English countryside. Part of the 9th Air Force Troop Carrier Wing was waiting for us at Cottesmore with the C-47s all prepared to take us on our intended journey. Each trip led to rumours of one type or another, but this time the older vets of Sicily and Italy were saying that this was it! We did not pay much attention to them because we had heard all that Jazz before in the windy currents of swirling rumours around the Camp and airdrome.

'We had an MP escort via a motorcycle troop of snappy looking GIs with their official arm bands on their uniforms and as we arrived at the base they ushered us into the base grounds, right up next to the hangars that would be our homes for the next several days. It was quite a struggle for us to exit from the close quarters of the buses and form up into company formations to march into the hangar assigned to us. Marching was probably not the best description for this manoeuvre, because we practically dragged ourselves and equipment to our places. There were cots all over the hanger floor with barely room to walk, which compounded our travel. It appeared that there were about 500 cots. I wondered who they were expecting. In reality, it was the whole third battalion of the 505th Parachute Infantry Regiment. Each company had an area assigned and commanded to organize their gear and await the call to chow. They even had that area ready for us! After chow we had a preliminary briefing about our conduct on the base and general cleanliness rules to be observed while there. Location of latrines, constant calisthenics, area boundaries and all that important stuff every GI needed to know.

'With the morning chow and calisthenics out of the way, we were ready for our first briefing regarding our new mission. We were issued several new pieces of equipment that were not issued on previous sorties. We received new gas masks and K-rations. Following those items we were handed, after an appropriate demonstration, a grenade composed of some new explosive called Composition 'C' which had been manufactured by the British. It was a mass of clay like material about the size of a softball to which one added a wrapping of elastic sock like covering and then implanted a detonator. It was explained that we would carry this item in one of our pant leg pockets and when this wonder unit was properly used against a tank, it would blow a hole in the side of the vehicle imploding on impact scattering metal fragments in the interior of the tank, or it could disable the treads. I heard what sounded like a 'whooppee' in the rear and several of the Sicily veterans who had witnessed Tiger tanks in action at Biazza Ridge, expressed some doubts about the value of this new grenade. It appeared to us that we would be vulnerable toting this unit in our pant leg pockets.

'The rumours that had persisted since we arrived at the airdrome began to take on a more serious tone when we were issued ammunition for all our weapons. The invasion was imminent. The final touch was the explanation of 9-inch Hawkins land mines to be used for road blocks by all our units and these would be issued to all individuals prior to take off. They would be packed in our mussette bags along with our rations, miscellaneous items and extra clothes. We were reminded to insert the stiff cardboard piece between the case and the detonator to prevent premature explosions during transit to our destination. We would secure the mine in between rations to keep it tight in the mussette bag. Jolly, what!

'Training exercises were constant to avoid stagnation from our cramped quarters within the confines of the hangers. On June 1st after the usual chow and calisthenics, the hanger was buzzing with activity as groups of troopers toted into our briefing area large models about the size of ping-pong tables, which showed towns, bridges and terrain of some unidentified land. All the contours were in place along with wooded areas and grassy fields and in some cases animals. We correctly concluded that this was where we were going to land in the very near future. The briefing began at 9 am sharp. We were called to attention by our officers into Company formations all sounding off for attendance roll call. Instructions were given about the models and who should gather about which model and listen to the explanations of the tasks to be performed in those areas. The whole Third Battalion was present and Colonel Ekman introduced 'Overlord' in general terms, but not noting at that time where or when, but reviewing the 505th Regiment's important objectives and responsibilities and the proposed link up with seaborne forces within a scheduled time frame. He signified the terrain models around him and indicated that we would receive further indoctrination shortly regarding our company objectives. He then revealed that these were places in Normandy that we would be expected to take and hold until the beach forces linked up with our units, which he indicated was approximately 12 hours, or at least that was the intended schedule. He then ordered Company Commanders to take charge of their units to complete their specific parts in the invasion plans. Our earlier indifference began to fade as the situation appeared to be serious.

'Within a short time we were ordered to assemble around those tables which indicated the objectives assigned to Company 'H', as part of the third battalion. I marvelled at the excellent workmanship that had created those units. Our model had a small village at its centre with roads leading out in different directions with labels indicating other towns such as Chef du Pont and Montebourg. North, east, south and west directions similar to maps were indicated. It was difficult to absorb everything at one glance and I was fascinated by the details. I saw the rivers and the fields bordered by hedgerows and other vegetation. A Lieutenant from G-2 gave the initial presentation to our group outlining the areas of main concerns, then turned the discussion over to our platoon lieutenant, Lieutenant Alexander Townsend and he emphasized our responsibility to support the third battalion companies in the capture of Ste- Mère-Église. We were to hold road blocks around the village to secure it until the beach force reached our lines in about twelve hours. They would probably be units from the Fourth Division which was scheduled to land on the beach opposite us called by code name 'Utah'. We learned that this peninsula was called the Cotentin. Being unfamiliar with the geography of France, we wondered where that was. Never heard of Merderet River, Ste-Marie-du-Mont, La Fière, Neuville, Montebourg, Coquerie, Beuzevillle au Plain, or Chef du Pont to name a few of the titles thrown at us in the review. Some names! Who's going to remember all that data? I surely hope that all the officers and non-coms were listening. Take the bridges, ford the rivers, take the towns, set up road blocks, take prisoners for enemy position information and above all hold until the beach forces reach us. I asked where the code name 'Utah' came from, but no answer was given.

'At last a break came and we had time to mull over all the information we were given. I could hardly tear myself away from the models as I went around to each of them. One of the officers was still standing by one and he showed us the map of the area of Normandy pointing out the areas depicted on the models and I then began to understand better what I heard earlier. We could see the names of all those places. 'Oh', I said, 'There's 'Utah' Beach, Ravenoville, Fourcarville, Ste-Germain-de-Varreville and Ste-Martin-de-Varreville just inland from the beaches.' It appeared that with quick success they would reach us in a short period of time right through Baudienville, Beuzeville au Plain, Mesieres, Turqueville, or Ecoqueneauville. That last name was a tough one to pronounce. French was a difficult language for me in High School and with all these odd titles I began to question the French people and their language pronunciations. Well it was soon time for chow, so we headed for the mess area with our standard GI mess kits, after a quick latrine visit.

'We finished our meal, dipped our mess kits and utensils in the two 55 gallon drums of boiling water outside the mess tent soaped, cleaned and aired dried the cleaned kits and headed back to the hangar area. Crap and poker games were already in progress by those who had completed their meals first, since we had some free time before the next briefing. Money was laying all over one army cot that was being used as the crap game table, while another cot was available for poker. Everyone who was willing, or had the dough, was involved either directly, or in side betting at the crap games.

'The airdrome was a crowded place these days and the games had been in progress as continuously as free time would allow since we arrived at the base hangars. On several occasions air corps personnel sauntered in to be included in the round robin. A quick road to poverty, I thought to myself. I wanted no part of the actual gambling, but I became a watcher. I supposed that some troopers figured that they had little to lose, because they would not need the money where we were headed. Perhaps they had a premonition of impending disaster for after all, hadn't we been repeatedly told way back in jump school, that few of us would return alive. We had been indoctrinated into the brevity of a paratrooper's life span and most of us did not believe that meant us.

'The crowded conditions of our hanger life and the endless formations for briefing, mess, calisthenics and waiting for the uncertain future began to get under our skin. We were getting agitated with each other and more than one fight had broken out in the hangar and environs. If we could carry this energy of fight to the enemy, wow!

'June 4 arrived; the eve of our departure for Normandy. Just after midnight we would jump. The situation was now made as clear as possible in order to insure our success. All the towns, rivers, streams, railroad bridges and roads were thoroughly reviewed on the models and maps, with the officers coordinating the information for us as well as for their own recall. There was some mention of possible flooding of certain areas by the krauts and that some fields were strewn with obstacles that might thwart our efforts. We would board the planes sometime after 2000 for takeoff. All equipment not already issued, would be distributed by 2000 hours and then we would assemble for our trek to the reliable C-47s. Earlier we had been issued some French invasion currency for use if necessary. For what purpose, we couldn't fathom. In addition to our main chute, we carried a reserve chute strapped across our chest, added to this equipment were the following items that I carried : one M1 Garand rifle, belt loaded with 30 calibre ammo, two bandoliers of extra 30 calibre ammo, two fragmentation grenades, one smoke grenade, one orange smoke signal grenade, one 20-foot rope, trench knife with brass knuckles, several days of K-Rations, canteen filled, clothing changes - first aid pack - water purification tablets - toilet articles - misc. equipment such as pencils, notebook - mess kit and utensils - and heavy duty belt and suspenders to help support the load. I put my New Testament in my breast pocket close to my heart. It was a gift from my mother.

'I carried my M-1 in three pieces in a special pouch designed for that purpose which was set behind my main chute. I was just about ready to start putting my equipment on and head for the planes, when the order came to us to assemble without our gear. The invasion was postponed for twenty four hours. This announcement was greeted with many groans. Uncertain weather conditions over the Channel made it necessary to hold for later developments. This only added to the agitation that already prevailed. It meant another period of waiting which increased the foreboding of the unknown. June 6 would be the assault date!

'This postponement provided additional time to review assignments which sharpened our focus on the impending events. Third Battalion Companies which included Headquarters, G, H and I Companies of the 505 PIR were to take Ste-Mère-Église which was situated along N-13 the main road running basically north and south through the Cotentin Peninsula. A strategic objective along this highway, which ran from Cherbourg east to Bayeux in the area of Normandy through towns such as Valognes, Montebourg and then through Ste-Mère-Église and Carentan and eastward, this vital road, if cut, could deny the Germans control of the western portion of the peninsula and our beach forces could then succeed in establishing a strong beach-head from which they could support the landings with additional forces and supplies. If the invasion was to be successful, we needed as much area as we could take for all the troops and equipment to make it so.

'June 5 was a day to ponder about our immediate future and all the data that was pumped into us for the past several days. Who's going to remember all the right things?

I hope I remember the sign and counter-sign and where I secured that cricket sounding device for the purpose of recognition signals. I hope that I do not get separated from my squad and platoon. We had some light recreation and rechecking of our gear, the ever present card and dice games, constant treks to the latrines and early in the evening our chapel service led by Chappie Wood, whose prayer is still part of our life.

'Almighty god, our heavenly father: who art above us and beneath us within and around us drive from the minds of our paratroopers any fear of the space in which thou art ever present. Give them the confidence in the strength of thine everlasting arms, endue them with clear minds and pure hearts that they may participate in the victory which this nation must achieve in thy name and through thy will. Make them hardy soldiers of our country as well as thy son, our saviour, Jesus Christ. Amen.'

Pfc Leslie Palmer Cruise Jr., Company 'H', 505th Parachute Infantry Regiment, 82nd Airborne. General von Schlieben had his HQ in Valognes. As far as he was concerned, the holding of Montebourg 30 kms south-east of Cherbourg, was essential to his plans to defend Cherbourg and prevent the vital port falling into the hands of the Allies.

'We were loaded on a train and went to Swindon. There, we went by truck to Aldbourne Wilkes. We hit it off with the people in the village, but they didn't understand the way we spent our money. We told them we couldn't take it with us where we were going, so we might as well spend it and enjoy it. We were at our highest pitch in training by the time D-Day came that we would go into town just spoiling for a good fight. It didn't matter who it was, just so we could blow off some steam. One day we were loaded onto trucks and we were taken to an area that was all fenced in and guarded by MPs. We were told to behave ourselves and start checking our equipment for the big jump. We got instructions and started studying maps and photographs of the whole area where we were going to jump. By the time it came time to jump, I think every man could have run around the whole area where we were supposed to jump blindfolded, but it didn't work out like it was planned. On June 5 the officers told us we could go to a show that was close by. We didn't suspect anything, so we went. When we got back around 18:00 they told us to get our things together, whatever we were going to jump with. I had all this stuff packed in a bag that looked like a barracks bag that was tied to a rope about 20 feet long and tied to the bottom of my harness. There were two straps that went around my leg and I was supposed to pull a cord to release the bag after my chute opened. In all, it weighed around 110-150 pounds and it was loaded with: three boxes of machine gun ammo (each box had 250 rounds in it), six hand grenades (they would later come in handy), all my toilet equipment and change of underwear, 35 packs of cigarettes, 100 sticks of chewing gum that my mother had sent me and 12 candy bars. On top of the bag, I had a banana knife called a machete, to be used to cut telephone lines or anything that could delay the enemy. On top of the bag I had a land mine for tanks or trucks and ten clips of rifle ammo. I had a knife strapped on my leg and a belt full of ammo, which held nine clips. All the pockets on my jump suit were filled with K-rations and hand grenades. I had long underwear plus my dress uniform on because it was damp and chilly. We went out to the planes about 20:00 and lay around and smoked and talked.'

Bill Oatman, born in Lancaster, Pennsylvania, on 20 May 1924. He signed up on 28 July 1942 for the paratroops and was sent to the newly formed 506th Parachute Infantry Regiment.

'The 439th Troop Carrier Group was assigned to Balderton airdrome near Newark, until a month or so before the invasion, when we were moved to Taunton. It was time to invade Hitler's Festung Europa. We could feel the tension in the air. Then came June 3 and we were herded into a block of barracks behind barbed wire. Uncle Sam wasn't about to let any of his invasion party troops wander off downtown and give away any secrets that we might have had. And that's not to say that a single one of us knew our exact destination along the coast of France. Only Ike knew the landing spots and he didn't disclose them until sealed orders were brought to commander and flight planners 24 hours in advance. The briefings for the aerial invasion of 'Utah' Beach, our particular destination, were serious matters, but not without a little pressure-relieving levity upon occasion. Our Chaplain, Father Whalen, had probably heard about all the profanity known to mankind because he was a prison chaplain at Joliet, Illinois prior to volunteering for the service so he wasn't shocked at one of the briefings to hear some profanity which included the Lord's name. Upon looking around his listeners, the briefer stopped to apologize to the good Father. 'Don't worry about what I think,' said Father, 'worry about what the Lord thinks.'

'One of the briefers was our own 91st Troop Carrier Squadron's captain named Merriman. As I listened to him, I recalled that he was a former school teacher but quite a roughneck when he wanted to be. I remembered the time when he took a carbine to the shower in North Carolina to see if its charge would penetrate the wall of wood and galvanized steel. It did. It went clear through, crossed half the barracks and lodged in a four by four of hard timber. I remember hoping that the American armament would be that good on the beach. The conclusion of the captain's briefing went something like this: 'Glider pilots will release when the pilot of the C-47 leading the formation starts a gradual turn to the left to return to the coast. If any C-47 pilots cuts his glider off during an invasion without sufficient reason and there shouldn't be any, he'd better keep on going because if he comes back here, I'll be waiting for him.' I never heard of any tow pilot needlessly cutting his glider off during several invasions on the European continent.

'Speaking of C-47s - they were actually underpowered for many of the jobs they were called upon to do, including pulling heavily weighted gliders. One of our C-47s carried a radio crewman who must have weighed nearly 300 pounds. Nobody knew his exact weight but he was heavy enough to upset the trim of the C-47 as he walked to the rear. His pilot, a Captain Anderson, joked to a buddy that he intended to tie the sergeant to the seat at the radio because he didn't want to worry about keeping his plane trimmed straight and level during the assault on D-Day. My group briefing was sombre right up until the final moment. 'Sir,' asked the glider pilot, 'what do we do after we land our gliders?' There was a brief period of silence, after which the briefing officer, a non-flying person, admitted, 'I don't know. I guess we never really thought of that.' Perhaps it was true. I thought then and there amid a lot of laughter, that maybe glider pilots really were originally meant to be expendable in war. The best answer to the question came from a glider pilot sitting next to me. He said, 'Run like hell.'

Flight (Warrant) Officer Charles E. 'Chuck' Skidmore, Jr., combat glider pilot, 91st Troop Carrier Squadron, 439th Troop Carrier Group, who was born on 17 January 1920, in Columbus, a small town in Cherokee County, Kansas, just across the line from Joplin, Missouri. Following graduation with a journalism major from Kansas

University in June 1941 he enlisted in the aviation cadet program but was eliminated from the flying program due to 'flying deficiency.' Finally, in July 1942 he enlisted in the glider programme as a Class-A glider pilot, because he already had a private pilot's licence. Only a limited number with no previous flying experience were accepted for a few weeks during early 1942.

'In December 1943 I'd become Chief Gunnery Instructor at HMS *Turtle*, the Combined Operations training base at Poole in Dorset. So I trained the support craft - LCT(R)s and LCG(L)s - for all five landing areas, ready for Normandy. We used to go out every day and bombard the nearby Studland range, till there wasn't much of it left! When we'd finished training all five forces I was told to take the School back to Wales, where it was to remain until we could begin preparing people for the Japanese war. However, I thought this was a rotten idea. So I persuaded the CO of the last of the forces to come through, Captain Lorenzo Sabin, USN [senior officer of the Close Gunfire Support Group destined for 'Omaha'] to take me with him. I said to him 'Don't you think, having trained all your people, I'd better come along as your Gunnery Officer?' He said 'Very good idea. Come along'. So I did! In a LCH (Landing Craft, Headquarters), which was an LCI(L) converted to accommodate a signals staff.

'We sailed from Poole the first time, but then they had to halt this whole gigantic operation for a day because of the weather, so we had to go back. Not to Poole; to Salcombe, in Devon. The LCT(R)s we were with had only a short range. They made the Germans get their heads down pretty quickly! We had quite a lot of them and they were all firing at the same time, which was a terrifying sight. They must've had a terrific effect on morale. My God, they frightened me! And then came the turn of the LCG(L)s. I'd given them targets and then told them to fire on targets of opportunity, which they did. We had wonderful detailed maps with all the defences marked in blue and purple. We couldn't really be sure our 4.7-inch guns, two of which formed the main armament of each LCG(L), were going to penetrate some of these concrete emplacements, so we just had to fire on them and hope we were doing some good. Because the defenders were all dug in, of course and prepared for this kind of stuff. The rockets were out of range after D-Day. The LCG(L)s went on popping away at various things, but even they were out of range after a few days.

Patrick Wall, an officer in the Royal Marines who inveigled his way into the American assault on 'Omaha' Beach. [26]

'Preparations were endless. My 19th Birthday was only 3 month's past and I had been assigned to the 115th Regiment as an Infantry replacement after arriving in England in January. Obviously something big was about to happen. Considerable barracks talk was of an impending invasion of France, but when and where was all conjecture. Our Battalion Commander was Lieutenant Colonel Richard Blatt, a tall imposing West Pointer who, when forming the battalion for a lecture would refer to us Company Headquarters' chaps as 'you specialists'. Each Battalion had in its HQ

---

26 *Invaders: British and American Experience of Seaborne landings 1939-1945* by Colin John Bruce (Chatham Publishing 1999).

Company a reconnaissance or intelligence platoon, an anti-tank platoon and an ammunition pioneer (or the A&P) platoon, to which I was assigned. It was responsible for laying mines, finding and removing enemy mines, laying barbed wire obstacles, supplying all ammunition needed by the battalion, blowing up or destroying obstacles and in general doing the work required by engineer troops.

'We were not allowed to keep diaries or cameras. About the middle of May, we were told to send home all non-essential things that we could not, or did not want to carry. At this time we turned in our green HBT fatigue uniforms. We wouldn't be wearing them again. We were given anti-gas impregnated ODs. I wore a pair of smooth leather hobnailed shoes - just like the World War I shoe. Others had the regular rough shoe. All wore canvas leggings and the tan or khaki field jackets. Our packs were virtually the same as the World War I infantry pack. Entrenching shovels strapped into their canvas cases were the new folding type shovel. In my pack were six boxes (two day's supplies of K-rations). We also had a raincoat, a pair of socks, one change of underwear and a cloth bag containing shaving stuff and a toothbrush. My pistol belt contained a carbine magazine pouch with two magazines for my M1 carbine. (The early version with the 'L' type sight set for either 150 or 300 yards and no provision for the bayonet, as did the later version that was introduced at the war's end). The M3 was attached to the belt along with the usual canteen and first aid pouch. I had two fragmentation grenades attached to my pack straps. About this time we were issued waist type CO_2 inflatable life belts. They worked by squeezing a pliers-like-grip releasing the CO_2 bottles.

'There was much activity in camp but we were told nothing specific. We were simply moving or what? One morning we boarded trucks that took us the ten miles into Plymouth into a Naval Base named Sir Walter Raleigh. When the gates closed, no-one was allowed out. We were quartered in the Navy barracks and a detachment from the 5th Armoured Division prepared our meals on a grand scale that had not previously been enjoyed. Steaks and delicious menus were not seen since the states. The wags quipped that they were 'fattening us up for the kill'. Here we were issued French language books and paid the equivalent of four dollars in French invasion currency. Outside we were marched one platoon at a time into a specially fenced off building where large photo maps were displayed of a panorama of the French coast and we were told of the invasion sometime in the next few weeks. Colonel Blatt pointed out our Regiment's objective, a little village a mile or so from the coast. 'Ste-Laurent-sur-Mer', he called it. The map revealed the draw we were to try to use to get off the beach. Our platoon leader was told to have his men set up a road block on a road leading south, just east of the village. We were told that our Regiment would not be the assaulting regiment, which was up to the 116th Regiment, along with some elements of the First Division. We would be in the second wave and would be loaded down with extra ammo and explosives. We had a lot of invasion training on the English coast, so I suppose we considered ourselves as prepared as we'd ever be. The many hedgerows were pointed out and we saw they were very similar to those in England. We checked the functioning of our gas masks in the usual gas filled building and were issued new OD wool uniforms that had been soaked in a gas resistant oily chemical.

'It was the ending days of May, days of beautiful spring sunshine and as I looked over the vast Plymouth harbour, the sun glistened on the waves as hundreds of invasion type boats silently rocked in their moorings. That night a lone German plane flew high over Plymouth. The great searchlights went on and would reveal the plane for a moment while anti-aircraft fire filled the sky. I was amazed no bombs were dropped and the plane disappeared into the night. We thought about what a target all those invasion ships anchored in the harbour was, yet they were left entirely alone. Surely they'd be back and this time with lots of friends - but the remainder of the night was only an eerie silence. The next day we were marched from the Naval Base to the docks, where rows of ships were waiting. Sleek looking craft they were, not those boxy little infantry landing craft we trained with. These ships had the appearance of private yachts; long and slender but bristling with 20 mm guns. We walked aboard on ramps just wide-enough for a single company of men. I believe it held our entire company minus the anti-tank guns. The ship's captain greeted us from a miniature bridge and identified his ship as a landing craft infantry (LCI), with '455' in big white letters painted on its hull. I took a special note of this and wrote a letter to my folks mentioning the number in the event they might see such a ship in the newsreels or papers that would surely cover the invasion.

'Once aboard and assigned to our bunking areas, we were free to relax, read a few armed forces paperbacks or listen to phonograph records on the portable phonographs provided by the navy. Rations were 10-1 prepared by navy cooks. A sailor brought a case of unusual grey-painted soup cans, made in England, about twice as tall as a conventional soup can with the unique feature of a self heating device activated by a pull-wire to ignite a heating mixture. I took a couple with me. We sailed out of Plymouth and several hours later assembled at another harbour someone said was Weymouth. D-Day was set for the morning of Monday June the 5th. Leaflets containing a message from Eisenhower were distributed explaining the great task ahead. I carefully folded the leaflet and put it in my shirt pocket. I would include it in my next letter home. I still have it with the scrap book my folks had begun to assemble.

'Church services were conducted that night of June 4th. I was assigned to guard duty which amounted to nothing more than standing on deck for two hours at a time looking at the night. It seemed to me a rather senseless thing to do with the hundreds of ships anchored there. Our equipment was rechecked. Our gas masks, which included a large green plastic bag with a clear plastic end, forming a 360° window were folded into a compact package about 4x8 inches. When opened it would completely cover the soldier and presumably protect against any vesicant type chemicals the Germans might use.

'That evening we began moving out into the Channel. The sea was quite rough and our little ship rolled and pitched uncomfortably, but shortly we turned back towards Weymouth harbour. It was announced that the invasion had been postponed for another 24 hours. The weather we learned was not favourable for what we had to do. We relaxed again and wondered about tomorrow. I sat on my bunk and wrote another letter. I guess I slept some too. About this time the Lieutenant in the Communications platoon made a rather startling announcement. Addressing his platoon sergeant and all within speaking range 'Sergeant, I want you to understand you have my permission to shoot any orders given from here on out.' I thought that is hell of a pompous statement to make. We're soldiers and

soldiers are conditioned to obedience. Why make such a remark?'
John Hooper, 29th Infantry Division, HQ Company, A&P Platoon, 1st Battalion, 115th Regiment.

'In April I was in charge of two squads of riflemen. We were billeted in a house in the village of Broadstone in Dorsetshire. The house belonged to a widow whose husband had been killed at the battle of El Alamein. He had been a soldier in 'The Queen's Own'. We got along well with the people of Broadstone and shared our rations and food parcels with them. An orange was worth its weight in gold to us and to them. We spent May in a marshalling camp near the harbour town of Poole on the south coast of England. Our camp was ringed with armed guards and barbed wire to keep spies out and us in. At the end of May word came down that the invasion was imminent. Barbers cut off all our hair so we would not need a haircut for months. My buddies and I wanted to grow long, drooping moustaches like the Chinese villain Fu Manchu in movies to frighten the Germans, but our officers said 'no'. By June 3 my battalion boarded a LST or Landing Ship (Tank) at Poole. There was nowhere to go, few pastimes but card games and shooting craps, the weather was foul, the meals were 'character-builders', the ship stank of a thousand men packed like sardines and overworked plumbing. We slept on decks, vehicles, in passageways, maybe a bunk bed, but only the ship's crew had berths. We left Poole after nightfall on June 5. Once we were out of the harbour swells in the Channel made a lot of us 'green at the gills' in spite of seasick pills. We did not know whether there were U-boats or torpedo boats waiting for us as had happened during Operation Tiger in April. It turned out there were none. Nobody slept well that night, except the Germans. At maybe 2 o'clock on D-Day morning our officers awakened us sergeants and we awakened our squads. We were offered a breakfast of beans and bacon along with a hot drink (coffee or cocoa), smoked cigarettes and collected our gear. Each man carried 50 to 80 pounds: his weapon, its ammo, maybe his share of ammo for a machine gun or mortar or bazooka, pack, K-rations for three days, gasmask, entrenching tool, raincoat, life-jacket, canteen, shelter-half, first-aid kit and so on. We also carried rope and toggle ropes. The latter was a short rope with a wooden handle (toggle) at one end and a small loop at the other end through which the toggle was pulled to make a big noose. These came in handy. Morale was good, all things considered. It would get better at dawn when we could see our ship surrounded by others and smaller landing craft from horizon to horizon.'
Sergeant Jim McKee, Rifle Company 'K', 3rd Battalion, 12th Regiment, 4th Division.

'In April 1944 I was a Typhoon pilot on 197 Squadron at Needs Oar Point near the Beaulieu River overlooking the Solent and the Isle of Wight and became part of the 2nd Tactical Air Force; along with 257, 266 and 193, then became 146 Wing, all operating from the same airfield in preparation for D-Day. The Typhoons were equipped with bomb racks under each wing to take 500 or 1,000lb bombs. In May our main operational work was attacking radar targets along the coast of France and V-1 sites, as well as being on escort and standby duties. On 3 June we made a high level dive bombing attack on the radar site at Cap d'Antifer, not far from Le

Havre. We crossed over the French coast, high enough to avoid the light flak and then turned 180 degrees in a dive bombing attack with a final burst of our cannon fire before levelling out over the sea at approximately 500 knots. Then we formed up in sections of four in battle formation for our return home. Total flying time was 1 hour, 15 minutes. Later in the day, orders were received to paint the broad black and white invasion stripes on the wings and fuselage of our Typhoons, hopefully to identify friend from foe, both in the air and on the ground. Needless to say, a lot of paint was splashed around by both pilots and ground crew and a great sense of anticipation was felt by everyone.

'On 5 June I started off by air testing one of our new four bladed Typhoons, which had just been delivered. In the evening of D-1, we carried out another operation over the French Coast. I noted in my log book 'large convoys of LCTs seen heading toward Cherbourg.' In fact, the Channel was covered with boats of various kinds, a fantastic sight and it seemed impossible that the Germans did not know what we were up to. On our return all squadron pilots were told to attend a large mess tent where a covered blackboard was set up. We were then informed by the senior officer present that tomorrow, 6th of June, would be D-Day. The blackboard was then unveiled to reveal the proposed landings, etc. We were told to turn in early, as we should be on call from approximately 4 am the next morning. Needless to say, the roar of aircraft going overhead towards France made sleep almost impossible in our tents.

'We all took an early breakfast and reported to our various dispersals, where the ground crew were already running up the Sabre engines of our Typhoons and then refuelling them while we awaited the first calls to briefing and also listened to the BBC radio broadcasts. My squadron was first involved at 07:10, eight aircraft being led by Wing Commander Baker, who later lost his life over Normandy on 16 June. They attacked targets in a low level attack south of Bayeux and all returned safely at 08:20. As soon as the aircraft from the first operation of the day had landed and taxied in, they were surrounded by both ground crew and the other pilots on standby, who were checking firstly to see if the muzzle (the mouth of the cannon) covers had been blown off, which would indicate that each of the four 20mm cannons had been fired and then if there was any flak damage to the aircraft. As soon as the pilots had climbed down, we all wanted to know what it was like over the beachhead. 'Any enemy aircraft seen? How much flak? The weather conditions? What targets had been attacked?' Meanwhile, the Squadron Intelligence Officer was hovering around, wanting to speak to each pilot who had taken part in this, our first operation of D-Day. Having slung their parachutes over their shoulders, many walked away to light a cigarette before giving way to the countless questions still coming from all sides. The aircraft were now surrounded by the ground crews, busy refuelling and re-arming to get them ready as soon as possible for the next operation. I was not involved in the first operation of the day, but was requested later in the morning to fly the Wing Intelligence Officer to a meeting at Thorney Island airfield not far from Portsmouth using the Auster aircraft. While waiting, I observed a great deal of aerial activity; Typhoons on standby and light bombers overhead from airfields further away. On my return to Needs Oar Point I remained on call until 1750 hours when eight of us were briefed to carry out a reconnaissance south of Caen. This involved low level bombing on an emergency supply dump, which was left with black smoke and flames coming from the target area. We all returned at 1920. The third operation by my squadron took off at 2105, this time led by our commanding officer, Squadron Leader Taylor. Again, eight aircraft were involved, the operation being an armed reconnaissance in the Caen/Bayeux area. They landed back at 2215.'

Pilot Officer Kenneth Trott, born in Ilford, London on 28 December 1922. 'From D+1, we continued at standby until called upon to provide close support to the Canadian Army, as well as specialist operations on selected targets. 146 Wing only lost one pilot that day, although my best friend failed to return from an operation in the area of St. Lô, the following day and was later reported killed in action. In all, during the ten weeks of the Battle of Normandy, 150 Typhoon pilots lost their lives, while many others were taken prisoners of war, myself included. To commemorate this battle and in particular the part the Typhoon played, a memorial has been erected near the village of Noyers-Bocage about ten miles southwest of Caen.'

The 6-inch gun cruiser HMS *Belfast*, flagship of Fire Support Force E and the 10th Cruiser Squadron, which left the Clyde on 3 June and arrived in the Eastern Task Force area at 0500 on D-Day where she engaged the batteries at Ver-sur-Mer and Courseulles-sur-Mer in the sector of the 3rd Canadian Division, opening fire at 0527. (IWM)

HMS *Rodney* blasting targets ashore

HMS *Warspite* blasting targets ashore with its 15-inch guns. This veteran battleship, which had taken part in the Battle of Jutland in 1916, arrived in the Eastern Task Force area at 0525 on 6 June and provided notable gunfire support (Bombardment Force D) (Assault Convoy S6), expending 219 rounds of main ammunition by 1600. She suffered superficial blast damage on the 7th and returned to the Solent. (IWM)

Right: On the eve of D-Day the first Allied aircraft to cross the enemy beachhead were B-17 Flying Fortresses of the 422nd Night Leaflet Squadron, which dropped copies of this leaflet over France warning of an impending invasion.

Below: A joint statement signed by Dwight D. Elsenhower and the Dutch Prime Minister Pieter Gerbrandy was dropped over Holland on D-Day by Leaflet Squadron Flying Fortresses and advised the civilians of the D-Day landings.

Message urgent

du Commandement Suprême des Forces Expéditionnaires Alliées

AUX HABITANTS DE CETTE VILLE

Afin que l'ennemi commun soit vaincu, les Armées de l'Air Alliées vont attaquer tous les centres de transports ainsi que toutes les voies et moyens de communications vitaux pour l'ennemi.

Des ordres à cet effet ont été donnés.

Vous qui lisez ce tract, vous vous trouvez dans ou près d'un centre essentiel à l'ennemi pour le mouvement de ses troupes et de son matériel. L'objectif vital près duquel vous vous trouvez va être attaqué incessament.

Il faut sans délai vous éloigner, avec votre famille, pendant quelques jours, de la zone de danger où vous vous trouvez.

N'encombrez pas les routes. Dispersez-vous dans la campagne, autant que possible.

PARTEZ SUR LE CHAMP !
VOUS N'AVEZ PAS UNE MINUTE A PERDRE !

Z.F.4

Geallieerde troepen landen!

GENERAAL EISENHOWER SPREEKT TOT HET VOLK VAN BEZET EUROPA:

VOLK VAN WEST-EUROPA!

Troepen van het Geallieerd Expeditie Leger zijn aan de Fransche kust geland. Deze landing maakt deel uit van het gemeenschappelijk plan der Vereenigde Volken voor de bevrijding van Europa, in samenwerking met onze groote Russische bondgenooten. Zelfs al heeft de eerste aanval niet in Uw eigen land plaatsgehad,
nadert toch het uur van Uw bevrijding.

Alle patriotten, mannen en vrouwen, jong en oud, hebben een rol te spelen in het behalen van de beslissende overwinning. Tot hen, die lid eener geheime verzetsbeweging zijn, binnenslands of van buiten af geleid, zeg ik ,,Volgt de instructies die gij hebt ontvangen". Tot de patriotten, die geen lid van een georganiseerde verzetsgroep zijn, zeg ik ,,Brengt Uw leven niet noodeloos in gevaar ; gaat voort met Uw lijdelijk verzet totdat ik U het sein geef om op te staan en vijand aan te vallen. Er komt een dag, dat ik Uw vereende krachten zal noodig hebben." Tot de dag aanbreekt, moet U de harde taak van
discipline en zelfbedwang blijven opleggen.

BURGERS VAN FRANKRIJK!

Ik ben er trotsch op wederom de dappere Fransche soldaten onder mijn orders te hebben. Schouder aan schouder strijdend met hun bondgenooten zullen zij hun rol in de bevrijding van hun vaderlandschen bodem waardig vervullen.

Omdat de eerste landing op Uw grondgebied is geschied, herhaal ik voor U met des te méér nadruk de boodschap, die ik tot de volken van andere bezette landen in West-Europa richt. Volgt de instructies die Uw aanvoerders U geven. Een ontijdige opstand van alle Franschen zou U kunnen verhinderen om Uw Vaderland later, als het critisch oogenblik daar is, op de meest doeltreffende wijze te hulp te komen.
West geduldig. Maakt U gereed !

Als Opperbevelhebber van het Geallieerde Expeditie Leger rusten op mij de plicht en de verantwoordelijkheid om alle maatregelen te treffen die noodig zijn voor het voeren van den oorlog. Het is van het grootste belang dat mijn bevelen vlug en bereidwillig worden uitgevoerd.

Het effectieve burgerlijke bestuur in Frankrijk moet door Franschen in handen worden genomen. Ieder moet zijn tegenwoordige werkzaamheden doorgaan tenzij hem andere instructies worden gegeven. Zij die gemeene zaak met den vijand gemaakt en hun land verraden hebben, zullen worden afgezet. Als Frankrijk van zijn onderdrukkers bevrijd is, zult gij Uw vertegenwoordigers kiezen en U zelven de regeering geven, waaronder gij wenscht te leven.

In den loop van dezen veldtocht, die den beslissenden nederlaag van den vijand ten doel heeft, is het mogelijk dat gij nog meer verliezen en schade zult lijden. Hoe tragisch deze ook mogen zijn, rij maken deel uit van den prijs die voor de overwinning betaald moet worden. Ik weet dat ik op Uw standvastigheid mag rekenen, niet minder dan in het verleden. De heldhaftige daden van de Franschen die den strijd tegen de Nazis en hun satellieten to Vichy hebben doorgezet, zijn voor ons allen een voorbeeld en een inspiratie geweest.

Deze landing is slechts het eerste stadium van den veldtocht in West-Europa. In de toekomst zullen groote veldslagen worden geleverd. Op allen die de Vrijheid liefhebben doe ik een beroep om aan onze zijde te staan. Blijft vol vertrouwen -onze strijdkrachten zijn vastberaden -tezamen zullen wij zegevieren.

Dwight Eisenhower

DWIGHT D. EISENHOWER,
Opperbevelhebber der
Geallieerde Expeditie Legers.

Z.H.1

Opposite page: The camera catches a stark and dramatic picture as Flying Fortresses return to base after making their third flight over over enemy territory in support of the Normandy landings. The long neon-like streamer is the landing lights from a Fortress that has just landed - the arched flares fired from the ground are signals to other aircraft to stay clear of the runway and in the sky are flares fired from a aircraft coming in to land with wounded aboard. Sillouetted in the foreground are the medical officers who wait for the flare-firing B-17 to land.

Above: German view of the invasion fleet off one of the D-Day beaches. Below: a pair of German machine-gunners look for targets.

Opposite page: Low level PR sweep of the invasion beaches.

How the invasion was reported!

Above: An American gentleman reads his copy of the *Detroit Times*.

Below: The *Los Angeles Examiner* being read avidly by ladies eager for news of their loved ones.

Opposite page: The *Evening Standard* reports Churchill's announcement, along with civilians and servicemen who study the dramatic news on the streets of London

Still the Best! **BIRD'S CUSTARD**

Evening Standard

37,357 BLACK-OUT 10.57 pm to 5.0 am   MOON Rises 9.50 pm; Sets 6.29 am.   ONE PENNY

FINAL NIGHT EXTRA

THE SPIRIT OF A GREAT RACE
LONG JOHN SCOTCH WHISKY

Churchill Announces Successful Massed Air Landings Behind Enemy in France

4000 SHIPS, THOUSANDS OF SMALLER VESSELS

"So Far All Goes to Plan"— 11,000 First Line Airplanes

An immense armada of more than 4000 ships, with several thousand smaller craft, has crossed the Channel, said Mr. Churchill to-day, announcing the invasion.

"MASSED AIRBORNE LANDINGS HAVE BEEN SUCCESSFULLY EFFECTED BEHIND THE ENEMY'S LINES," HE SAID.

MR. CHURCHILL DESCRIBED THE LANDINGS AS THE FIRST OF A SERIES IN FORCE ON THE EUROPEAN CONTINENT."

"The landings on the beaches are proceeding various points at the present time. The fire of shore batteries has been largely quelled, said Churchill

'LANDINGS ON JERSEY

Thousands Of Fighters Strafe The Nazi Guns

Since the invasion began, Allied fighter-bombers have been dive-bombing, glide-bombing and strafing German defences and communications.

'They do literally into the mouth

SHELLED BY 640 GUNS

The Supreme Headquarters of the Allied Expeditionary Force state that over 640 naval guns, from 16in. to 4in., are bombarding the beaches and enemy strong points in support of the armies.

About 200 Allied mine-sweepers, with 10,000 officers and men, are engaged in the operations.

The weight of minesweeping material used amounts to 2800 tons, and the amount of sweep wire in use would reach almost exactly from London to the Isle of Wight.

The Press Association learns that enemy destroyers are reported coming into the operational area,

'Tanks Ashore on Normandy Coast'

Opposite page: A 10th Photo Group F-5 Lightning passes King Sector on Gold Beach.

The DUKW (colloquially known as Duck) was a six-wheel-drive amphibious truck that was designed by a partnership under military auspices of Sparkman & Stephens and General Motors Corporation (GMC) for transporting goods and troops over land and water and for use approaching and crossing beaches in amphibious attacks. The designation of DUKW is not a military acronym; rather, the name comes from the model naming terminology used by GMC: "D" indicated a vehicle designed in 1942, "U" meant "utility", "K" indicated driven front wheels, "W" indicated two powered rear axles. Here one is seen approaching the loading ramp of a landing craft during the Normandy invasion.

James Gabler, a pilot in the 388th Bomb Group.

Barry Roberson and his fiancée Elizabeth who he married on his return from the war.

Members of the Beach Group at Juno. The two Royal Navy officers (centre) have radios and a loudspeaker for issuing orders.

Men of 6 Commando having tea while waiting to embark for the assault on Ouistreham as part of the 'Sword' Beach operations. The soldier in the foreground is a member of a 3-inch mortar detachment.

Landing craft heading out.

A Navy LST boat with its yawing doors is pictured on the Northern Coast of France unloading its supplies, vehicles and men to keep up the constant flow from England. These boats shuttle back and ofrth day and night under an air cover and close support by the AEAF.

A German anti-aircraft gunner is sillouetted against the setting sun while on duty above part of Hitler's famed 'Atlantic Wall'.

Lieutenant Bob Midward briefs the pathfinders of the 22nd Independent Parachute Company.

On the first day of the invasion, the 9th AF played a great supporting job in the landing with water proofed vehicles on this scene at the beachhead while 88 mm shells burst around them. In the background on the cliffs smoke soars from the devastated German positions which was hit by the 9th Air Force.

British Landing Craft are hauled up to the main deck of a liberty ship (IWM)

Left: Members of the 351st Fighter Squadron, 353rd Fighter Group load their necessary equipment onto trucks and Jeeps which will transfer them to their aircraft already out on the field ready to participate in the D-Day Invasion

Aerial view of Omaha Beach, Normandy, taken 6 June 1944, showing landing of two infantry regiments (18th and 115th), vehicles, and landing craft.

Men and assault vehicles storm the beaches of Normandy as Allied landing craft make a dent in Germany's West Wall on 6 June 1944. As wave after wave of landing craft unload their cargo, men move forward and vehicle surge up the roads.

This is how the beaches of Normandy looked on D-Day from one of the 9th AF Marauder medium bombers which went out in close support of Allied ground troops. Bombing from lower-than usual altitudes, the Marauders struck behind the lines at gun positions, troop and tank positions, and vital road and rail junctions. Bomber crews returned with stories of 'the channel filled with every kind of ship ever built' and the beaches 'as crowded as Fifth Avenue'.

Chapter 3

'This Is It!'

They spent the morning killing the enemy. Their bombing target was a defended area on the French coast south of Calais. This was no railroad bridge or marshalling yard, but a German stronghold - enemy troops dug in behind guns that pointed west across the English Channel. There was no way of telling how many dead and wounded lay beneath the billowing smoke over the target. But the bombs from the B-26 Marauders had walked right through their pillboxes, bunkers and artillery.

At least a dozen 88mm guns protected the area. Nothing unusual these days. For months, the Germans had been stiffening their positions in anticipation of an allied invasion. Fortunately, on this mission, the B-26 Marauders had help from their little friends - strafing P-47s that drove the flak gunners into their holes before the bomb run. By late morning, all 36 Marauders returned to their base in England with only minor flak damage.

That afternoon, June 5, a few young men from the 323rd Bombardment Group assembled in the situation room. They were lead crews mostly-the pilots, bombardiers and navigators who led formations of bombers to the targets. Some had been up since 0430 hours for that earlier mission to Ambleteuse, which was delayed three hours by stormy weather. Their talk was about the unusual activity in the English Channel. Many more ships floated and steamed off England's coast. Some towed huge, strange floating objects, barges maybe.

As soon as this small group realized that they were the only ones called to the situation room, they knew something big was up. The briefing officer told them that soon - maybe tomorrow - 54 Marauders from the 323rd would join streams of aircraft in the skies over England in support of the invasion of France. Their role, along with hundreds of other Marauders from five other groups stationed in England, was to knock hell out of the German coastal defence positions along the Cherbourg Peninsula, just behind a place code-named 'Utah' Beach. Destroy minefields, tank barriers, barbed wire, guns, bunkers and personnel. There wasn't much time to do the job right. They would be among the last bombers in before low flying attack bombers, the A-20s, laid a smoke screen on the beach to protect thousands of Americans coming ashore. Bombs away had to be between 0605 and 0624 hours. At 0630, the landing craft would hit the beach. Leave big holes in the ground so that those guys have a place to duck as they battle their way inland.

In the meantime, the young men in that afternoon briefing were removed from flying status. They were a privileged few sharing one of the greatest secrets of the century. They knew where the long awaited invasion would take place. A crash landing or bailout would lead to interrogation by German intelligence. The last order was to go to bed early every night to be fully prepared for the call.

When the briefing was over, no one left the room. So the bombing that morning at Ambleteuse, far north of the invasion beaches, was a distraction. Make the Germans think that when the Allies finally mounted an invasion, they'd be crossing the Channel at its narrowest point. For the past few months the group's bombers had been hitting targets up and down the French coast and even further inland near Paris-airfields, ports, bridges, rail yards and the most difficult targets of all, camouflaged sites from which the Germans planned on launching flying bombs against England. As far as these Marauder men were concerned, this invasion was long overdue.

This would be a story to pass on to their kids and the generations to follow. But the responsibility weighed heavily on them. Thousands of American lives depended on their skill as pilots, bombardiers and navigators. They spent the rest of the afternoon reviewing flight plans and studying the detailed maps depicting gun emplacements - thick concrete bunkers, mostly buried in the earth within yards of the beach. Here the enemy hunkered down with powerful guns ready to massacre any who dared approach from the sea.

For 1st Lieutenant Frank Burgmeier, an experienced navigator for the 456th Bombardment Squadron, this mission would be his 39th. His job was to guide a Marauder formation, which could be as many as 54 aircraft, to the target and keep everybody out of harm's way. He rode up front where a co-pilot usually sat. For him and the crews he flew with, every mission carried extra risk. Flak gunners and enemy fighters targeted lead aircraft. Blow a leader out of the sky and the followers lost their bombing accuracy.

Burgmeier's focus that afternoon was on the areas where they could expect the heaviest concentrations of anti aircraft fire. He also reviewed enemy airfields near the target where the Germans would launch their fighters. What worried him most was every navigator's nightmare: getting lost and leading the formation through a barrage of flak. It happened a few months ago to a classmate of his. This navigator mistakenly directed his ships over Boulogne, a heavily defended area on the French coast. Three crews in three aircraft never came back. Paralyzed with anguish, he was unable to fly again. Shortly after, they sent him home.

It could happen to anyone. The lousy European weather and the frequent course changes every 15 to 20 seconds to evade the flak complicated the task of navigating with precision. Usually Burgmeier shed his flak jacket and helmet so that he had more mobility to check his flight plans, maps and the terrain below.

With him in the situation room that afternoon were his pilot and his bombardier, both good friends. Captain J. B. Stirling, the son of a Navy admiral, loved partying as much as flying. In the evenings, he and Burgmeier often headed to a local pub or a movie together. Their bombardier, 1st Lieutenant William 'Hutch' Hutchens, was Burgmeier's singing partner after they'd downed a few scotches at the officers' club.

Outside the situation room, the ground crews worked quickly to paint the black and white stripes on the wings and fuselage of every Marauder. For easy identification, the 323rd's Marauders already sported a wide, white stripe on the tail, which gave them the nickname, 'white tailed marauders.' The added zebra look was to help the Americans on the ground in France sort out friend from foe.

At 2000 hours, Burgmeier tried to go to sleep. His usual routine was to hit the sack between 2200 hours and midnight after he'd written letters home-most of them to Tedi, his bride of 10 months. They spent only a couple of nights together before he shipped out. How he missed her! But tonight he lay on his cot thinking about his next mission. For the past two weeks, he'd flown 13 box or group leads, sometimes two in one day.

All that target bashing was reaching a climax. 'Let's get it over with,' he thought. The invasion meant the beginning of the end of a dragged out affair that kept him - kept all of them - from their homeland, homes and loved ones.

It might have been 2230 hours when he dozed off. At midnight the wake-up call came. Burgmeier dodged heavy rain and deep puddles to join the hundreds of other men in a smoke-filled Quonset hut. Suddenly the sound of 'a- ten-hut' stilled the voices and brought the men to their feet. Colonel Wilson R. Wood, the popular base commander from Chico, Texas, made his way down the long aisle to the front. The time was 0115 hours.

With a wide grin, he announced in his Texas drawl. 'Boys, this is it.' Months of anticipation erupted into deafening cheers, whistles and applause. Only six years before, Col. Wood had been a private in the US Army. He joined the Air Corps in 1940 and after earning his wings, quickly rose through the ranks. At 25, this handsome colonel had the respect and trust of enlisted men and officers alike. He had a way of making all of them feel important. 'Chico' or the 'Old Man' as his men affectionately called him, had flown the first mission of the group in July 1943 and had led many others. Now he was full colonel, a hands-on commander, who watched from the tower as his men returned from their missions. Once he even wielded an axe to free one of his men trapped in a crashed Marauder.

After Colonel Wood uncovered the map showing the targets of the day, the weather briefer subdued the crowd by reporting low clouds over the target areas. Then the colonel spoke the words nobody wanted to hear. 'For our men to come ashore, these defences must be knocked out,' he said pointing once again to areas with pretty sounding names like Beau Guillot and Madeleine. 'We are to go in at any altitude necessary to strike the targets visually and effectively. I repeat, any altitude necessary.'

Colonel Wood emphasized that thousands of aircraft would be headed for France. 'Don't screw up times, make turns or sightsee,' he said. Then he added, 'Let's kick the hell out of everything Nazi that's left!'

Outside, rain still penetrated the darkness. Under any other circumstances, this would have been a scrubbed mission. Burgmeier piled into a crowded jeep and headed to the line where he joined Stirling and Hutchens and their three gunners. A seventh man, an Army Air Corps photographer, also climbed aboard and joined the gunner in the open waist position at the rear of the plane.

The sky was lightening just a little when the Marauders following Sterling lined up behind his aircraft. Sitting in the right seat, Burgmeier always felt this mixture of fear and pride as he scanned the long line of Marauders following their lead.

As rain pelted the windscreen and streamed off the wings, Stirling pushed the throttles full forward. The time was 0430. At 500 feet, he entered a cloudbank and relied on his instruments to break out of the gloom. Instinctively, Burgmeier tensed. Suddenly they emerged into an opening between the thick layers. There, less than 100 feet away at the eleven o'clock position, a yellow-tailed Marauder from the 386th crossed their path. There had to be others following, significantly raising the odds of a midair collision.

'We're going to die up here,' he thought as he tried to slow his breathing. As quickly as the sky opened up, it closed around them. Burgmeier strained his eyes looking for ghostly shapes passing in the fog. They had to be all around. But there was no escape. Nothing to do but keep climbing. A bad start to such an important mission. Then came the blessed breakout.

What glorious chaos surrounded them! Planes, planes and more planes everywhere. Formation after formation, above, below, beyond. Off in the distance, clouds of dots headed east. Above, contrails streamed across the heavens. Stirling slowly circled, looking for the other 11 Marauders in his formation. They were wasting precious time and fuel. At some point, ten planes fell into place behind his Marauder, three from other groups.

As they joined the swarms of aircraft headed over the Channel, Stirling led his Marauders lower and lower to stay beneath the cloud cover. He levelled off at 4,000 feet as they neared the Cherbourg Peninsula, where Navy destroyers belched fire from their giant guns at the shore defences. In response, the Germans fired away from their positions making bombardier Hutchen's job a lot easier.

Never before had Burgmeier flown a mission 'on the deck' and been chased by 'light flak,' intended to destroy low flying invaders. As they neared the target, green and yellow streaks climbed into their path then veered off at the last moment. For Burgmeier, they were scary and distracting and he wondered how Hutch kept his concentration up there in the nose as he guided Stirling along the bomb run.

Never before and never again would Burgmeier have a box seat on such a spectacle unfolding beneath him. As they held steady on the bomb run, low level attack planes, the A-20s, laid parallel smoke screens that obscured the white sand beaches and dark, churning waters lapping the shore. Beyond 23,000 men in countless landing craft drew inescapably closer to the shoreline. Over the intercom, tight-throated crew uttered, 'God bless 'em!' 'God bless 'em!'

Then 'bombs away' and the crew experienced another first. As Stirling pulled away, turbulence rocked the Marauder tossing it around like a toy. Concussions from their own bomb blasts violated their airspace. Clearing the target area and heading westward over the Cherbourg Peninsula, Burgmeier checked his watch. 0630 hours. Contracting chicken skin sent a chill through his body.

Over the Channel, Hutch crawled out of his compartment in the nose to assure them their bombs walked right through the target. The crew revelled in their success until Stirling told them to hold the applause until they reached the base. They'd been airborne nearly four hours-their longest mission yet-and they were almost out of fuel.

Back at the base, the returning crews were jubilant. Everyone landed safely. There'd been no emergencies calling for red and orange flares. The official debriefing turned into hundreds of informal debriefings as crews shared their experiences. The bombing was good. The troops had landed. No way could the Nazi bastards hold their positions after today. Piece of cake. Burgmeier and the others agreed that the broken gliders and different coloured parachutes sprawled over the landscape just meant our troops were everywhere. The enemy was surrounded. The men of the 323rd couldn't wait for the next mission!

The celebrations that day at Earls Colne near Colchester, northeast of London, reflected the Group's own limited view. Their efforts had spared the lives of thousands of men landing at 'Utah' Beach that morning. Of the 23,000 who came ashore that day, there were fewer than 200 casualties. But to the east, at a beach called 'Omaha', a different story unfolded: hundreds of bodies lay dead on the beachhead and floated in the Channel. American casualties numbered 3,000. Something had gone terribly wrong there. But only the generals saw the whole picture and they were not talking.

***D- Day and the White Tailed Marauders** from Marauder: Memoir of a B-26 pilot in Europe in World War II by Louis S. Rehr with Carleton R. Rehr.* [27]

'...I went round to Norfolk House where... Admiral Ramsay took one look at it, signed it. Air Chief Marshal Sir Trafford Leigh-Mallory insisted on reading the whole bloody thing from start to finish, trying to correct commas. I had to say, 'You know it impossible to alter anything more, it's all been agreed.' Finally he signed it.'

Major Goronwy Rees, 21st Army Group Planning Staff who after finishing the Overlord operation orders, visited Montgomery at St. Paul's School for him to sign the document before taking it to Admiral Ramsay and then Leigh-Mallory the Air C-in-C of the Allied Expeditionary Air Force, for their signatures. In late 1943 it had soon become apparent to Leigh-Mallory that the air forces available to him for the invasion of Europe (Second Tactical Air Force (RAF), Fighter Command and the US Ninth (Tactical) Air Force) were entirely insufficient to undertake phase two and three of the air plan. He had no heavy bombers at his disposal and without them he could not hope to attack and immobilise the large list of targets regarded as essential to success. These views he made known forcibly and, as he was of the opinion that the heavy bombers of RAF Bomber Command and the US Eighth Bomber Command would have to be used, he planned accordingly.

'Overlord must now presumably be regarded as an inescapable commitment and it is therefore necessary to consider the method by which our most powerful offensive weapon, the heavy bomber force, can be brought to bear most effectively in support of it... It is clear that the best and indeed the only efficient support which Bomber Command can give to Overlord is the intensification of attacks on suitable industrial centres in Germany. If we attempt to substitute for this process attacks on gun emplacements, beach defences, communications or dumps in occupied territories, we shall commit the irremediable error of diverting our best weapon from the military function for which it has been equipped and trained to tasks which it cannot effectively carry out. Though this might give a specious appearance of 'supporting' the Army, in reality it would be the greatest disservice we could do to them. It would lead directly to disaster.'

Air Marshal Sir Arthur Travers Harris CB OBE in a letter to Marshal of the RAF Sir Charles Portal, Chief of the Air Staff, 13 January 1944. In February 1942 Harris had been directed by Portal to break the German spirit by the use of night area rather than precision bombing and the targets would be civilian, not just military. The famous 'area bombing' directive, which had gained support from the Air Ministry and Prime Minister Winston Churchill, had been sent to Bomber Command on St. Valentine's Day, 14 February, eight days before Harris assumed command. In February 1944 'Bomber' Harris and Lieutenant General Carl 'Tooey' Spaatz of the US Strategic Air Forces In Europe (USSTAF) were informed that preparations for Overlord would require their bombers to be diverted from the strategic bombing offensive against the Reich. Harris wanted none of it. He always maintained that bombing alone would defeat Germany and to his critics he once said: 'There are a lot of people who say that bombing can never win a war. Well, my answer to that it has never been tried yet and we shall see. Spaatz too, who wished to continue attacking oil targets and German fighter production, also shared Churchill's concern about the dangers of killing large numbers of French civilians and Churchill could not believe

27 McFarland & Company Inc., 2004.

that the bombing campaign might succeed in isolating the battlefield. Harris, who claimed that his heavy bombers would not be effective against tactical targets such as railways and bridges said, 'I have neither planes nor crews to spare for useless side-shows' but he and Spaatz were forced to give way when Air Chief Marshal Tedder went to Eisenhower and told him that he must get control of the bombers or he must resign. And Eisenhower threatened to take the matter to President Roosevelt.

25th May, 1944

Dear Harris,

I have of course been familiar with the overall strategic effort against Germany from the air, but since you showed me last night the photographs and charts portraying the extensive damage inflicted upon the enemy within the boundaries of his own country, I am more impressed than ever.

I would feel derelict in my duty if I did not tell you and through you every member of your Command, of the appreciation and gratitude which I and all of us hold for the contribution of Bomber Command toward eventual victory.

Now, by combining the efforts of air, sea and ground forces, I hope we can capitalize on the work already done and press on soon to bring the Hun to his knees - and keep him there.

Sincerely,

Eisenhower.

Letter from General Eisenhower to 'Butch' Harris after Ike's visit to Bomber Command on 24 May. Between 1 April and 30 September 1944 whilst Bomber Command was under the direction of Eisenhower, Harris dispatched 82,411 sorties, of which more than 90 per cent were at the request of Supreme Headquarters and these aircraft dropped no less than 304,072 tons of bombs. In addition Harris dispatched 2,923 aircraft on mine-laying sorties and these dropped 10,223 mines in enemy waters.

'... with the approach of D-Day a rapidly spreading paralysis was creeping over the railway network of the Region Nord. When that day dawned, 21,949 British and American aircraft had cast down a total of 66,517 tons of bombs on eighty chosen targets... The movement of German troops and material by rail had thus become a matter of very great difficulty and hazard and this well before any landings had been made. Such trains as still ran moved very slowly, were forced to make long detours and travelled only at night. The enemy had no freedom of movement in a large part of France and Belgium... The 'Transportation Plan' had proved singularly successful.'

The Royal Air Force 1939-1945 by Denis Richards and Hilary St. George Saunders (HMSO 1974).

'The amazing thing is that Harris, who was even more resistant than the Americans to the idea of AEAF domination, has in fact thrown himself whole-heartedly into the battle, has improved his bombing performance enormously and has contributed more to the dislocation of enemy communications, etc., than any of the rest.'

Professor Solly Zuckerman, diary entry, 9 July 1944. Zuckerman was a leading member of the Allied Expeditionary Air Forces Bombing Committee under the chairmanship of Air Commodore E. J. Kingston-McGloughry, an Australian.

'Everyone knew the invasion was close at hand and we were going to the marshalling yards as part of the pre-invasion offensive against the enemy transportation system. There had been a heated debate among the planners of our war strategy as to which would be the better use of our heavy bombers. One group thought the 'Transportation Offensive' was urgent to break the Germans' ability to supply their Western front once the invasion had taken place. Another equally vocal group said the Strategic Oil Offensive should take first priority. To me it seems now that we did both, we were knocking out Hitler's oil capacity and at the same time striking at any form of transportation.'

Second Lieutenant John W. McClane, navigator, 44th 'Flying Eightballs' Bomb Group, Shipdham, Norfolk.

'The invasion tension is growing. You can almost feel it in the air. I'm convinced that things are going to pop any day now. The Officers Club on the post has been closed, also the theatre, until further notice. We flew over the Thames Estuary the other day and it was packed solid with invasion barges all set to go. One of these days they won't be there. I've never seen so many boats in my life. They stretched as far as the eye could see.'

Lieutenant John A. White, a pilot in the 448th Bomb Group at Seething in Norfolk. In April he and his crew had flown the Southern Ferry Route to England. He had said his goodbyes to his wife Vangie and young son, Jackie in Lancaster, Tennessee a few months before. He was not afraid of dying and he enjoyed life. It did not seem possible that he might never get back to the USA and he hoped that he 'could make the grade'.

'In between training and the invasion we were sent out to France to drop supplies to the Maquis. That also gave us training for map-reading at night. A typical exercise was to go to somewhere where the mountains start, in the middle of France, where the Resistance were. We would flyover from England to Fecamp and then gradually reduce our height from about 6,000 to 2,000 feet and descend to about 1,000. I used to aim for three little islands in the middle of the Loire, which always reflected in the moonlight and gave me the confidence of having a pinpoint, then we would come down to 500 feet. 'All the searchlights would be out looking for something, but at 500 feet they couldn't get you, because as they came down, they would go out and you could duck underneath the lot. Usually we would be over the top of the flak before they could get organised, but there would be quite a lot of things shooting behind. Then you would come to the rendezvous and the dropping zone, where there would be the reception party. We would go round and acknowledge the fact that we were there and then we would lower the flaps and the wheels, reduce speed to about 80 or 90 mph and go 600-800 feet above the line of torches to drop the goods. Then up again, go around, flap our wings, wish them good luck and away.

'When it came to D-Day we were given lots of pictures of the French coastline. I had to look at this panorama all day long. I had it in my room, when I woke up in the morning with my cup of tea - I tried to memorise it. What we had to do was to take a glider over there. On D-Day we had to fly somewhere up to Newcastle to start with, because that take-off was between two and three minutes and you had 40 to do, so it's quite a long time. We had to go up north for about 50 minutes, come back over the airfield and by then the rest of the gliders were airborne to go across together. When we got there, there was nothing happening. We saw the area and we had a wire through the tow rope to talk telephonically to the glider pilot without going through the air. We circled over the area and asked the glider pilot if he could recognise his landing zone and he said he could. So we asked him to let us know when we should release them. He said, 'It's OK, you can release us right now.' This was at about 2.00 or 3.00 in the morning that the drop took place, some eight or nine miles inland. There was a battery three or four miles up the coast, of heavy German 'Atlantic Wall' stuff and that was being bombed very heavily by about 80 Wellingtons.

'It wasn't until three or four in the morning, when you saw the dawn, that you could see the fantastic sight. The air was full of aircraft going in every direction. I've never seen so many aeroplanes in all my life. Of course at night, when you were flying, you never thought of that. You just took your course and went ahead.

'I wasn't aware of anything at sea until the return journey, when dawn broke and the pilot said, 'Come up and look at this' and you saw all these ships coming in, the bombing and the fighting. I have to say the operation didn't worry me at all - you get used to it, don't you? It's like driving a new car you've never driven before but after you've had it for about six months it becomes second nature. I went to the Loire so many times, looking for these three islands, that I knew what was going to happen. The only thing that would have been frightening would have been if we had lost an engine - then we'd have problems. There again, I planned for all exigencies. I used to pack everything up in my room in case I didn't come back and I used to take with me all sorts of things. Just before I left the mess, I used to tear the front page off the Daily Mail and stuff it in my back pocket. This was because if I had to land in France, the Germans were setting up decoys to pretend they were British airmen trying to escape, to try to find out the French families who were helping them, then rounding them up and shooting them. So to let anybody know I am a British airman, I would have that day's date on a newspaper.

'I thought of everything for survival - I carried yards of string and had razor blades stitched into my trousers. They gave us one or two pieces of survival equipment - a handkerchief with a map of France on it, some French money. I had a pipe which had a compass built into the bowl and that sort of thing and I also took a pair of shoes, because if you bailed out, I'd heard people say that they lost their flying boots. Most of this was my idea. But on D-Day I didn't do anything at all. I felt it was a mass organisation and we'd all be back in five minutes. It didn't worry me one little bit.'

Flight Lieutenant David Warner, a navigator on 296 Squadron, had returned from North Africa late in 1943 and started to train in towing gliders, dropping paratroops and supplies in accurate zones and using Gee radar. All this was in preparation for the D-Day assault.

'During the winter of 1944, the [82nd Airborne] Division was stationed near Leicester. To hear the kids talk of Leicester you would think it was a combination of Venice, Paris and home. For after all, they are mainly kids and they had seen nothing to date except home and a lot of ruins. In Leicester, people spoke almost understandable English and were friendly, clean, and civilized. They gave the girls their glider wings and the parachute wings now decorated with two combat jump stars, and went jitterbugging at the Palais de Danse. They polished their boots until they shone, pressed their baggy pants, set their high peaked caps at the fashionable angle and strolled the streets: for, in the language of the day, they are very sharp troops and they take the greatest pleasure in this. Some 12,000 of them, experienced soldiers and younger than you would believe, took over that corner of England and the English actually liked it.

'There were a certain number of pub fights and a certain amount of resultants disciplinary action. The English accepted this all calmly. If you take very young men and teach them to hold their own lives lightly and to kill, and then expect them to go out and kill on your behalf, you cannot be indignant in case they raise some hell outside the combat zone.

'They were having a wonderful time, but they did not think Leicester was journey's end. They had proved the extraordinary value of an airborne division and the war was a long way from won.

'No one was surprised when the sand tables and the maps appeared again and they were briefed on Operation 'Neptune,' the invasion of Normandy; and no one was surprised to learn that they would be the first men there.'

Martha Gellhorn, writing in *Collier's Magazine.* **General James Gavin commanding the 82nd Airborne, had suggested that reporters cover the action and Martha had been one of the first to accept the challenge. Martha had grown up in St Louis, an only daughter in a family of four children. Spending much time in Germany in the 1930s acquiring background material for a new novel she had observed 'the strutting storm troopers and frightened people with despair.' In her story** *'Rough and Tumble'* **she struck up a close friendship with the 37-year old Gavin; something which had not gone unnoticed by Ernest Hemingway who she had married in November 1940; they had both covered the Spanish Civil War. With her 'tawny blond hair and long legs, her easy, knowledgeable conversation sprinkled with expletives and punctuated by puffs on a cigarette'. [28]**

'Upon arrival at Upottery airfield on May 31 we were placed in a closely guarded area. After getting settled, we spent most of our time in the large briefing tent. In this tent there were wall maps, sand tables and aerial photographs. We listened to lectures did an intense study of the maps, sand tables and aerial photographs. We learned that we would land on drop zone 'C' just west of Ste-Marie-du-Mont, inland from a beach labelled 'Utah'. The food served while at Upottery was better than any we had since leaving the States. We had ice cream, white bread, steaks and many other food items not usually served to us since arriving in England. We joked that we were being fattened for the kill. We were issued our parachutes, ammunition, gas mask, life preservers, etc., a day before the expected departure for Normandy. This was June 3 since we originally were taking off from Upottery at about 23:00 on the evening of the 4th of June. As we now know, D-Day was delayed one day due to weather conditions.'

David 'Buck' Rogers 1st Sergeant, HQ Company, 1st Battalion, 506th PIR, 101st Airborne Division.

'The operation on D-Day morning was probably one of the most thrilling and significant flights although the easiest we have probably made in this theatre. Everything went according to plan and it was planned thoroughly by the higher echelons. We took off as

28 *The Women Who Wrote the War* by Nancy Caldwell Sorel (Arcade Publishing, New York 1999).

briefed at just about dawn and gained our height over the field and finally set a southerly course which was to take us down to the invasion area. Everything went as planned. We reached the Channel on time. We looked down and could see a few barges. They looked like they were standing by, ready to go in. As we approached the French continent we could only see scattered areas of the French coast. At one point we could look down and see a considerable hole in the clouds and see what looked like hundreds and hundreds of fighters milling about in that area, although we could not tell at that time whether they were friendly or enemy. We searched the areas constantly, knowing that we were going independently and we anticipated a pretty good fight when we got over there. However, searching, we couldn't see any enemy fighters, found no enemy flak of any sort and we wondered for some time just what was going on down below. However, we finally made up our minds that it must have been that the enemy was too well engaged down below to have any fighters to divert to our height. We finally came back out of French territory after hitting about six targets and coming back over the Channel we saw swarms and swarms of boats making their way southerly and it was very thrilling to look down and realise that we were seeing first hand the initial start of this Great Crusade. We came back to base and landed all very thrilled; glad to have had the chance to take part in this great operation.'

Major Earle J. Aber of Rancine, Wisconsin, a B-17 pilot and CO of the 422nd Bomb Squadron at Chelveston, which flew bombing missions by day and leaflet missions by night, dropped hundreds of thousands of leaflets over France on the morning of D-Day. The unit moved to Cheddington on 9 June and became the 406th Night Leaflet Squadron. Major Aber was promoted to the rank of Lieutenant Colonel. On the night of 4 March 1945 Aber was returning from a 'milk run' news leaflet drop over Holland (his 51st mission) when his personal B-17 *Tondalayo* was shot down in error off Clacton, Essex by British shore batteries that had opened fire on a German intruder detected in the same area. Aber and his co-pilot, Maurice J. Harper, remained with the aircraft long enough for nine crewmembers to bail out but both pilots were killed when the aircraft crashed into the sea off Harwich. Only a hand that belonged to Colonel Aber was found and that was only identified by his class ring. He has graves both at Madingley (Cambridge) and Arlington National Cemetery.

'There have been all sorts of rumours about an imminent invasion of the enemy coast'.

Lieutenant Abe Dolim, a navigator in the 94th Bomb Group, recorded in his diary at Rougham.

'Every day we'd heard the bombers go out and every evening we head heard them return. But there was something different enough to send us, at dawn, from our beds to windows that looked out on chimney pots and slates and beyond to the clear blue sky with tiny white clouds. The bombers seemed to come from nowhere in perfect, geometric formation. They kept coming and coming; as if the whole sky belonged to them as they roared away to deal death and destruction. It was D-Day.'

Jean Lancaster-Rennie, an English schoolgirl.

'D-DAY! We were called to briefing at 11pm June 5.'

Wallace Patterson in 1st Lieutenant Albert L. Northrup Jr's crew at Seething, writing up his journal.

'Some of the things they said started the boys thinkin'. Speculation ran thru the field like wildfire and nobody slept. We had 15 to 20 guys in our hut all night long up to the time we took off and they all seemed to have inside information on the thing. The idea that we were to have a bird's eye view of in probably the most enormous military effort ever attempted by man was very thrilling indeed.'

Lieutenant John A. White, 448th Bomb Group who was awakened for a 2300 briefing for a pre-dawn take-off. That night he added: 'Our Group flew four missions and rumour has it that two more are to go out tonight. A lot of boys will get in two of them today. We are sweating out the German news broadcasts and midge ['Axis Sally'] now. I'm anxious to hear what they have to say about the thing. Boy! If this goes right, we'll have this thing over with before long. It's got to go right.'

'...We work all day and night preparing our aircraft for the invasion support. As dawn approaches on the 6th, the sky is filled with a myriad of aircraft forming for their missions. It is an unbelievable panorama of seemingly endless waves of planes, a sight which will probably never be repeated. Our base puts up three missions during the day. A respite between missions comes at noon and I catch a few winks while resting on a pile of lumber near a hardstand despite the bright sun shining overhead.'

Thomas A. Nelson, a ground crew member, [29] who recorded those words in his diary.

'The day before D-Day the German local command had a concert for the officers and troops in the garden behind the house. In the evening they had a big dinner and the party was finishing after midnight, when suddenly the alarm came. All the officers then rushed out down the garden to their bunkers which were in the woods. About one hour after the alarm, very heavy bombing began. It seemed to be all over the country. The first waves of planes were very, very high in the sky but as the night went on they came lower and lower and the bombing around us became more intense.

'At dawn I went to the little village of Tracy, where happily, nobody had been killed during the night and I went along to the top of the cliff. The cliff itself was mined so I couldn't go right up to the edge but I climbed on to the top of a wall - there I saw a sight on the sea that has remained part of my life.'

M. de Bourgoing, whose family had been allocated a single floor of the 17th century château of Philippe de Bourgoing near Tracy-sur-Mer, requisitioned by the Germans.

'I shall never forget that night or the thrill of knowing the Allies were coming to expel the Nazis at last. My mother woke up in the early hours when she first heard the noise and said: 'It must be the landings.' But I dared not confirm it, even to her because I knew that the Germans thought it might be a diversionary tactic. So I told my own mother nothing. In the morning a friend called and told me the sea was black with ships. Then the bombing began. I was helping to take the injured to our local hospital in the convent of the Bon Sauveur, which was run by nuns, but there was nothing to distinguish it from other buildings the Germans had been using. We couldn't paint a red cross because the Germans had requisitioned all the paint so the nuns brought out the sheets, red with blood, that had been in use in the operating theatre and we spread them out in a cross.

'I'll never forget the next RAF plane to fly over us. It waggled its wings and we all

29 *UK Memories* by Thomas A. Nelson, writing in the 2nd AD Journal.

knew it had worked. The bombing stopped in our area.'
André Heintz, 23, a French Resistance fighter.

'I was the wireless operator on night duty from 1900, 5 June to 07:00, 6 June. Our radar installation was some miles south-west of Rennes (Brittany) and I had to listen in to the whole company wavelength all over Brittany. At times this could be very boring through non-action, so sometimes I used the spare communication set to listen in on the wavelength of our sister company in Normandy. In the early morning hours I seemed to get some weird Q groups (signals which, translated, gave us certain events in certain sectors). Amongst many others about hundreds of planes, came 'Battleships, cruisers, etc. off the coast', 'shelling' and the one which opened my eyes to events, 'tank battle in Bayeux'. All of a sudden, I realized that the invasion must have started.

'But in our sector everything was quiet and peaceful. The question was - what to do, as it was against regulations to listen to any other wave-length than your own? So at 06:30 our Company Commander came in to ask for the latest report which I gave him 'Nothing to report but...' and he said, 'But?' So I had to tell him the truth; that I had listened in to the wavelength and believed, according to my Q groups, the invasion had started. After a severe ticking off by him, he got interested in what I had taken down on scrap paper about the events.

'After he studied it he went to the phone to contact regimental headquarters in Rennes and enquired after the position. For a while he listened quietly and then all of a sudden he blew his top at the person on the other end of the telephone and said in no uncertain tone: 'I suppose if my wireless operator had not listened in, you would have waited till the Yankees nabbed us, still in slippers and pyjamas and then told us about the invasion.'
Obergefreiter T. W. Hausdorfer of the Luftwaffe Signal Corps.

'I was at Quineville when the invasion started. The number of ships, aircraft and tanks thrown in against us defies any description. The guns of the Allied warships pulverized one position after another. Planes overhead reported on the accuracy of the guns, quite undisturbed and with uncanny precision. Every moment we expected our own fighters to appear. The whole sky was darkened by planes, but they were Marauders, Typhoons, Liberators, Flying Fortresses and Mustangs, attacking our posts, our machine-gun nests and artillery positions with their bombs and guns. As far as I could see, there was no anti-aircraft fire with the exception of a few two-centimetre rifles.'
An Obergefreiter (German corporal) recalling the invasion for the benefit of BBC listeners. At Quineville there were four 105mm guns in casemates, some of them disguised as houses with fake gabled roofs with tiles. This battery was shelled by the 8-inch cruiser USS *Tuscaloosa*. The fortified positions surrendered to the 3rd Battalion, 39th Infantry on the evening of 14 June during the battle for Quineville.

'Here we were in a foreign land where they drove on the wrong side of the road, where 'knocked up' meant they were busy that night and where the great Normandy Invasion Landing was happening.
Lieutenant Ed Wanner, pilot, B-24 Liberator *Asbestos Alice*, 700th Bomb Squadron, 445th Bomb Group, 2nd Bomb Division, Tibenham, Norfolk, whose crew were recent replacements.

'*Stars and Stripes* gave American losses over Europe in the five months preceding D-Day as 1,407 heavy bombers, 673 fighters and 100 medium bombers. These figures do not include those killed or wounded when the planes returned to their home base or crashed in the United Kingdom. Over 14,000 men were lost in the heavies alone. The British had parallel losses.

'In June, after 6 months of intense training, we were assigned as a crew, to a B-17G at Kearney, Nebraska. We flew it overseas to England where we started flying combat missions immediately, just in time to join the D-Day invasion support flights. The first few short haul sorties were milk runs, giving us the false impression that this combat flying was a piece of cake. But that was to change quickly…It was apparent to all of us that the long-awaited invasion of Festung Europa was imminent. We knew that we would be involved, but expected all-out opposition from the Germans. The night of 5 June we saw the RAF aircraft and gliders coming over, wave after wave. We knew we would be going in the morning and thought there would be hell to pay. We didn't sleep much that night. At briefing we heard Eisenhower's inspirational message to the departing troops. At least it was supposed to inspire. Churchill could have done it with a lot more class.'

'**Chicks Crew' by Ben Smith Jr, radio operator-gunner on Anthony 'Chick' Cecchini's crew, 303rd 'Hell's Angels' Bomb Group, 1st Bomb Division, 8th Air Force, Molesworth.**

Phantom Fleets

2130 5 June First aircraft take off from British airfields. (More than 10,000 aircraft are involved in the invasion).

By midnight 5 June 1,333 heavy RAF bombers drop 5,316 tons of bombs on radar stations and the ten most important German gun batteries in the assault area. In the 24 hours between the night of 5 and 6 June. The RAF drops 15,000 and 20,000 tons of bombs.

5/6 June Operations 'Taxable' and 'Glimmer', both devised by Wing Commander E. I. Dickie, create 'Phantom Fleets' on enemy radar screens. 'Taxable' involves 16 Lancasters of 617 Squadron and is a joint RN/RAF operation aimed at making the Germans believe that an invasion force was attacking the French coast between Dieppe and Cap d'Antifer. Attacks on enemy radar installations had all but destroyed their effectiveness, but care had been taken to leave enough operational to allow the Germans to deceive themselves that their radars were showing an invasion fleet. The RN uses 18 small vessels as tugs to tow 'Filbert' balloons containing a special reflecting device, which would show up as large ships on the German radar screens. This 'convoy' occupies an area of sea that measures 14 miles by 15 miles and appears to move at seven knots towards the coast. It is known subsequently that the German High Command has plotted three invasion forces arriving on the French coast.

Eight Stirling aircraft (including two reserves) of 218 Squadron and a few boats mount Operation 'Glimmer', whose 'convoy' is aimed at the beaches of Boulogne. German searchlights are turned on and guns open fire on the 'convoy'. Luftwaffe night fighters are directed towards the jammers and spend hours in the area, as do E-boats searching for a fleet that never sailed.

Operation 'Titanic I-IV'

34 Stirlings, Halifaxes and Hudsons of 90, 138, 149 and 161 Squadrons, giving the impression of a much larger force, drop dummy parachutists called 'Ruperts' equipped with sound and light simulators to mimic a small arms battle, through a screen of 'Window' between Rouen and Le Havre; in the Yvetot area, 30 miles south-

west of Dieppe (11 Halifaxes and four Stirlings) about 5 hours before the first Allied troops are due on the beaches, 200 dummies are dropped; Maltot area (three Stirlings of 149 Squadron) and the Marigny area in the base of the Cherbourg Peninsular (15 Stirlings and one Halifax of 90, 138 and 149 Squadrons). The first 'Titanic' drop is made in the early hours of 6 June between Coutances and St. Lô. Two parties of SAS men have already been dropped in this area and as the dummies touch-down they attack despatch riders and lone vehicles. The SAS men are briefed to allow enough of the enemy troops to escape to spread the news that there has been a paratroop landing. The object of this diversion is to retain enemy forces north of the Seine and, with luck, to draw reserves from south of the Seine. 'Titanic II' uses 50 dummies, which are dropped east of the River Dives. It is intended to prevent German reserves from moving out of this area to join the troops defending the beaches in the west. 'Titanic III' also uses 50 dummies, which are dropped south-west of Caen to divert attention from the 6th Airborne Division and to draw local counter-attack troops away from Caen. 'Titanic IV' at Marigny uses 200 dummies to entice German forces westward from St. Lô. It too relies on the SAS to give life to the simulated attack. The sixteen aircraft, flying tracks 15 miles south of that taken by the invasion forces, simulate landings at Marigny and Villers Bocage and the operation also supports the genuine drop of the 101st US Airborne Division.[30] The Marigny decoy serves to relieve some pressure on US airborne forces around Ste-Mère-Église.

At 0400 the 915th Regiment, General der Artillerie Erich Marcks' LXXXIV Corps reserve, abandons 'Omaha' and sets off to intercept the dummies. It takes hours before the German reserve can be re-grouped and brought back to the beachhead.

24 Lancasters of 101 Squadron and five B-17 Flying Fortresses of 214 Squadron carrying 82 radio jammers between them, obliterate the German night-fighter frequencies for more than five hours.

16 Stirlings of 199 Squadron and four Fortresses of 803 Squadron USAAF establish a 'Mandrel' screen from Littlehampton to Portland Bill jamming all but 5% of the Freya radars between Cherbourg and Le Havre.

The Allies fly 14,674 sorties on D-Day, including 2,656 by 8th Bomber Command (approximately 20 aircraft lost) and 3,587 by 9th Air Force (26) and 2,249 by 2nd TAF (24) and 912 by ADGB (8). RAF Coastal Command flies 353 anti-U-boat and ship patrols without loss. Losses, 21.00 hours 5 June-sunrise 7 June are approximately 131 aircraft.

The Luftwaffe flies 319 sorties.

'Invasion fever was abound. On 25 May something occurred that made everybody really start talking about this invasion that should be coming up soon. All flight crewmen were ordered to carry their side arms, .45's, at all times on the base. The ground crews were issued carbines to carry with them as they worked on the airplanes, to have at the ready, in case enemy paratroops would attempt to foul up any suspected plans. With double summer time in effect, darkness came very late and the nights were much shorter than I was used to, growing up in Long Beach, California. I had been attending Long Beach Junior College day classes while working a night shift at a local

30 *Deception In World War II* by Charles Cruickshank (Oxford University Press 1979).

Douglas Aircraft plant, and saw the first B-17 go out the door of that plant in 1942. The date was 6 June 1942.

'In order to get some sleep, before the usual crack-of-dawn (or earlier) briefing for a bombing mission, it was necessary to close the blackout curtains to darken the room by shutting out the later evening light. But on the evening of 4 June we were called out to get ready just before darkness was fully upon us. Unusual. The rumours circulated once more. After some night formation flying and speculating, we headed for our target along the French coast sometime after dawn. It was a long day and again it didn't happen. Just a rumour. Little did we know. Must wait again. It was an even longer day for those in the intelligence unit. About 6 or 7 of them were placed under guard, food sent in, etc., until the dawn of the big day. Next evening, 5 June, we started early again, same as the night before. So, we felt this must be it for sure.

'At briefing, this was it. The Briefing Officer said, yes, this was the day. The invasion was going to begin and we had to be over the target and gone by 06.30. That meant that the last of the airplanes had to be gone by then, so some of us would fly earlier. Because this was invasion day, nothing was going to keep crews down. Those that usually hated to go to the regular targets, even the ones that normally might bitch and complain, this day they wanted to go. What a contrast when it was usually groans when we learned of the target. We were told in briefing that the airplanes over the target area would be all Allies and they didn't expect any German aircraft at all. Flak would be very light and it turned out that way. What animated talk and yippee! It took a while to get everybody calmed down before they could tell us exactly what we were going to do and where. What a different climate.

'The weather was better for the Channel crossing. It was a go! The pilots gave a few more details as we repeated last night's run and then to the shoreline targets at dawn before the landings were to begin in about an hour.'

Wilbur Richardson, 5 feet 11 inches, B-17 ball turret gunner, 94th Bomb Group at Rougham near Bury St. Edmunds.

'ENGLAND - You had to keep reminding yourself on the afternoon of June 6, 1944, that this day was something special and enormous. After all, the machinery that moved American Forts and Libs out of England and over Fortress Europa is no new thing, but an established and finished apparatus. Its movement from briefing to takeoff, bombing, return and late chow for the crew is something classic.

'D-Day did not change the routine.

'D-Day for the Eighth Air Force was a day of bombardment across the Channel in France, the same kind of bombardment that had been going on for a long time. The commanders and Operations officers and pilots of the Eighth Air Force are veterans. D-Day or not, Major Roy W. Forrest, a squadron commander at one of the bases covering 'our friends on the ground,' was relaxed, although busy, at operations with his feet perched on the desk; the ground men went through the thorough checking of aircraft; the pilots moaned about lack of sleep and long flying hours and got ready for another takeoff.

'Captain S. L. Burr, the briefing officer, busy giving bombardiers the detailed breakdown of the afternoon's target, asked about the chow he had missed at noon and stared sadly at his quick-lunch jam sandwich.

'At the briefing there was only one new touch-a bomb line; i.e., a line roughly outlining the area inland from the enemy coast which Allied penetration should have covered by H-Hour plus on D-Day.

'You will not,' said Captain Burr, 'under any circumstances drop your bombs within the bomb line.'

'Out on the stand the newer silver and the older green painted Forts waited for another raid. The pilots in the officers' lounge listened intently to a radio speaker talking an awful lot about D-Day but saying very little. The pilots were very interested even though they themselves were going to fly today and were in effect part of the invasion operation. They listened to somebody off in London giving them the low-down.

'They made a lot of interesting comments while waiting for the afternoon raid. They said: 'I called Calais, but was told the telephone line wasn't quite ready yet' and 'It's dangerous ditching in the Channel today. There's no room in the water.'

'They had nothing much to say about the early morning raid. There had been ten-tenths cloud cover. On the way back, landing barges and naval crafts had been seen in the Channel through a break in the clouds.

'Lt. Col. Chester C. Cox, of Superior, Wis., strolled around Operations with his hands in his pockets. This morning, flying in the lead ship of the earliest formation of American heavy bombers to cross the enemy coast on D-Day, had given him the honor of being the first US heavy bombardment pilot to drop bombs in direct support of landings in France. The event had taken place at 0700 this morning, but other mornings Col. Cox had seen more flak, more enemy fighters and more merry hell than he had seen today. He was taking it easy.

'But the man who was really taking it easy today was Lt. Robert H. Thompson, who had finished a tour of duty on D-Day's morning raid. The lieutenant had started with Berlin. He'd been over Berlin eight times and had gradually worked his raids closer to the French coast, ending up with a raid on France on Invasion Day. This was the reverse of the tour of duty when the Forts began to fly in November, 1942. You began at the coast in those days and worked into Germany.

'D-Day wasn't a good day for flying. There were clouds and very late in the day there was rain. Carefully controlled, but nevertheless very real were the signs of a sense of responsibility toward the men storming onto the French beaches. Short of a typhoon, the weather would not stop flying. At the briefing at 2100 hours the night before, they had been told the next day was invasion and there had been one long burst of cheering and then back to the business-like routine of plane check-up, take-off and bombing. The ground crews worked with a little more zest than usual. For more than a year now they had loaded bombs and checked engines and guns and had nothing to show for it except what it said in the papers. But this invasion made a milestone in two long years of bombing. It was as if the pin-ups in the barracks were beginning to stir out of their paper frames and would soon talk for real in the accents of the girls back home.

'At 2 o'clock there was a briefing, at 3 o'clock the mission was scrubbed; at 4:30 it was on again, leaving your chow halfway down your gullet. It might be D-Day, but it was just like any day at an airfield.

'I was assigned to the crew of Lt. James J. Gabler, of Pittsburgh, Pa. At the ground-crew tent the flyers sat around and gassed with mechanics. One of the ground crewmen is 43 years old and Lt. Gabler, squinting out at the clouded sky said, 'I wish I was 43 right now' and moved around trying to imitate someone with St. Vitus's dance but fooling nobody, for he is a big, healthy-looking young man.

'We took off at 1720 hours of a cloudy day and climbed up through the overcast to join our formation, which was led by Col. William B. David. Everything was shipshape except that you couldn't see much through the overcast and everyone aboard was very much interested in what 'our friends' were doing downstairs. Through an occasional break in the sky we could see the Channel. Over France was revealed the mystery of no flak and no enemy fighters. Moving into our target we could see smoke columns and fires clearly visible below, although you couldn't tell if they were the result of off-shore shelling or bomb damage. The navigator, Lt. David L. Me Gee, handed over a pair of binoculars and the fires really stood up big through the glasses.

'We dumped our load and the bombardier, Lt. Harry M. Hill, looked satisfied and relaxed. Lt. Gabler, the pilot, sounding slightly bored, asked his radio operator, T/Sgt. John T. Middleton: 'See if you can find out anything about this invasion on the radio.' 'I'll see what Jerry has to say,' said the radio operator.

'On the way home we followed the most ambitious traffic pattern over conceived for aircraft. For, in effect, the all-day trains of aircraft at all levels from England to France and home again meant a careful 'all-the-way-through' pattern that would not crowd the air over England to a danger point. So we swept wide on the return, making it a long trip home.

'There were broken clouds below us and through them the first real glimpse of invasion. You could see miles-long columns of ships moving like herds across the water. Long streamers of gray gun smoke lay near the water.

'We were above the overcast and letting down very slowly. The props of No. 1 and No. 2 whirled in the sunlight, but Nos. 3 and 4 were caught in the evening dusk. Over on the right the moon was up above the clouds. We let down through the clouds. The bombardier dozed off.

'Rain and almost night now. Another huge flotilla was moving toward the enemy coast below us. We looked down and could see them and we knew the men were looking up at us. We had nothing to say to them, except that perhaps it was understood between us that there is a thing called 'air support.'

'We were over England. Somewhere a light flashed a welcome mat for returning planes. We set down nicely at the home base at 0010 hours of June 7 or ten minutes after D-Day was finished. In the rain and cold wind we asked one of the ground mechanics, 'What's happening?'

'Churchill spoke, there's been hymns and prayers and casualties are not as heavy as they expected,' he said and got to work on the Fort. The interrogation was smooth and over with quickly. One of the nurses grabbed hold of a gunner who had hurt his head in the flight by banging into something in the waist and ran her fingers through his hair to find the wound, scolding him like his big sister.

'Everybody was off to bed because today had meant fifteen hours of flying. Lt. Gabler said before going off: 'If you want to really do a job, why don't you come along with us to Berlin sometime?'

D-Day Bombing by Sergeant Saul Levitt, *YANK* Staff Correspondent who flew on the third of four missions flown by the 388th Bombardment Group at Knettishall near Thetford, Norfolk, to Pont L'Eveque.

'In April 1944 we attacked three targets in France and then began training to use a new type of Gee called GH. This would enable the navigator to direct the pilot to fly to within a few yards of a position on the ground to allow bombs to dropped blind. We practiced during May using Lincoln cathedral as our target and taking photographs to record the results. This work continued in the first week of June and then on 5 June we took part in Operation 'Glimmer' to simulate a naval attack on the Pas de Calais area in order to deceive the Germans into believing that the D-Day landings were there and not Normandy. This was achieved by flying a progressive square search pattern between Newhaven and Boulogne, dropping 'Window' continuously. The plan was successful and we shared the task with 617 Dam Busters Squadron with additional crewmembers to ensure that a continual dropping of the packets of Window was maintained. I understood that no aircraft were lost during this risky operation. We returned to Woolfox Lodge after five hours fifteen minutes of demanding flying. After the usual breakfast we slept for a few hours and awoke to find out on the 1 pm news, that today, 6 June was D-Day and the landings in Normandy had begun. In my diary I noted that it was cold and miserable at home.

Harry Barker, RAF bomb aimer, 218 Squadron. On 19 May Bomber Command had sent instructions to 218 Squadron commanded by Wing Commander Fenwick-Wilson DFC at Woolfox Lodge that it would be used in the forthcoming operation to augment 617. 218 at the time was the only squadron fitted and trained with 'GH' and 'Gee' systems. The crews were already skilled in precision flying and highly trained in the use of 'Gee' and 'GH' so 218 could complete the task satisfactorily without extensive training. Within 11 days the required standard was reached - crews who operated at this time would simply record 'special local flying' in. their log-books. Starting at 23.59 hours on 5 June 8 Stirlings (including two reserves) took off in two waves. Each aircraft carried a crew of 13 - two pilots, three navigators, one wireless operator, one flight engineer, two 'Window' droppers plus two replacements. The plan once airborne was for the Squadron aircraft to fly elongated orbits with the major axis of the orbit perpendicular to the coast. During the orbits 'window' would be discharged at a rate of 12 bundles a minute. Very precise flying was needed to achieve the desired affect; the timing called for an advance of 18 miles at a speed of 7 knots and involved the front line aircraft in a total of 23 orbits. As the operation commenced very near the English coast, the second line of aircraft came in 8 orbits later than the first and thus required to do 15 orbits only. The flying time for the first line was 2¾ hours and for the second 1¾ hours. There were three aircraft in each line. If the window was discharged on schedule and the aircraft remained on time an imaginary convey would be picked up by Freya radar crossing the Channel at 7 knots making straight for Boulogne. Each individual crewmember was only too aware of the importance of this operation, with the aircraft in their allotted positions and accuracy required measured in yards! For nearly three hours the six crews maintained their allotted positions with no recorded encounters with the enemy. The last aircraft touched down at 05.12 hours.

The German reaction to 'Glimmer' was immediate - official Air Ministry and Naval documents states that the Germans mistook this raid for a genuine threat. Long-range gun positions along the French coast opened fire on this imaginary convoy and searchlights were also used. E-Boats were sent into the area where the convoys were supposed to be sailing. The bulk of the German night fighter force was sent to intercept a RCM operation by 'Airborne Cigar' (ABC)-equipped aircraft of 101 and 214 Squadrons operating south of 'Glimmer'. The enemy mistakenly thought that the ABC patrol was also the cover for 'Glimmer'. At 19.30 hours on 6 June a message was received from the AOC HQ. 3 Group:

'I have received the following message from C-in-C Bomber Command for aircrews - begins - you did famously last night in the face of no mean difficulties, fire from the coastal batteries, which were your targets, have been reported virtually negligible.' A further message from C-in-C to OC 218 Squadron. 'It is already established that the operations on which you were engaged on the night 5/6th June were very successful and it may well be that when the full facts are known it will be found that you achieved results of even greater importance than can be known at present. This can only have been brought about by intensive training and attention to details, as a result of which crews concerned, acquitted themselves admirably. The Naval Commanders have expressed their great appreciation of the support of 218 and 617 Squadrons and it is now disclosed that this and the patrol carried out by 101 and 214 Squadrons succeeded together in delaying the enemy's appreciation as to the actual point of the assault thereby assisting the measure of tactical surprise gained for our main assault forces.'

'We were cruising on course at 30,000 feet, a brilliant moonlit night with 10/10ths cloud 5.000 feet below, the vapour trails from each wing tip standing out for all to see. Inside the Fortress aircraft 'N' with its crew of ten fully trained airmen all is silent just the steady hum of the four engines can be heard. There was a click as the wireless operator Flight Lieutenant Bill Doy switched on his intercom and spoke. 'Rear gunner,' there is a U/I aircraft approaching very fast from the rear, I confirm that I have it in sight some 2,000 feet astern and approximately 800 feet below.' I brought it in by commentary - 1,200 feet 1,000 feet - at 800 feet it started to disappear under the Fortress. I handed the commentary back to the W/O, who gave the skipper the order 'Corkscrew, starboard go!' On the word go, I fired one short burst blindly with both .5s fully depressed. The next second with the Fortress in a deep dive to starboard the attacking aircraft I now recognized as a Me 410. It was on my port quarter for a second. It appeared to just hang there with the glow of two cannons being fired. I fired two short bursts and also observed an accurate burst from the mid-upper turret. There was no doubt that the Me 410 was hit as I did see smoke. He then disappeared from my view and I did not see the aircraft again. The Me 410 was claimed destroyed.'

Flight Lieutenant Eric 'Phil' Phillips DFC MiD, 214 Squadron Gunnery Leader, 100 Group, 2250 5 June. Five Fortresses on 214 Squadron operated in support of the D-Day operation in an ABC ('Airborne Cigar') jamming role. A protective patrol lasting over 5 hours was flown at 27,000 feet stating just north and east of Dieppe and running almost perpendicular to the coastline carrying out jamming and 'Window' dropping in conjunction with 24 Lancasters of 101 Squadron of 1 Group. One Lancaster was shot down. The patrol was outstandingly successful and earned a personal congratulation to all concerned by Arthur Harris to whom he pointed out that 'the work carried out was of paramount importance in connection with the Invasion Forces.'

When Flight Sergeant Roland 'Ginger' A. Hammersley, Lancaster air gunner on Pilot Officer Ron Walker's crew on 57 Squadron went to briefing at East Kirkby in the afternoon of Monday the 5th of June the only information crews received was that they would be attacking three 170mm heavy gun positions at La Pernelle on the Cotentin Peninsula. The 5 feet 4½ inch WOP-AG from King's Langley had met his future wife, Nan Webber serving with the WAAF at Barford St. John. Walker was physically a well-built strong man. Since leaving school he had managed his father's farm in Sussex. Before the war young Roland had shared their three-bed-roomed council house with its fair sized garden in Apsley End with three brothers and a sister, Gladys. Their father had served in France in the First World War with the Royal Field Artillery. During the late 1930s Walter Alfred Hammersley was in and out of work plying his trade as a carpenter and joiner. In 1939 he re-mustered, enlisting in the Royal Corps of Military Police. His wife Elizabeth, who somehow had managed to keep the family well fed and clothed during the days prior to war kept chickens and introduced rabbits to supplement the rations as the war dragged on. Walter, the eldest child, had joined the Royal Artillery and Leslie, who was two years younger than 'Ginger' Hammersley, had joined the Royal Marines. Leslie, who was with the 541 Landing Craft Assault Flotilla aboard HMS *Empire Mace*, had been in Southampton for some time and was involved in moving mail from the dockside around the dock to the many units as they moved into place during the build-up of the invasion forces. The *Empire Mace* had a civilian crew captained by a Captain Smith, who had run a ship through the blockade during the Spanish Civil War. At last the move for embarking on assault craft day was called. The D-Day invasion, postponed by 24 hours because of bad weather, finally began with thousands of ships and aircraft setting out for five beach landing areas on the Normandy coast. It was a miserable wet morning as men trundled into Southampton's mean little dockside streets. It seemed that despite all the secrecy, everyone knew what was going to happen. There seemed to be nothing but Redcaps keeping troops and public apart. The dockside was a mass of organized chaos as vehicles, soft-topped and hard, manoeuvred to board their respective craft.

Leslie's landing craft was at the dockside and during a lull in the work he watched the flow of guns, tanks, lorries and troops with orders being shouted from all sides. Suddenly, amidst all the confusion, orderly as it was, alongside of his landing craft in a line of mobile field guns, came one with his brother. Sergeant Walter Hammersley was directing its movements. Leslie was hanging over the side of an assault craft. It seemed mutual that the brothers should stare at one another with a look of instant recognition. It was only a brief meeting, their first since the summer of 1942. They had only a few moments in which to chat and then Walter was away and being loaded onto a LCT (Landing Craft Tank). Walter and Leslie eventually moved out to their positions in line with what seemed like thousands of other vessels as the weather slowly got worse and they set off for Normandy, Leslie in the *Empire Mace*, Walter in his LCT with its four assault guns chained down. They were to fire onto 'Gold' Beach over the heads of the 50th Tyne Tees Division in front of them. It was terrifying in its majesty, with the flotsam of war everywhere.

Walter and Leslie's brother 'Ginger', in the tiny WOp/AG position in O-Oboe with its equally tiny side window to port had little time to look out at the invasion fleet as the Lancaster flew over the English Channel towards the Cotentin Peninsular on this momentous day. O-Oboe and fifteen other Lancasters in 57 Squadron had begun taking off from East Kirkby at 0140 hours with a bomb load of eleven 1,000lb AN-M and four 500lb GP bombs. As the Lancasters were crossing the English Channel the young WOp/AG's 'Fishpond' was swamped with blips. It was apparent that there was either a huge flock of birds, thousands of aircraft or a vast fleet on the sea immediately below their Lancaster. Hammersley reported this to Ron Walker and the navigator. Walker banked the aircraft to port and starboard and they could see that the water below was covered in a huge fleet of vessels heading towards the French coast. Thousands of men poured across 'Gold' beach where, Leslie Hammersley passed Walter and his gun. As the Royal Marine ran in towards the sandy shore, Walter told him that his unit was shelling the beaches and positions in front and that they were doing a good job too. At La Pernelle the Lancasters got their bombs away at around five minutes before 4am but the Cotentin Peninsular was cloud covered and they probably missed their target because at 0525, guns from two of the batteries fired on Allied minesweepers.

It was much the same story at Fontenay, Houlgate, Les Longues, Grandchamps-Maisy, Merville, Mont Fleury, Ouistreham and Ste-Martin-de-Varreville before the Lancasters headed for home. The ten batteries each received on average 500 tons of bombs. After the first landings Leslie Hammersley went back and forth to Southampton taking supplies and troops to 'Gold' and 'Omaha' beach heads for about six days before being withdrawn for a refit to the landing craft. Cloud interfered with the bombing all along the invasion coast and most of the bomb loads missed their targets completely.

'On the first day after the Allied armies had landed, their foothold on French soil was still precarious and they could have been in real trouble had the German armoured divisions been able to get there rapidly. Our squadrons were taken off the long flights into Germany and were kept busy attacking both the German tanks and their rail transport routes in and around the Normandy area. We went back to Normandy to destroy a rail and road junction at Argentan about 50 kilometres from the beachhead. I was Controller for this raid and as it would have been a vital transport junction for the Germans on the following day I was determined it would be pulverized with nil or absolute minimum damage to the adjacent village. At the planning conference I agreed to a bombing height of 6,000 feet but we all bombed lower. The target was accurately marked. I held up the attack for about five minutes to avoid confusion with another target under attack a few miles away. There were a few complaints but not many and it was another successful raid. Milling around the target in the dark and held back by their CO, the operational discipline was always excellent but the radio comments (always with no call sign) were typically Australian - pertinent, disrespectful, sometimes rude and usually funny. The raid report given by Squadron Leader Vowels, my most experienced Flight Commander in briefing session on return. 'Sortie completed. Cloud base 6,000 feet. Vis good. Cluster of green TIs 0127 hours. 2 x 1,000lb and 14 x 500lb bombs drop height 5,000 feet. Bomb bursts all around and on TIs - straddling and on road junction. Attack went very well, even though it opened about five minutes late through the Controllers order. Control very good and there was no hitch to original plan. TIs were practically bang on. Max error was about 30 yards. Was fired on by British Navy who ceased fire when colours of the period were fired.' Alec Vowels' comment of being fired on by the British Navy was not unusual around D-Day. The English Channel was full of allied Naval ships who continued to fire on us as we went across backwards and forwards - fortunately they were not as accurate as the Germans and I was not aware that they did any harm.

'I think I was the last to bomb at Argentan and my approach to the bomb release point was made on a shallow descending dive. Our bombs were always dropped rapidly one after the other and on this occasion they were dropped at about a micro fraction of a second intervals so they fell in a stick right across the target. I was possibly over keen and was too low, so when the first bomb exploded, its blast hit my aircraft with a really severe thump. In a flash I realised that as I was still losing height each successive blast would be harder and heavier. At this late stage being brought down by my own bombs may have showed my determination to press home the attack but it would have been a stupid way of finishing my career. My own report to the intelligence officer at debriefing states: Sortie completed. Thin layer cloud, base about 6,000 feet. Bombing appeared good and attack successful. Train on fire possibly ammunition train. 4,000 feet. 0140 hours. 2 x 1,000lb MC, 14 x 500lb GP. Attack delayed 5 minutes to avoid any possibility of the force bombing green TI's of the eastern target which were put down late. Markers quite good. Majority of bombs appeared to overshoot slightly and were to the west of the road junction - in the rail siding.' We landed back at base after a very short return flight - one of the best aspects of fighting so close to base. The self-inflicted damage the ground crew found was a fairly small dent under the tail plane.'

'The final raid of my tour of operations was a few days later on 14 and 15 June when we attacked a German Panzer (tank) force concentrated at night, hiding under cover of trees in a wood. With information from the French Resistance we knew exactly where they were. On 17 June my replacement, Wing Commander Donaldson RAAF, arrived and the next day I started my end of tour leave.'

Wing Commander Rollo Kingsford-Smith RAAF the Australian CO of 463 Squadron RAAF. [31]

It was almost daylight when thirty-five Lancasters from RAF Mildenhall attacked gun sites on the French coast north of Caen and west of Le Havre between 0500 and 0513 hours, just before the Allied landings. Red and green TIs were dropped by the PFF and spread for about 600 yards along the beach. The reds were believed to be in the right place but the greens were very scattered. 15 Squadron dropped 305 500 pounders and 622 Squadron, 288 500 pounders. All aircraft returned safely.

'On D-Day we operated twice in the one day. Once at dawn and another later on in the day, to Lisieux - a good prang. We did the job. They were only 1,000 yards ahead of our boys and so it was very accurate bombing. Once again the pathfinders did the job. They dropped TIs where they wanted us to bomb. You can imagine the mess it made to the armour. I'd reckon half of the fellows would be smashed with the shock just from the bombing, even if it didn't destroy the tanks. Imagine sitting in a tank and getting 1,000lb bombs dropped on top of you. It'd be a bit of a shock I think. It was very successful. Our boys were able to move forward. We didn't know it was D-Day. Nobody told us. It was kept a complete secret. Even to those operating. We were just told to bomb the defences along the shores of the D-Day landings. As we came back in the dawn, we could see the terrific mass of shipping going towards the French coast, so we realised it was D-Day.'

31 *Legend of the Lancasters: The Bomber War from England 1942-45* by Martin W. Bowman (Pen & 'Sword' 2009).

Flight Lieutenant Frank Hercules 'Herks' Dengate DFC RAAF from Tamworth, New South Wales, a 22-year old Australian pilot on XV Squadron who had trained on Wellingtons and the Stirling.[32]

One of the last Australian bomber crews out early on the morning of 6 June was a Lancaster crew captained by Flight Lieutenant F. L. Merrill DFC RAAF. To his crew it had been just another sortie in the pre-invasion softening-up when they took off in the small hours to attack a coastal gun battery. They were scheduled to be among the last of the night bombers to bomb that night and thus were among the first to see the invasion begin. They came down below the clouds on the way back, rounded the southwestern side of the Cherbourg Peninsula, passed over a then seemingly empty French coast and set course for home. Nearing Alderney Island, off the tip of the peninsula, the whole island seemed suddenly to burst into flame as the anti-aircraft defences opened up - unsuccessfully - on the Lancaster ahead. A few minutes later the invasion fleet came into view, filling the scene as far as eye could reach as ships of every kind moved across to Normandy.[33]

'When we went into combat in September 1943, there was a general policy that fighter pilots would be relieved from duty after 200 'combat hours.' However, when D-Day approached, the powers that be realized that most of the early pilots like me would be reaching that mark at about the time D-Day would probably happen. Whoa! The word came down that 'those pilots who had completed 180 combat hours' had two options. 1. To return to the US on R & R after completing 200 and then return to the group to be there for D-Day and fly a second full tour. 2. To complete their 200 hours and stay on board for an extra 100 hours and then return to the US after for a permanent change of station (or at least until needed in the Pacific). I opted to stay on for the 'long and short tours' did many others. We were there for D-Day. Those who went home on R & R did not make it back until about D-Day plus ten.

'The 352nd Fighter Group flew several missions on D-Day but these were probably some of the easiest we flew. Our job, like most of the Eighth's fighter groups, was to provide a: wall of aircraft from the deck to 30,000 feet in a semicircle about fifty miles south of the beaches to make sure no enemy aircraft reached the shoreline. In this we were successful (Hollywood be damned for indicating otherwise). No German aircraft reached the beaches that day.'

Robert 'Punchy' Powell, pilot, P-51B Mustang *West "by Gawd"*, 352nd Fighter Group at Bodney, Norfolk.

June 5th - INVASION. Target Montfleury-Cherbourg gun battery. Early morning take off. Almost a daylight operation. Heavy cloud and severe icing over Channel to target. We opened the 'Second Front' - D-Day - at about five in the morning. Saw the massive convoy formations in the Channel.

19 year old Sergeant Johnny Cook (later Flying Officer DFM) Halifax III rear gunner, 578 Squadron at Burn.

---

32   On 5/6 June Luftwaffe activity was almost non-existent, putting up just 59 fighters to intercept the invasion forces but only two Nachtjäger submitted one claim each. Finally, Oberleutnant Helmut Eberspächer, a fighter-bomber pilot of 3./SKG 10 flying a FW 190G-3 claimed three Lancasters at Isigny and Carentan while Feldwebel Eisele of the same unit claimed another Lancaster at Isigny-Lessay-Vire.

33   *Legend of the Lancasters: The Bomber War from England 1942-45* by Martin W. Bowman (Pen & 'Sword' 2009).

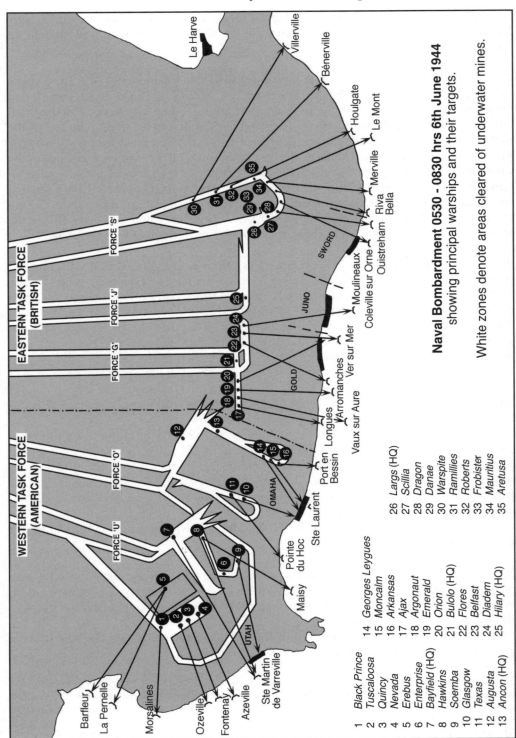

Naval Bombardment 0530 - 0830 hrs 6th June 1944
showing principal warships and their targets.

White zones denote areas cleared of underwater mines.

1 Black Prince	14 Georges Leygues
2 Tuscaloosa	15 Moncalm
3 Quincy	16 Arkansas
4 Nevada	17 Ajax
5 Erebus	18 Argonaut
6 Enterprise	19 Emerald
7 Bayfield (HQ)	20 Orion
8 Hawkins	21 Bulolo (HQ)
9 Soemba	22 Flores
10 Glasgow	23 Belfast
11 Texas	24 Diadem
12 Augusta (HQ)	25 Hilary (HQ)
13 Ancon (HQ)	
	26 Largs (HQ)
	27 Scillia
	28 Dragon
	29 Danae
	30 Warspite
	31 Ramillies
	32 Roberts
	33 Frobister
	34 Mauritius
	35 Aretusa

Chapter 3

'Off We Go Into The Wild Blue Yonder'

'We waited for so long it turned into a joke. Each time they woke us up in the night somebody would say, 'It's D-Day.' But it never was.

And then on the 6th of June it was.

The squadron waker-upper dragged us out of the sack twenty-nine minutes after the midnight of 5th June. Breakfast at one, briefing at two,' he said tiredly.

'Jesusgod,' I said.

'What the hell is this?' Sam said.

'We were sick of their war. We'd been in bed a half-hour.

When we went to chow there was a faint glow from the moon, curtained off by a low overcast. The line-men were pre-flighting the Forts, running up engines. There were a lot of RAF planes going over.

All the rank in the group made chow, tablesful of majors and colonels and captains.

'Late bridge party'," Bell said.

'Ground-gripping bastards,' somebody else said. 'They go to bed when we get up.

'Maybe this is D-day,' I said.

Nobody laughed. It wasn't worth a laugh any more. Too many times. I drank a lot of tomato juice and hoped it would be good for the deep weariness in my knees.

Doc Dougherty was there, looking charming. 'I'm going along,' he said. 'Maybe with you.'

'See you in Moscow,' I said.

Maybe it was a shuttle job. It was early enough.

The briefing-map was uncovered when we came in. France again, just south of Cherbourg.

'Good deal,' Sam said. 'Sack-time before lunch.'

Mac, the Public Relations officer, was there in white scarf and flying-clothes.

'You think this is D-day,' I said. He nodded.

The weariness was gone. For the first time I tuned in on the tension in that room. I grabbed the Doc and Bell and Sam in one handful.

D-day,' I said. 'Honest to God.'

They already knew.

We were in on it. We were flying in the big show.

Colonel Terry (CO), got up.'….This is invasion…were the first words I got. There was a lot of noise…you are in support of ground troops…'

1st Lieutenant Bert Stiles, co-pilot of a B-17 Fortress crew led by 1st Lieutenant Samuel 'Sam' Newton in the 401st Bomb Squadron, 91st Bomb Group, 8th Air Force at Bassingbourn. From the classic, Serenade to the Big Bird, which Stiles wrote while he was flying a 35-mission tour, 19 April-20 July 1944.

'To be awakened about 04:00 for a mission was pretty much routine but to be hauled out of the sack at about 0130 to report to briefing - well something unusual must be up, I thought as I groped sleepily for my clothes. The atmosphere at briefing was invariably sombre. Sitting quietly on benches dozing or languidly puffing on cigarettes that glowed eerily in the soft light of the starkly furnished rooms, there was very little talk while the fliers, officers and enlisted men, waited for the CO, Colonel Preston, to arrive.

'Tenshun!' someone up front bawled when the CO strode in. Everyone arose standing erect, eyes straight ahead.

'At ease', the Colonel said.

'The men sat down quietly, tensely awaiting roll call and the removal of the cover from the huge map of Europe on which the course to and from the target had been traced. If it showed a deep penetration of Germany that meant dangerous fighter attacks and flak encounters throughout the flight, a groan arose from the dry throats of the airmen that trailed off into excited whispers as briefing continued. But at 02:30, when the briefing officer announced, 'This is it - this is D-Day!' it was different; a lusty cheer shattered the quiet of a moment before. Whoops, whispers and yells echoed from the grey walls. It was an unprecedented and ecstatic vocal demonstration by the fliers who had doggedly been carrying the war to Germany for many months with considerable losses of men and planes. It was the day they had awaited to share with the ground forces and together they would assault the Nazi war machine, hopefully gaining a foothold on the mainland with the ultimate goal of driving the Wehrmacht back to the Fatherland and crushing it.

'We lifted off at 04:45. A 'fluffy' layer of clouds below hampered visibility but there were some breaks and I could see the choppy dark waters of the English Channel. Droning steadily toward the continent, I gasped when a huge opening in the clouds revealed ships and boats of all sizes dotting the water as far as I could see. Hundreds - no, there must be thousands, I thought. Although no one type of ship could be identified from nearly three miles high, I was to learn later practically the whole spectrum of powered vessels from battleships to motor launches made up the invasion fleet.

'Landing ships carrying thousands of troops, tanks, guns, vehicles and ammunition, were positioning for the dash to the Normandy beaches. Barrage balloons swayed lazily above the ships to which they were attached by stout cables.

'More holes appeared in the clouds and the awesome spectacle continued to unfold. I rose from my seat in the navigator's cramped work area in the left rear of the B-17G's nose to get a better view from the right waist window. Fascinated, I saw puffs of white smoke from the huge guns of battleships and cruisers aimed toward the mainland and a moment later massive explosions could be seen a short distance inland where the shells landed, kicking up a fountain of dirt and debris. That, I reflected, must be a mixture of steel and stones, flesh and bones when the targets were hit.

'The Fortress, swaying gently, throbbed on. No sign of Me 109s or FW 190s but our 'little friends' were out in force. The Lightnings, Thunderbolts and Mustangs, their invasion markings - black and white stripes on wings and fuselages - were very prominent, were providing an aerial umbrella for the landing forces. Strafing the enemy positions up and down the coast and for some miles inland, they were determined to help the GIs embarking on the great crusade. The white capped wake of hundreds of circling landing craft awaiting the order to head to the shore contributed to the drama of the scene.

'The cloud cover required a blind bombing technique using radar. According to my log we were close to the target; gun positions near Arromanches roughly midway between the Cherbourg peninsular and Le Havre. The bombs dropped from the bellies of the bombers, disappearing in the clouds to devastate and disrupt the enemy's fighting capabilities far below. The briefing officer was right. 'There would be meagre flak, if any at all,' he had said. There was none. The German guns were busily exchanging fire with the mighty invasion fleet massed in the Bay of the Seine and stretching for miles into the Channel. We touched down at 09:26 and I could sense an air of excitement on the base when I dropped to the ground from the plane after the pilot parked it in the dispersal area.

'How was it Lieutenant?' asked the crew chief in charge of keeping the Fortress flying, an intense look on his leathery face weathered by the winds of his native Texas.

'What I saw through the breaks in clouds was an unforgettable sight,' I replied.

'There was no time to say anything more. A truck pulled up to take the crew to interrogation after which we had to get ready for the afternoon flight, my 30th mission. B-17s continued to peel off from the formation and land as the sun shone brightly through the cloud covering that was breaking up. It was a good omen.'

Franklin L. Betz, B-17 navigator, *Old Gappy* in the 379th Bomb Group, 8th Air Force, Kimbolton.

'On June 5 we found the usual alert waiting for us, meaning we were to fly again the next day. There was something unusual about this alert, though. All of us felt it. At briefing time the next morning, June 6, we found out! Colonel Vandevanter addressed us. Everyone was tense with excitement, trying to catch every word. 'Gentlemen, you are about to embark upon a very important mission, the success of which will greatly affect the outcome of this war. Today is the day we've all been waiting for - D-Day.'

'A cheer went up.' This was it! Everyone was bursting with excitement and pride because we were all to be there to help those doughboys-assault the enemy beaches. We made two successful operations that day. One to bomb gun installations at Caen and one to bomb road junctions and railroad bridges. It was a great day. The Luftwaffe didn't dare show itself. We were all out; both the Eighth and Ninth Air Forces as well as the RAF. It was a day we will remember as long as we live.'

John Hibbard, left waist gunner and assistant radio operator aboard B-17 *Joker* in the 385th Bomb Group at Great Ashfield.

'We knew it was for real when we could see those battleships pouring shells into the beach... the awesome thing is the fate of our country was in the hands of nineteen- and twenty-year olds.

21-year old Staff Sergeant Perry Roberson, a southern farm boy born near Midland City, Alabama, flight engineer and gunner on B-24 Liberator, *Corky* in the 453rd Bomb Group at Old Buckenham, Norfolk. The target assigned to the 453rd was a defence position on 'Omaha' Beach near Ste-Laurent-sur-Mer. Zero hour was 06:28 hours; code word: *Maisey Doats*. A message sent by General Hodges, commanding the 2nd Bomb Division, 8th Air Force, which was read out at briefing said: The enemy defences must be destroyed... the success of all men of all nations participating will be profoundly affected by our efforts... we must not fail them now.' [34] Feldmarschall Erwin Rommel worked tirelessly to prepare the defences of the Atlantic Wall and urged commanders to improve

---

34 *An Emotional Gauntlet: From Life In Peacetime America to the War in European Skies* by Stuart J. Wright (The University of Wisconsin Press 2004).

defences and it was only in March 1944 that Seventh Army began fortifying 'Omaha' with beach obstacles and 15 cliff-top fortresses (Wiederstandnesten 60-74).[35] (When the beach was chosen originally - by COSSAC - it was undefended). The defences included eight artillery casemates, 35 pillboxes, six mortar pits, 18 anti-tank guns, approximately forty rocket-launcher sites, 85 machine-gun nests and six tank turrets, nearly all set in a heavily reinforced concrete position. Also, there were four artillery batteries on call in the vicinity. The slightly concave shape of the coast meant that the mutually supporting artillery and machine guns on the 30 metres high bluffs could enfilade the whole length of the five-mile long beach, which was sewn with concertina wire and minefields.

'Our first mission on June 2 we were briefed to bomb an airdrome, Bretigny, southeast of Paris and then a secondary airdrome north of Paris. Bombing results were good, especially on the secondary. We blew the fuel dump, flames shooting up about 1,000 feet. On the entire trip, from the coast to the target area and five miles out into the Channel, we experienced heavy flak. We lost one plane in our group. Flak hit the No. 3 engine of Evans, from Rochester, New York. He went down and was never seen again. I had a lump in my throat and stomach the whole trip.

'We must have been amongst the first fighter aircraft over the beachhead as dawn was just breaking upon our arrival. The invasion armada was enormous. Most of the landing craft were still heading towards the beaches. It really was quite a spectacle. There was flak everywhere though, mostly from the fleet and that was quite frightening. Watching the start of Europe's liberation was a fantastic experience, particularly the naval bombardment. You could see the guns fire and the shells landing on the coastline, getting further inland the more our troops advanced. It was amazing'.

Flying Officer Kazik Budzik KW VM, Spitfire IX pilot, 317 'City of Wilno' (Polish) Squadron, which flew four separate patrols over the invasion beaches.

'We started about 15:00 hours on June 5 with routine maintenance of the plane plus painting the stripes. When we painted the invasion stripes we used a British paint that was very heavy in texture and hard to spread. We had to hurry the job; even so it took us about four hours to complete. I thought it was a sloppy job, but I guess it answered the purpose. Then we did a special inspection, went to late chow and only got about one hour's sleep before it was time to do the pre-flight checks and warm-up at 02:30. The sky was full of aircraft - bombers, transports, gliders, etc. At dawn our planes took off and to me that was the longest day.'

Ralph Safford, Lieutenant Colonel Francis S. 'Gabby' Gabreski's crew chief.

---

35 The Wiederstandnest (WN, resistance nest) was a self-contained fortified position which usually included bunkers and was garrisoned by a squad or sometimes two squads with one or more anti-tank guns supported by machine-guns and mortars. Some were no more than field works with added concrete fortifications. All the positions within a Wiederstandnest were interconnected by communications trenches and supported by fire trenches, surrounded by barbed wire and anti-tank and anti-personnel minefields. Some nests were positioned to funnel attacks into killing zones. Often Wiederstandnests were located on the flanks of a Stützpunkt (strongpoint) to protect them and to give each other supporting fire. The Stützpunkt was the most numerous defence position and several were grouped together to form a Stützpunktgruppe. The majority of the strong-points were infantry positions though some were light or medium artillery or light anti-aircraft (20mm cannon) batteries that were housed in casemates or open emplacements. Command and fire-control posts usually formed part of the artillery strongpoint. See *Hitler's Atlantic Wall* by Anthony Saunders (Sutton Publishing 2001).

Battle for the Sky

England at this time was gripped with 'Invasion Fever' as the long awaited 'Second Front' approached and Duxford lost most of its 'country-club casualness'. Security was tightened and when passes at Duxford were cancelled even the Newmarket to Royston road, which separated the airfield from the domestic site, was closed and all civilians were barred from the area. Blackout restrictions were tighter than ever and special wardens patrolled the base to see that they were enforced. Airfield personnel worked flat out to prepare the Thunderbolts for 'the big one' as guards were posted and a permanent alert force of forty-nine men and one officer was maintained around the clock. Pilots were ordered to carry their .45s at all times and ground crews were issued carbines, gas masks and helmets to have at the ready, in case German paratroops attempted to sabotage any suspected plans. With double summer time in effect, darkness came very late and the nights were much shorter.

All the P-47s were removed from the far perimeter area at night and some of the enlisted men had to sleep in the dispersal areas. The Thunderbolt's low-level performance made it ideal for the ground attack role and thirty-four Jugs were transferred to the 9th Air Force, which was tasked with tactical missions in France before and after the invasion came, cutting each squadron back to twenty-eight aircraft, or sixteen per mission. During all of these precautions on 30 May Duxford airfield was rocked by the concussion of exploding bombs when an ammunition dump near Great Chesterford exploded. The explosions lasted until mid-afternoon and personnel had to keep all the windows opened in case of a new and bigger blast. At 1613 hours Major Harold Stump led a second 'Droopsnoot' mission to the railway bridge at Beaumont-sur-Oise. The Thunderbolts dropped fifty 500-lb bombs from twenty to fifty feet altitude and good hits were claimed on both ends of the bridge. During take-off from Duxford a 500-pounder with an eight-second-fuse dropped from one of the P-47s blew a four-foot crater in the grass runway. When the mission returned, another bomb that had failed to release over target, fell from a landing Thunderbolt, but failed to explode. A RAF bomb disposal team later safely defused the UXB. By the end of the month the 78th Fighter Group had flown twenty-five missions, suffered the loss of nine P-47s and had claimed twenty-five aerial victories, four ground victories and twenty locomotives destroyed.

On the first five days in June the field sent out six missions, all uneventful bomber escort jobs. On 4 June Captain James W. Wilkinson, the acting CO of the 82nd Squadron, who had recently been quite successful in strafing locomotives on the continent, was invited by the RAF to demonstrate his strafing technique against a locomotive in Wales. Tests on locomotives disproved that they were put out of commission permanently after strafing attacks even though penetrated by numerous bullets. The effects might have been spectacular but it was demonstrated that the holed engines could be repaired fairly rapidly and back in service within short order,' The thirty-one-year-old airman pilot was of the opinion that strikes in the right place could put a locomotive out of action for months rather than days. Bad weather en route held up his flight clearance so in order to get airborne, Wilkinson said that he was going up for a local test flight and then he headed for South Wales. On arrival the landscape was covered in mist and Wilkinson hit the mountainside near Llandovery, Carmarthenshire and he was killed. A few weeks later his attractive English widow was presented with his Distinguished Service Cross and Silver Star, which had been awarded for the two occasions when, single-handedly, he had fought off and broken up entire formations of enemy fighters attacking the bombers. A model Thunderbolt containing the chronometer from the P-47 was made by Wilkinson's crew chief, Staff Sergeant Ismal W. Boase and this was also presented to Mrs Wilkinson. The distraught widow was found dead in London a month or so after the presentation. A photograph of her husband was near her body. Captain Benjamin I Mayo, twenty-five years old from Little Rock, Arkansas, later took permanent command of Wilkinson 's squadron.

On Monday 5 June - D-Day minus one - there were all sorts of rumours about an imminent invasion of the enemy coast. At 1545 hours top secret orders were flown into Duxford for Brigadier-General Murray C Woodbury, commanding 66th Fighter Wing at Sawston Hall. On 5/6 June the sky was overcast and an occasional mist made it even darker. At Sawston Hall the 66th Fighter Wing HQ night staff watched the plotting table and knew that something big was in the offing. The betting was 'Dollars to doughnuts, this is it'. At some airfields towards midnight the sky above the low clouds was filled with the continual throbbing drone of aircraft. It was too steady and lasted too long to be RAF Bomber Command going out on another night operation. Personnel saw and heard RAF aircraft carrying paratroops or towing gliders filled with more of the same going over, 'wave after wave' and many knew that they would be going in the morning. The constant sound of aircraft flying overhead made sleep impossible for many. Betty's tearoom was closed that evening for the only time during the war. (It was re-opened next morning.) Enlisted men in their huts listened alternately to the BBC and the enemy propaganda station. Finally, mechanics, armourers, radiomen, pilots, ground officers and enlisted men who had not been on night duty were roused from their sacks. Hours before daylight they completed the long preparation for the first of three D-Day missions. Admin staff were given paintbrushes and told to help ground-crew paint black and white invasion stripes under and over the wings of the aircraft and around the rear fuselage. A South African RAF squadron leader who was visiting Duxford to make arrangements for the 'Thunderbolt All-American Swing Band' to play a dance at his airfield discovered next morning that his Spitfire had also received the black and white stripes!' Other personnel were pressed into service as truck drivers and ammunition linkers. Red Cross workers made piles of sandwiches and gallons of coffee, which were taken around to the men as they worked or walked their guard posts. Because of the sentries, it became an accomplishment to drive around the perimeter track. D-Day had arrived!'

By 0330 hours the 83rd and 84th Squadrons, with pilots who had slept only an hour or two that night, were ready and the first of the three 8th Air Force missions of the day took off. VIIIth Fighter Command code-named the three fighter missions, Full House, Stud and Royal Flush, which either by design or coincidence was in keeping with the giant gamble the Allies were taking. It could also be said that the Allies held all the aces for they had surprise and superiority in numbers.' The first mission flown by the 8th Air Force was primarily concerned with neutralising enemy coastal defences and front-line troops. Subsequent missions would be directed against lines of communication leading to the bridgehead. The bombers would be in good company with no fewer than thirty-six squadrons of Mustangs and

Thunderbolts patrolling the area. Initially, they would protect the 'Big Friends' but would later break off and strafe ground targets. It was evident that there could be no delay and that any stragglers would be left to their fate. Any aborts were to drop out of formation before leaving the English coast and then fly back to base at below 14,000 feet. It was a one-way aerial corridor and the traffic flow intense. Aircraft would fly to and fro over the length of England dropping various coloured flares to denote the aerial corridors. If an aircraft had to be ditched, only those ships returning to England from the bridgehead would stop to pick up airmen. They were told that if they were shot down they were to wait in uniform until they could join their own troops in France. The Thunderbolts' task was to provide cover for the Normandy landings.

Over the landing beaches the P-47 pilots reported seeing flashes over the coastal area and ground rockets being fired in the distance. After the first mission was completed the P-47s returned to Duxford where they were re-armed and refuelled, ready to go again. The 82nd Squadron, which had remained behind, went out on the second mission to relieve the earlier aircraft and bombed and strafed railway lines in the area near the invasion area. Single squadron fighter-bomber sorties were flown from midday from 0945 hours to 1430 hours with eight P-47s bombing and eight more providing top cover before the roles were reversed. A railroad bridge forty miles north-west of Paris was bombed and the P-47s also glide-bombed the marshalling yards at Alençon with fourteen 250-lb bombs, which damaged two locomotives, thirty to forty-five box cars, eight to ten coal cars and ten flat cars loaded with motor vehicles. One truckload of soldiers was reportedly left burning and three others damaged. Two locomotives were destroyed by bombing and the P-47s machine-gunned five freight cars. A large explosion was also caused in a nearby ammunition dump. This frenetic activity lasted all day. The only contact with the Luftwaffe came on the third mission, a fighter bomber effort to St-Valery aerodrome and the marshalling yards at Mayenne, which was led by Colonel Fred Gray. Near Mayenne the Thunderbolts bounced eight FW 190s and shot down two of them. The P-47s also bombed and strafed two locomotives and shot up a few other rail targets.

Duxford's last mission of D-Day took off at 18:22 hours when thirty-two P-47s plus spares were despatched to patrol the northern and southern sectors in the area of Chaillone Coulonche. The Jug pilots looked in vain for enemy aircraft reported by the controller but they failed to find them in the dusk and they departed for Duxford at 21:30 hours. Some others had better luck. They strafed a twelve-car petrol train, which exploded sending debris into the air and pieces hit three of the low-flying Thunderbolts. 2nd Lieutenant Wallace R. Hailey had to abandon his damaged Thunderbolt over the Channel and ASR picked him up unhurt. The two other damaged P-47s landed safely at Ford on the south coast. The rest began arriving back at Duxford at around 2300 hours. Altogether 2,362 American bomber sorties and 1,880 VIIIth Fighter Command sorties were flown with claims for twenty-eight enemy fighters shot down. An indication of the success of the operation was contained in a message from Lieutenant General Doolittle. 'Today the greatest effective strength in the history of the 8th Air Force was reached; an overall effectiveness of approximately 75 per cent of all crews and airplanes assigned. Please extend my congratulations to all members... for their untiring effort in achieving this impressive strength.'

Duxford and the Big Wings 1940-45 by Martin W. Bowman (Pen & Sword 2009).

'I am proud to be able to say 1 took part in the Normandy invasion. But to be perfectly honest, D-day itself was something of an anti-climax for most of us fighter pilots who flew cover over the beachhead that day.

'We had been watching the build-up for the invasion all spring long. Our targets had gradually switched back from Germany to France and all the papers were full of speculation about when the Big Day would arrive. I figured we fighter pilots were in for the air battle to end all air battles. The weatherman, however, had other ideas.

'We weren't briefed on any of the details of the invasion until early on the morning of the sixth. We knew that it was programmed to occur soon, but we also knew that the weather was a real stinker over England and Normandy right then. There was solid overcast in layers, with the bottom about 2,000 feet. This was enough to get the fighters off, so we were given specific sectors to patrol.

'It was still quite dark when we went out to our planes for the first mission a little after 0300. During the night, all of the P-47s had been painted with black-and-white bands around the fuselage and wings to help with identification. My P-47 was heavily loaded for that early mission and I couldn't see very well as we flew across the Channel, but I could tell that the water was literally covered with ships between England and France. It was one of the most spectacular sights that I have ever seen; a massive demonstration of power. I think I flew four times that day. We would go out and patrol our area as best we could until we were about out of fuel. Then we'd come home, load up again and go back out. We flew between layers of clouds. Sometimes I could barely make out the ground through light spots in the overcast, but that was all. I don't suppose we were very effective at cutting the Germans' supply lines to their defenders at Normandy, but at least our own guys weren't bothered by German air attacks. The weather must have kept the Germans from putting up their airplanes almost entirely.'

Lieutenant-Colonel Francis S. 'Gabby' Gabreski, 61st Fighter Squadron, 56th Fighter Group.[36] On 7 June 'Gabby' Gabreski destroyed a Bf 109 and a FW 190 east of Dreux to take his score to 24 confirmed victories. Gabreski was downed by flak on 20 July and taken prisoner. He was the top scoring American fighter ace in the ETO with 28 victories and he added six MiG-15 victories and one shared in the Korean War.

'Our job was covering the ships in the Channel. The P-38s were assigned to that because not even the most trigger-happy ack-ack gunner on the ships could mistake the twin-tailed Lightning. The clouds were low and we couldn't see far. I was disappointed at first. It didn't look like the show was so big after all. But as the limited horizon unrolled we kept seeing ships, ships and more ships. Big and little ships. They were spread from England to within 15 miles of the French coast, creeping under the cloud cover as darkness came. Out in front were the destroyers, cruisers and battleships and behind moved the concentration of troop and supply ships.

'We flew at 3,000 feet, under the cloud cover. We couldn't see much because we were blinded by the broadsides from the Channel below. The ships were throwing everything they had at the beaches. Those huge flashes would come and then the explosions inland. We were flying on instruments and the glare of gunfire hurt my eyes and made it tough to see the little navigation lights of adjoining planes in the formation. Collision in the air

---

36 *Gabby: A Fighter Pilot's Life*, Francis Gabreski as told to Carl Molesworth (Schiffer Publishing 1998).

was a danger. The sky was full of planes... I didn't see any answering gunfire from the beach. There didn't seem to be any big guns there.

'On my squadron's third mission the weather was better. We came over at five in the afternoon and the water off the French coast looked like the jam at Piccadilly Circus on a Saturday afternoon. The coast was black with ships and landing craft. A thousand craft were heading back for England, streaming across the Channel and a thousand were heading for France.

'One Me 109 carrying bombs appeared. We dived for him but somebody else got him; he didn't last long. The only other enemy plane we saw was another '109, which dived out of the clouds. Three Spitfires screamed into view after him. He swooped down toward the water and up into the clouds again, the Spits right on his tail.

'Over the beachhead tanks were crawling in, streams of them like an invasion of beetles. Gliders that had carried our men were lying all over the landscape. Some of them were broken. The ground was spotted with coloured parachutes, which had dropped guns and supplies. Five squadrons of Lightning's flew cover all the time over the ships.

'This was the big show, but we weren't doing anything. We all thought the Jerry would throw up every plane that would get a wheel off the ground. And it was just a milk run for us. Coming back I saw a big ship concentration moving out of the Thames estuary behind a smoke screen.

Robert P. Tibor, P-38 Lightning pilot, 55th Fighter Group, 8th Air Force.

'It was still dark. The red and green navigation lights dotted the taxi-way as each ship cautiously found its way into position. One or two roared as pilots checked engines for power. Ground crews stood around their planes while waiting for their pilots to take-off. The pilots get a little bit of a boost out of that; sort of a cheering section to urge them on. But the pilots are not grandstanding for attention - they are only appreciative of the concern shown by the crews for their safety.

'The first two started down the runway. Gaining speed, they staggered into the air with extra belly tanks full of gasoline and a 1,000lb bomb under each wing. We were off to play our part in the show.

'Our Thunderbolts circled the field once to get everyone in formation and then set course for the invasion beach. Formations were flown much closer than usual. It was still dark and wingmen had only a vague outline of each flight leader's plane. They had to tuck in close to stay together.

'In a few minutes we were over the Channel. We could see the moon's reflection on the water broken by countless vessels which, up to now, had rarely ventured far beyond the English coastline. Still too dark to observe the rest of the water's surface, we concentrated on our course to the beach.

'The sky was quite gray but brightening rapidly as the definite line of the French coast moved toward us. Preparing to dive bomb our primary targets, shore gun batteries, terse commands came from the squadron leader, 'Relic Squadron, echelon right - flights in trail.' Inching slowly over into formation, we stole a quick look down at the beach as often as we could and at the same time we looked around for any enemy aircraft which could be very troublesome during the crucial forming of the beachhead.

'Below us, for a three or four mile stretch, we could pick up innumerable water craft of all sizes, shapes and types. There seemed to be thousands of them! Battleships standing off-shore were firing broadsides over the other craft. Their firepower was helping pin down and hamper return fire from the enemy shore. At the shore line, landing craft were spewing out men and equipment at an astonishing rate. We could see them scattering like kids from school.

'Target in sight - turning left. TALLYHO!' The squadron leader's call that he was diving on his bombing run jolted our attention back to our own mission. One by one we peeled off after the leader.

'Somehow we felt more daring on that mission. We went dangerously low in our anxiety to hit the target accurately. The target was knocked out by the first two flights and the third, already diving, had to add its bomb load to the devastation rather than harm the wings by a quick pull-out with 1,000-pound bombs.

'Hello, Gimlet. This is Relic Red Leader - primary target destroyed. Have you anything else for us? Over.' By radio our squadron leader reported in and waited for instruction from the Air Controller who was broadcasting from a battleship in the Channel.

'Hello, Relic Red Leader. This is Gimlet - no, no targets for you right now. Seek out targets of opportunity as ordered. Over.'

'Roger, Gimlet. Relic out,' called our leader in acknowledgement.

'We gazed at the beach fascinated by it and the realization that this was D-Day. However, it was no time to go glassy-eyed. We had to see what we could do to help the boys advance. Reducing altitude to 2,000 feet we split into flights of four to facilitate greater independence of operation and manoeuvrability. We could see that heavier guns were firing now and the artillery bursts were dotting the beach around our men. Without hesitation we pulled around inland to try to locate enemy batteries and if possible strafe them out of existence.

'Unknown to us we were beginning the employment of air coordination right then. It was a logical way to use our armament when the Luftwaffe was conspicuously absent. 'While attempting to locate the enemy artillery batteries, another bug-bear came to light - hedgerows. Surrounding every French field in Normandy, they ranged from three to fifteen feet in height and two to ten feet thick. Enemy personnel, artillery and tank took advantage of such cover and fired accurately at our troops without being seen. If the fields in Normandy had not been so small it wouldn't have been so bad, but most fields in that area are between fifty and one hundred and fifty yards square. Consequently, hedgerows literally covered the terrain.

'Still searching for enemy artillery batteries, we noted one battery just as it fired. Expertly camouflaged, we would never have seen it had not the concussion of the gun blown the surrounding shrubbery and camouflage nets to attract our attention. We peeled down on the artillery position and hammered at it with all guns. Although the heavy gun itself may not have been destroyed, the firing mechanism and crew were surely knocked out, for the gun did not fire again.

'Proceeding back toward the beach, we noticed tracer streams leaving numerous hedgerows toward the advancing troops. Unable to pick up specific targets, we sprayed all the hedgerows in the area from one end to the other. No more tracers came out.

'We had to imagine the din of battle made by the firing, shouted commands and roaring tanks. Our two thousand horsepower engines drowned out any and all other noise. Only our eyes could be used to seek out targets, whereas ground troops were able to call on both sight and hearing...

'Depending on eyesight alone to pick up enemy installations put us at a disadvantage that day. In time, we were able to detect man-made attempts to conceal positions or equipment. Our eyes sharpened with each mission and we learned a few tricks of our own as well. Flying along at tree-top level often revealed equipment and troops which could never have been picked up at a thousand feet. At the same time we learned what types of terrain were used by enemy troops, that the Nazis often used houses and châteaux for 88mm guns as well as for armed personnel and that anti-tank weapons usually chose positions just around road curves, at intersections or camouflaged positions on commanding ground affording good fields of fire along roads and adjacent fields.

'Such targets were very much in evidence on D-Day, so much so, in fact, that in the heat of battle we emptied our guns long before they should have run out of ammunition. We had not yet learned to conserve ammunition for the next target and also save a little for the trip home in case the Luftwaffe surprised us with a sudden appearance.

'Our first flight home on D-Day was a little more hurried than usual. All of us wanted to get back, refuel, re-arm and get in another sock at the Nazis.'

Lieutenant Colonel H. Norman Holt, CO, 366th Fighter Group, 9th Fighter Command at Thruxton. Holt had been an infantry lieutenant before transferring to the Air Corps in June 1941 and later served in the Canal Zone as Squadron Ops Officer and Flight Commander, 1942-43, before becoming CO of the 390th Squadron of the 366th Group in 1943 and Group Commander in May 1944. From his unpublished history, 'Column Cover'.

'General Eisenhower visited the 4th Fighter Group at Debden airfield just before the invasion and asked whether we could prevent German armour and trucks coming up on the beachhead. The Germans had kept most of their forces back, but as soon as the Allies landed they could bring them up. I replied to Eisenhower that I thought during the daytime we could stop anything that was moving on the roads but couldn't do it at night. I thought we could ·create enough havoc on the roads so we could jam them, preventing reinforcements from getting through. I was pretty sure we could prevent the Luftwaffe from attacking the beachhead, spraying machine gun and cannon fire on landing troops. On D-Day, only two German fighter planes got through. After the war I talked to one of the pilots who did penetrate and asked how they did it. He said, 'We were right down among the weeds and when I got back the tips of my propeller were bent where they struck the ground. Only my wingman and I got through. We got over the beachhead and saw several thousand troops on the beach, several thousand ships at sea and looked up above at several thousand aircraft above. My wingman asked what do we shoot at and I said, just spray and we'll go home.'

James Goodson, CO, 336th Fighter Squadron, 4th Fighter Group.

'It was zero hour for us at this United States advanced fighter bomber base. A general call was sent round to all operational barracks half an hour before calling all men to attend a special briefing. We could only guess what this meant. The D-Day secret had been kept so well here that it was not until a few hours before that their commanding officer himself knew that to-day's operations were to be in support of our Forces landing on the Continent.

'Some of us were awakened by the roar of aircraft, the strength of which had never been heard before, passing near the field. We have been watching one or the most thrilling sights in history - a stream of transport airplanes towing gliders, their navigation lights ablaze and speeding towards the assault beaches loaded with airborne troops and equipment.

'Colonel Gilbert Meyers, Commanding officer of the station, tells us: 'This is it' and then outlines the plan of attack. He reads a message from Air Chief Marshal Sir Trafford Leigh Mallory, Air Commander-in-Chief, A.E.A.F. It says:

'I have every confidence that you are up to the great work that lies before you. I am proud to be with you as a member of the team to fight this great battle. I have every confidence in you all and I wish you God speed and the best of luck.'

'The Commanding Officer tells us that airborne infantry units have already made a landing on the Continent and British and US army units will have made landings along the shore. For this group there is one new order. They must destroy their target at all costs.

'We are not going to get two 'cracks at them' Colonel Meyers says. 'Any mission assigned us we must complete first time.'

'One squadron gets an immediate target - road bridge. The road bridge is an important link between German reinforcements and our invading forces.

'Within 20 minutes or the termination of briefing all aircraft are airborne and on the way to the first daylight mission of D-Day.

'The squadron did not need two cracks at that bridge. Several bombs dropped smack on the target.

'On the way out several of the fighter-bombers found an enemy convoy stretching half a mile along the road. They swept down, shooting up 20 or 30 trucks. All the aircraft returned safely.

'I met some of the pilots when they got back. Twenty-eight year old Lieutenant Colonel Frank S. Perego of New York, told me: 'We just smothered that bridge. The main trouble was to keep in our line of traffic. There are literally hundreds of Allied aircraft over the whole invasion area and there was no doubt at the time we went over that the Allies had complete mastery of the air.'

'In operations room here we are waiting for the next mission. From now on it is an 18-hour day job for these men. They have been promised no more than an hour's rest between missions.'

Philip Grune, *Daily Mirror* **Tuesday June 6. What Grune was unable to say was that he was with Colonel Gilbert L. Meyers' 368th Fighter Group, 9th Fighter Command at Chilbolton equipped with P-47 Thunderbolts. Grune had been with the American army since they first arrived. He went to Northern Ireland to meet them when they landed and had been covering their operations ever since. Colonel Perego took command of the 368th Fighter Group on 1 November 1944.**

'We expected D-Day to happen but didn't know when. We just crawled out of bed, got into the briefing room in the early morning, maybe two or three am. There on the big board in big soft letters it said, THIS IS IT. We had a briefing from Hub Zemke. Meanwhile, we hadn't realized it but the ground crew had spent all night painting these white stripes under the wings to avoid friendly fire from the ground. Around 0400 we took off, just going back and forth, shooting at anything that moved toward the beachhead. We kept coming back, eating an egg sandwich, waiting around the ready room while they gassed up your plane. I had four missions over France that day.'

Herbert Holfineier, 56th Fighter Group.

'Weather was bad, but there were some holes in the cloud over the Continent. We beat up everything we could see. We came over an airfield and seven planes were lined up. We'd developed a new strafing technique, which entailed diving instead of coming in level. This made us harder to hit. When we got down to about 3,000 feet we started to pull out of the dive and open up with those eight .50-calibre guns at the same time. As the nose of the plane swung in the pull out, the guns swept the field. We plastered those sitting planes and went on.

'We ran into some Mustangs strafing a convoy of motor trucks. There were about 25 trucks lined up and when we got there the P-51s were sweeping across giving them hell. We joined in. Some of the trucks carried gasoline and some munitions. When we made our first pass we had to circle around waiting for another. So many of us were after that convoy that we had to queue up for our turn. The truck crews were running for cover as the gas was going up in flames and the munitions exploding. The flaming gas spread over the ground under the trucks and a great column of black smoke billowed up. Up ahead, some Jerry planes hit the Mustangs and there was a dogfight. We only saw one and Zemke chased him.'

Robert J. Rankin, P-47 Thunderbolt pilot, 61st Fighter Squadron, 56th Fighter Group, Boxted.

'Leading the 61st and 62nd Squadrons on a Type 16 mission on 6 June we were vectored to investigate something near the ground at Evreux aerodrome. The aircraft intercepted proved to be P-51s of 4th Fighter Group and we returned to 12,000 feet. Upon circling Evreux aerodrome, there were spotted about fifteen aircraft parked on the ground in the northwest dispersal. I don't know where my hits were registered, but saw several of the other pilots following me register strikes in and on the parked aircraft.

'As we were about to make our second run, I noted a bogie aircraft to the west-northwest and told the boys to follow me. On the bounce, this turned out to be one of several P-51s of the 352nd Fighter Group (Blue noses) who were doing a beautiful job of burning up a motor convoy on the ground. We joined the traffic pattern of their P-51s and I destroyed a truck in the convoy. Aerial PRU pictures were taken during the strafing. The entire convoy was soon afire so I began looking for other targets of opportunity and soon picked two trucks parked on a road some five miles west of hew originally strafed convoy. Two passes were taken at these trucks and though I hit them, someone else set them afire.

'As we recovered from this, I looked up to the east and saw the 352nd Fighter Group engaged at 3,000/5,000 feet in aerial combat just north of the original convoy. The P-47s were opened up and I gave orders to climb and engage the enemy. As we climbed, I saw one P-51 shot down and three FW 190s descend in flames and hit the ground. They had been shot down by P-51s.

'When just about in position to bounce, I saw a single FW 190 dive down on two of my boys below, so I turned right and down to attack him. He must have seen me for he changed his mind and dove towards the west. Because of my superior altitude and dive, I began overtaking him rapidly and he turned abruptly to the right to engage me. After about a 180 degree turn, during which time I was closing fast on his tail, he spun to the right and went straight into the deck. Since I had not fired a shot I took a PRU picture of his fire.

'Upon recovery, the four aircraft then with me were led back toward the original encounter. As I picked out a single FW 190 just ahead and began to race for position on him, a P-51 came slicing out of the sky to fire upon the enemy at close range, from directly astern. The FW 190 immediately broke in flames and the pilot bailed out. Since I was still about one-half mile away, I continued straight ahead and killed the German pilot while he parachuted down. It may be noted that the pilot's shoulders and head were on fire before I hit him, so I may have ended his misery.

'Recovery was made again and no further aircraft were seen. The Group then returned home.'

Combat Report, 6 June, Colonel Hubert 'Hub' Zemke, CO, 56th Fighter Group, Boxted, P-47D Thunderbolt *Oregon's Britannia*. On 12 August 1944 Zemke was appointed CO of the 479th Fighter Group at Wattisham, Suffolk and on 26 September he claimed two Bf 109s for his first P-51 victories. On 30 October, when his score stood at 17¾-2-9 and 6½ ground victories, north of Hannover his P-51D was thrown over on its back by violent winds and it entered a dive in which the wing parted from the fuselage. Zemke bailed out before the Mustang disintegrated. He was soon captured and sent to Stalag Luft I at Barth, Silesia where he became the SAO.

9th Air Force

By May 1944 the 9th Air Force had grown very nearly to full strength and dispatched an average of more than 1,000 aircraft daily against enemy lines of communication leading into and supporting the Atlantic wall defences, both in the Calais and the Normandy areas and against all types of enemy transport on rails, roads and rivers, to prevent supply, reinforcement and re-fortification of the vital sectors. As the invasion approached IX Bomber Command and the IX and XIX Tactical Air Commands were given full responsibility for a systematic programme of interdiction which called for the destruction of all major railway and highway bridges crossing the Seine from Paris to the English Channel, from Normandy and Brittany in the west and from Pas de Calais and the Low Countries' coast in the east. This programme was pursued until only one road bridge was serviceable between Conflans and Rouen and the enemy was forced to follow circuitous, slow and costly routes to move troops and supplies to the beaches. At the same time the bombardment force began late in the spring to carry out difficult precision bombing attacks against the large anti-invasion guns in use or under construction on the French coast'.

Reconnaissance, daily becoming increasingly important in the tactical sphere of operations, was fitted into the total air force operational scheme in order to provide vast quantities of detailed intelligence to the ground forces for the assault stage, as well as to furnish clues for most effective bomber and fighter-bomber employment. High reconnaissance, for instance, revealed extensive beach defence construction on the French shore, while low (10 to 50 feet true altitude), extremely hazardous 'dicing' missions undertaken by the 10th Photo Reconnaissance Group accomplished possibly the war's most remarkable and valuable photography, by providing close-range, easily interpreted photographs of the intimate details of the beach defences along the full length of the potential invasion coast, including the Calais sector.

On D-Day major air assignments for IX Bomber Command were to attack three coastal batteries at first light, three more 20 to 5 minutes before H-Hour and to attack seven defended localities in the 'Utah' area. IX Bomber Command dispatched 1,011 aircraft, of which 823 made attacks. This averaged five-plus boxes per group and for the first time more aircraft were dispatched than there were crews available and so many crews flew on two missions. Coastal batteries in the British area and on the northwest tip of the Cherbourg peninsula were attacked. Road junctions or highway bridges were visited in both the British and US areas and B-26s and A-20s attacked four marshalling yards east of the Seine in the afternoon. Takeoff of IX BC aircraft was accomplished between 0343 and 0500 hours, but weather and pathfinder difficulties reduced the effectiveness of the attacks considerably. Of the first three batteries attacked only one B-26 was over the battery at Beneville and eleven were over the two batteries at Ouistreham. Results at the other three batteries were unobserved for one and good to excellent at two. Owing to weather conditions the attacks on the seven defended localities were made at extremely low altitude, from 3,500 to 7,000 feet. A total of 269 aircraft dropped 523.63 tons of 250lb bombs. Results of all attacks were difficult to determine, but the ground commander in the 'Utah' area stated the pin-point bombing of the beach targets was excellent. The light resistance encountered by a 101st Airborne unit in occupying a battery west of Ste-Martin-de-Varreville was assessed as 'due to the excellent air force bombing.'

By the end of the day the B-26s and A-20s had contributed over 1,000 sorties to the 4,656 flown by all elements of the Ninth Air Force in support of the greatest invasion in history. The AAF official history said. 'Where the effects of part of the 'mediums' effort on 'Utah' Beach could be later followed, 35 per cent of the bombs were reported to have fallen to seaward of high water mark, but 43 per cent [were] within 300 feet of their target'. To quote Herman Goering: 'The Allies owe the success of the invasion to their air forces. They prepared the invasion; they made it possible; and they carried it through.' Medium and light bombers, taking off before dawn, carried out eleventh-hour attacks against powerful German defensive gun batteries on 'Utah' Beach and later in the day switched to communications centres; command posts, supply depots and other targets in the enemy's immediate rear. First US Army reported that enemy coastal defences were much less formidable than had been expected and it attributed much of this surprising weakness to the power of tactical air attacks on the shore before and during D-Day.

Flying approximately 2,300 sorties in 20 hours fighter-bombers had the general commitments of protecting the cross-Channel movement, preparing the way for landings by neutralizing beach defences, protecting troops actually on the beaches, reducing the enemy's ability to mount an effective counter-attack by denying him the use of roads into the battle area and, finally, providing co-operation in the advance of ground forces inland from the assault areas. Scores of reports from captured German commanders described the difficulty of travelling on all roads leading to the front in daylight, the necessity of using aircraft spotters on all vehicles and the failure of troops to reach their positions in the line at full strength, on time or in an orderly fashion. General Fritz Bayerlain, commander of the Panzer Lehr division said that his unit took 80 hours to reach the front and arrived with only 50 percent of its original firepower. Von Rundstedt complained too that the incessant fighter-bomber attacks on roads and rails, as well as the bomber attacks on larger communications centres, prevented the shifting of reserves which could have defeated the Allies on the beaches.

Apart from its strike aircraft, the 9th Air Force was the operator of the most formidable troop-carrying force ever assembled. On D-Day, no less than 56 squadrons in fourteen troop carrier groups were in action carrying paratroops or towing gliders.

Almost all the aircraft were C-47 Sky trains and the gliders mainly Waco CG-4s, plus a number of British-built Horsas. Under the Ninth Air Force the IX Troop Carrier Command organized, planned and successfully executed the greatest troop-carrier operation in history, the delivery of paratroops and airborne units behind the German lines on the Cherbourg Peninsula and maintained resupply and medical evacuation operations for several months after D-Day. IX Troop Carrier Command was transferred to the First Allied Airborne Army about three months after D-Day.

The first units of IX Engineer Command landed on 'Utah' beach on D-Day and on 'Omaha' beach on D+1. An emergency landing strip was completed on 'Utah' by 2115 hours on D-Day. The build-up of aviation engineer units proceeded approximately on schedule: by D+5 four battalions were ashore and construction was well under way on three fighter-bomber airfields on 'Omaha' and one on 'Utah'. By D+6 five fighter-bomber groups were based in Normandy and participated in the all-out air assault on the outer defences of Cherbourg. By 30 June (D+24) nine all-weather airfields had been completed on the continent and seven others were under construction. From 6 June to 24 July the Ninth Air Force concentrated upon maintaining undiminished operations against the enemy in cooperation with ground forces and upon transferring tactical units to the continent as rapidly as possible. By 24 July 13 fighter-bomber groups and one reconnaissance group had crossed the Channel and a highly efficient and effective radar control system had been established on the beach-head without losing a single day of operations. Continuing to operate from Britain, medium and light bombers relentlessly smashed bridges over the Seine and Loire Rivers, attacked railway yards and communications centres and destroyed fuel and ammunition supply points serving the Germans along the entire Allied front in Normandy.

At Woodhall Spa in Lincolnshire on 5 June everyone on 617 'Dam Busters' Squadron was confined to camp. One of the pilots was Flight Lieutenant Hubert C 'Nick' Knilans. The American, who had flown a first tour on 619 and who would finish the war with both the DSO and DFC, had joined 617 Squadron at Woodhall on 14 January. On 1 June, when Avro experts had installed new automatic pilots in sixteen Lancasters for the D-Day operation, Knilans at last found out why his much-cursed R-Roger flew like a lump of lead and had so often frightened his crew. The elevators had been put on upside down at the factory and Roger needed longer elevator cables than the other Lancasters on the station. Knilans had been flying the aircraft for months like that and, as Wing Commander Leonard Cheshire VC DSO** DFC said 'only you and God, Nicky, know how you stayed up.'

'Not me, sirrrr,' Knilans drawled... 'Only God. I didn't know.' [37]

At dusk, with guards on the doors of the briefing room, Cheshire told his assembled crews that the invasion was about to start. Most everyone had known for several weeks that the invasion was imminent but only the Chiefs of Staff knew when and where. Postponed by 24 hours because of bad weather the D-Day

37 *The Dam Busters* by Paul Brickhill. On 4/5 June 259 aircraft of all groups bombed four of the gun batteries, three of which were deception targets in the Pas de Calais. But the fourth battery at Maissy, which was covered by cloud and could only be marked by Oboe sky-markers before being bombed by 52 Lancasters of 5 Group, was in Normandy between what would soon be known as 'Omaha' and 'Utah' beaches.

invasion finally began with thousands of ships and aircraft setting out for five beach landing areas on the Normandy coast. Cheshire outlined the operation that the Dam Busters would be required to fly. He explained that the object of Operation 'Taxable' was to induce the German crews manning the radar installations on a part of the French coast, designedly left intact for the purpose, to believe that a large convoy was proceeding at seven knots on a fourteen mile front across the narrowest part of the Channel between Dover and Cap d'Antifer and heading straight for them. The necessary reaction on the radar screen was to be reproduced by the sixteen Lancasters and by eighteen small ships, of which some towed balloons fitted with reflectors to simulate echoes given off by a large ship. [38]

The Lancasters, flying at 3,000 feet, in a series of elliptical courses, were to circle these ships again and again, at the same time releasing 'Window' cut to a special length and pattern to produce a response similar to that created by an aircraft or a ship. Intense rehearsals, in which the crews of the Lancasters flew fifty hours, were exacting enough. 'The tactics' Cheshire explained later, 'were to use two formations of aircraft with the rear formation seven miles behind the leaders, each aircraft being separated laterally by two miles. Individual aircraft flew a straight course of seven miles, turned round and flew on the reciprocal one mile away. On completion of the second leg it returned to its former course and repeated the procedure over again, advancing far enough to keep in line with the convoy's speed of seven knots'.

The first wave of eight aircraft would take off at about 23.00 hours with twelve men in each aircraft, an extra pilot, extra navigator and three men to drop the bundles of 'Window' out. At around 3am the second wave of eight aircraft would take over. The task set the navigators was one of extreme difficulty. A ship cannot suddenly alter its position on the sea but an aircraft, flying at three miles a minute or more has only to maintain its course for ten seconds too long for it to be seen much too far forward on the screen and thereby to ruin the deception. 'Window' had to be

---

38 The naval element in 'Taxable' (and 'Glimmer') consisted of three lines of small craft. In 'Taxable' the first line had 8 motor-launches, spread across a front 14 miles wide. Their job was to jam the coastal radar stations, just enough to confuse their pictures. If the radar was put completely out of action the operators would be unable to see the approaching 'convoys'. The launches also carried radio transmitters, which exchanged signals simulating the preparations for a rocket barrage. This traffic would not normally be coded, so the Germans would have no difficulty in understanding it. The operators had the usual detailed scripts, but because of inadequate rehearsal and the fact that 'Taxable's own radar countermeasures made radio communication difficult, their performance was less convincing than it should have been. Two more lines of motor launches came 8 and 13 miles astern, each carrying a reflector balloon and towing a float with another balloon; and in line abreast with them came pinnaces [manned by American signals personnel] equipped with 'Moonshine' electronic equipment, which also carried balloons (9 craft in all). 'Moonshine' had been developed in 1942 [to be used against German Freya radar] but was virtually unused [just 30 occasions, 6 August-October 1942, all by the Defiant Flight of specially modified Defiant II aircraft], so it had a good chance of success. It received the pulse sent out by enemy radar stations and sent it back to them in magnified form [to give the appearance of an extremely large target or a compact formation of several aircraft]. The total effect of this electronic armada, which advanced towards the French coast at precisely 7 knots, was to simulate a huge fleet on the German radar screens. The picture was further enhanced by 8 Lancaster bombers which flew round and round the launches dropping 'Window' from an altitude of between 2,500 and 3,000 feet. Their orbits carried them towards the French coast at 7 knots, to keep in step with the ships beneath them. *Deception In World War II* by Charles Cruickshank (Oxford University Press 1979)/ *Confound and Destroy; 100 Group and the Bomber Support Campaign* by Martin Streetly (Macdonald and Jane's 1978).

discharged with the same accuracy and twenty-four bundles were to be thrown overboard on every circuit at twelve second intervals. It would take an error of only four seconds in timing to make the convoy suspiciously change position on the German radar.

Operation 'Taxable' began soon after dusk and 'went steadily and mercilessly on through the night'. With curtains drawn and nothing but instruments to guide the navigators, the Lancasters moved round and round their orbits. At the same time, in order still further to heighten the illusion, the German radar was jammed but not too heavily.

A similar operation ('Glimmer') was carried out by eight Stirlings on 218 Squadron, off Boulogne, while Halifaxes and Stirlings on 138, 149 and 161 Squadrons dropped dummy parachutists, rifle fire simulators and other devices such as squibs and fireworks, which produced the sound of gunfire. [39]

'Taxable' successfully created the impression that an airborne landing near the village of Yvetot in north-west France was taking place. Hour after hour the Lancasters flew in the blackness over the Channel, turning on stop-watches up and down on reversed courses while the 'Window' was tossed out at four-second intervals. Right on cue at about 3am the second wave of eight aircraft took over. This was the trickiest part of all because they had to come in directly behind with split-second timing to carry on. They saw nothing of the invasion. Seven miles off the French coast they broke away just before dawn, before the light was good enough for the Germans to see from the shore that they had been tricked. Crews had their reward as they turned for home; the German coastal batteries opened up... not the flak but the big guns, aiming 12-inch shells by radar prediction at the ghost armada. Enemy E-boats came out from Calais and Boulogne but they would have needed aerial torpedoes to do any damage. [40]

39   Glimmer was on a smaller scale. It had 6 launches in the front line, and in the second and third lines 6 balloon-carrying launches and a single 'Moonshine' pinnace. Overhead circled 6 aircraft, edging nearer and nearer to France. Both operations concluded when those balloons which had not been carried away by the high winds were anchored off-shore, to simulate a great fleet preparing to disgorge an assault force. A smoke-screen was laid to delay the dawn. The wire recorders were switched on to play back the noises of landing-craft approaching the shore. Unhappily the amplification was so poor that it could not be heard above the wind and although the launches went to within two miles of the coast their performance passed unnoticed. Taxable and Glimmer, perhaps the most ingenious tactical deceptive operations in the whole of the War, made virtually no impact. On 13 June, when it was still not certain that the Allies had gained a firm foothold in France, a diversionary attack was simulated against the coast north of Granville in the Cotentin Peninsular, to take the pressure off the Americans at 'Omaha' and 'Utah' beaches. Code-named 'Accumulator', it was mounted at short notice and carried out by two Canadian destroyers, *Haida* and *Huron*. *Deception In World War II* by Charles Cruickshank (Oxford University Press 1979).

40   At 19.30 hours on 6 June a message was received from the AOC HQ 3 Group: 'I have received the following message from C-in-C for aircrews - begins - you did famously last night in the face of no mean difficulties, fire from the coastal batteries, which were your targets, have been reported virtually negligible. A further message from C-in-C Bomber Command to OC 218 Squadron. 'It is already established that the operations on which you were engaged on the night 5/6th June were very successful and it may well be that when the full facts are known it will be found that you achieved results of even greater importance than can be known at present. This can only have been brought about by intensive training and attention to details, as a result of which crews concerned, acquitted themselves admirably. The Naval Commanders have expressed their great appreciation of the support of 218 and 617 Squadrons and it is now disclosed that this and the patrol carried out by 101 and 214 Squadrons succeeded together in delaying the enemy's appreciation as to the actual point of the assault thereby assisting the measure of tactical surprise gained for our main assault forces.'

Nineteen year old Phil Stonehouse was an instructor in an Aircrew School (3 Group) where they revised navigators before they went on their second or third tours. 'The call came through at our roll call at 8am on 5th June when we were called for volunteers for a 'job' that night. Twenty men were asked for and two of my navigators were accepted. The next day [D-Day] we found out that our boys had been sent on a trip over the Calais area dropping 'Window'. Neither of my boys came back and I, with an officer had to go to their bunks and retrieve their personal belongings. It was the most distressing period in my whole life in the forces. To pick up their pictures of their wives or girlfriends was very heart-breaking. We then had to sit together, read all their letters received and destroy any that in our opinion would cause distress. I had to remove bodies, sometimes burnt, from crashed aircraft, strapped them on to stretchers and carried them to where an ambulance could receive them, but that was nothing compared to removing things belonging to absent aircrew.' [41]

Overhead, massive aerial support was given before dawn to the Normandy landings. [42] Flight Lieutenant Charles Owen of 97 Squadron wrote: 'The Army had pulled its finger out at last and D-Day was on. We bombed at 05.00 hours just as it was getting light and had a grandstand view of the Americans running in on the beach.' [43] Allied intelligence had pinpointed 73 fixed coastal gun batteries that could menace the invasion. In Operation 'Flashlamp' just over 940 aircraft dropped more than 5,000 tons of bombs on ten coastal batteries in the Bay of the Seine along the fringes of the Normandy landing beaches. It was the greatest tonnage in one night so far in the war. Only two of the batteries were free of cloud, at Le Pernelle on the Pointe de Barfleur and at Ouistreham; all other bombing being carried out

41   218 'Gold' Coast Squadron Newsletter No.57 January 2010. The two Stirlings with nine man crews were on 149 Squadron at Methwold on D-Day Support. One complete crew was lost without trace and only three survived on the other aircraft.

42   For the landings in Normandy, 100 Group contributed both jamming and fighter support. Its three jamming squadrons, 199, 214 and the American 803rd, had been held in reserve for this event. On the night of 4/5June 199 and the 803rd set up their first Mandrel screen in a line from Littlehampton to Portland Bill to give cover to the advancing invasion fleet. 199 contributed 16 aircraft to this operation while the 803rd supplied four, the 20 aircraft being divided between ten jamming centres. 214 Squadron despatched five B-17 aircraft to join 24 [ABC-equipped Lancasters on 101 Squadron which patrolled all known night fighter approaches] in an 'ABC'/'Window' barrage along the line of the Somme estuary. This force, with its total of 82 ABCs, was designed to distract enemy night fighter attention from 1,000 Allied transport aircraft on their way to drop paratroops on the Cherbourg peninsula and to the east of Caen. The 214 Squadron aircraft were airborne for 6½ hours, patrolling back and forth along 90-mile beats at an operational altitude of 27,000 feet. The airborne jamming was backed up by ground stations in the UK and the Mandrel screen, Ground Mandrel and 'Window' were all aimed at the early warning radars in the 90 to 200 MHz band. The Window employed was type MB, which was used for the first time during this operation and was the first of the family to be aimed at the Freya device. The Mandrel screen used what was known as the Racecourse Pattern. The idea was to fly circuits up and down the Gee lines most nearly perpendicular to the enemy coast... The fighter elements of the Group were equally active on the night of the invasion, despatching 21 'Serrate' sorties to France and 26 'Intruder' sorties to Dutch and Belgian airfields and over the beach-head between 10pm on the 5th and 10pm on the 6th. Confound and Destroy; 100 Group and the Bomber Support Campaign by Martin Streetly (Macdonald and Jane's 1978). In all, 110 aircraft of 100 Group carried out extensive bomber-support operations. Two enemy night-fighters were claimed destroyed by two Mosquitoes. Two Intruders were lost and one ABC Lancaster ditched off Beachy Head. 58 aircraft of 3 and 5 Groups flew diversion operations.

43   An outstanding operational captain, Owen was a squadron leader by 1944 and he ended the war as a Master Bomber with a string of decorations.

on 'Oboe' marking.

The attacks opened at 23.31 hours on 5 June when 92 Lancasters of 1 Group, with two 'Oboe' Mosquitoes, began dropping bombs on the Fontenay-Crisbecq (Ste-Marcouf) battery, part of the 1261st Army Coastal Artillery Regiment, which covered 'Utah' beach on the east side of the Cherbourg Peninsula. [44] C-47s carrying the 82nd and 101st US Airborne Divisions were due over the area an hour later, so it was essential that 8 (PFF) Group aircraft marked on time using Musical Parramatta. In the ensuing ten minutes, 1 Group's Lancasters, bombing through solid cloud and rain, dropped 534 tons of high explosives, mainly 1,000-pounders. The bombing attack destroyed the guns and killed many of the men who were off duty in billets in adjoining houses. Ten minutes later, a further 94 Lancasters of 1 Group dropped 547 tons of bombs onto the casemates of the Ste-Martin-de-Varreville battery a few miles further south, between the beaches and the 101st US Airborne Division's dropping zone. The target had been well marked by five Mosquitoes. American paratroopers who captured the battery positions soon afterwards reported that, although the bombing had been accurate, the guns had seemingly been moved prior to the raid.

The first wave to attack was led by Flight Lieutenant W. E. G. Humphrey DFC with Squadron Leader J. F. C. Gallacher DFC who left at 22:04 hours for Crisbecq, about 3.5km south of Quineville. Humphrey marked the occasion with a note in his logbook stating 'Ops. Crisbecq - Dropped first TI on night the second front started.' Flight Lieutenant Geoffrey H. 'Taffy' Gilbert DFC* who flew as navigator with Wing

---

44 The official German title for this position was Marine-Küstenbatterie Marcouf after the village of the same name just to the south. It was referred to as the Crisbecq battery by the Allies. Built in 1941 for the Kriegsmarine, its personnel were absorbed into HKAR 1291 already at Ste-Marcouf but under Kriegsmarine command. Originally, the battery had six 150 mm guns in open emplacements but these were upgraded in 1943 to four 210 mm guns, retaining only one of the 150mm weapons, the rest being reassigned to Fontenay-sur-Mer. The 210mm guns had a range of 20 miles. By D-Day, two of them had been encased in casemates with another casemate under construction. A fourth had yet to be started. The sole 150mm was to be housed in a type M272 but this was still under construction. The battery was protected by Flak (six 75 mm and three 20 mm), 15 machine-guns, barbed wire and anti-tank and anti-personnel mines. There were various other bunkers including the fire-control post for the battery at Azeville, located here because there was a better view of the coast from Ste-Marcouf. The battery was bombed regularly from April 1944 to the night preceding D-Day, which destroyed the Flak and killed some of the battery personnel. *Hitler's Atlantic Wall* by Anthony Saunders (Sutton Publishing 2001).

At full strength the battery consisted of three officers, seven NCOs and 287 men commanded by Ensign First Class Walter Ohmsen. Construction work had begun in 1941 for a battery of six 15cm (5.9 inch) guns. All but one of these guns had been moved to Fontenay-sur-Mer and it had been rearmed with three more powerful Czech-built Skoda K52 21cm (8.26 inch) guns with a range of 20 miles. Their Type 683 casemates allowed them to cover an arc of 120 degrees. However, they had a slow rate of fire because to reload they had to be at an elevation of 8 degrees and then re-aimed. On D-Day, only two of these guns were operational. Regular air attacks had delayed the construction of the three remaining casemates that would house the other guns and protective armour plate had not been delivered to cover the embrasures. The battery was protected against air attack by six 7.5cm (2.95 inch) and three 2cm (0.78 inch) flak guns that could also be used in the ground role. The perimeter was surrounded by a double barbed wire fence and minefield with 17 machine guns in tobruks. (Many batteries were defended by a ring of machine-gun positions, or tobruks, so-called after the town in Libya where they had been first used during the North African campaign. At its simplest, a tobruk was a concrete pit large enough for one man to stand in. Some were fitted with turrets taken from captured French tanks while others housed mortars.) It had an Observation and Fire Control Post that also provided range data for a battery at Azeville, 1.2 miles to the south-west. *D-Day; The First 24 Hours* by Will Fowler (Spellmount 2003).

Ste-Martin-de-Varreville

'The Americans were nervous about the long-range heavy gun battery at Ste-Martin-de-Varreville behind what was to be 'Utah' beach. This presented a threat to Allied shipping approaching Normandy and also to the troops landing on 'Utah' beach. It was decided that 5 Group would attack this precision target, so on the night of 28/29 May, a force of 64 Lancasters, led by a flare force from 83 and 97 Lancaster Pathfinder Squadrons and four Mosquitoes of 627 Squadron, flew to Ste-Martin-de-Varreville. The flare force identified the gun battery on their H_2S sets and laid a carpet of flares over the target. At Zero Hour minus five minutes, the Mosquitoes roared in at 2,000 feet and identified the gun battery visually. The first pilot to see the target called, 'Tally Ho' on his VHF radio to warn his companions to keep out of the way and then proceeded to dive at the gun, releasing a red TI at the appropriate point in the dive. His companions followed suit, making individual dives on the battery and creating a box of red TIs around it.[45] The Master Bomber now called in the Main Force, with each aircraft carrying several 1,000lb armour-piercing bombs and the target was obliterated. On 6 June the 101st Airborne Division landed behind 'Utah' beach as planned, but amid a certain amount of confusion. However, by 0600 hours Major General Maxwell Taylor had mustered one sixth of his force and with this he captured the exits from 'Utah' Beach. An element of the 502nd Regiment had orders to overrun the battery and to crush the garrison if necessary but Captain Frank Lillyman, the first [sic] US soldier to land in Normandy on D-Day, [46] reconnoitered the battery and discovered that it had been bombed and abandoned as a result of the 5 Group attack on 28/29 May. A document captured soon afterwards revealed that the Officer Commanding, Heer Kust Artillerie Regiment 1261, reported the bombing attack had begun at 0015 hours, parachute flares having been dropped first in great numbers. He said that the battery had been hit 'with uncanny accuracy', approximately 100 bombs of the heaviest calibre having been dropped in addition to several hundred smaller ones. Very large bombs had made several direct hits on the gun casement and it had burst open and collapsed. As a result of the destruction caused by the attack he had cleared the remainder of the battery out of the position into three farms in the Mesier area.'

Flight Lieutenant J. R. 'Benny' Goodman DFC (later Group Captain DFC* AFC AE), Mosquito pilot, 627 Squadron in 5 Group RAF at Woodhall Spa, Lincolnshire.

45 The target was found by Flight Lieutenant Ronald L. Bartley who after dropping his red spot fire 50-60 yards 245 degrees from the Marking Point was followed by Benny Goodman, who laid two further reds which fell 200 yards 360 degrees and could not easily be seen as they landed on the edge of a wood near the gun battery. Flight Lieutenant D. W. Peck DFC then backed up the original marker with two red spots, which were assessed as being 100 yards 240 degrees. Finally, Flight Lieutenant J. F. Thomson DFC RNZAF laid a green TI on the reds and this was assessed as being 300 yards 240 degrees from the Marking Point. See *At First Sight; A Factual and anecdotal account of No.627 Squadron RAF.* Researched and compiled by Alan B. Webb. 1991.
46 As with the 82nd Airborne Division, the pathfinders of the 101st departed from North Witham. They would be the very first American troops to land in France the Base Stick from the 502nd Parachute Infantry Regiment, bound for DZ 'A', was to be the very first to jump. Captain Frank Lillyman, the commander of the 101st Provisional Pathfinder Company intended to be the first man out at 1220 hours. His C-47 arrived over the DZ ten minutes early, but the pilot overshot and had to go round again. The delay led to the jumping order being changed and, although Lillyman later claimed to be first, he was actually second or third. First man through the door was Pfc John G. McFarlen and, as he said later, 'unless Captain Lillyman found a way to beat me to the ground, I was the first to land'. *D-Day Then And Now Vol 1,* (After the Battle 1995).

Commander F. A. Green DFC remembers the night Overlord began: 'I flew on 5 June for an NFT and went to bed early, in preparation for another flight that night [to Maisy - take-off 01:55 hours]. I was woken up by my batwoman to say my leave was cancelled and that the Second Front was open! The remarkable thing about the invasion was that I knew nothing about it until it happened. It was obvious from pre-invasion targets that something was happening. Things got a bit more hectic once we reached D-Day.' [47]

Elements of the 502nd Parachute Infantry Regiment of the 101st Airborne attempted to seize the Crisbecq battery on the night of 5/6 June but failed despite only being faced by middle-aged Kriegsmarine reservists. At H-Hour on D-Day, the 8-inch cruiser USS *Quincy* opened up on the battery which returned fire on the Nevada, which later turned her guns on the battery. At about 07:30 hours the battery's 155mm guns sank the destroyer USS *Corry* although there is some doubt about this as the ship may have hit a mine. At 08:00 hours one of the battery's guns was damaged and put out of action. An hour later, a shell entered the second casemate's embrasure and destroyed the gun. But before the battery was silenced it had sunk several landing craft and damaged a number of ships. The next day, the damaged gun was back in action and the battery was pounded by three cruisers until it was silent.[48]

There then followed a lull in Main Force operations until 03:14 hours on 6 June when the positions at Maisy was the first of the remaining seven batteries attacked, by 101 of the 110 Halifaxes of 4 Group. A 77 Squadron Halifax lost an engine on take-off at Full Sutton and crash-landed six minutes later, injuring everyone on board. Although silenced during the actual seaborne assault, most of the bombs fell east of the target, which had been bombed already on the night of 4/5 June and the gun crews recovered to fire and be fired on by the US Navy. This went on until 10 June. The seven-gun battery at La Pernelle, which commanded the approaches to the American beaches, was the target for 1,000lb bombs of 108 aircraft of 5 Group, which dropped 600 tons between 03:31 and 04:44 hours. The attack opened with marking by four 'Oboe' Mosquitoes of 8 Group followed by four Mosquitoes of 5 Group dropping ground markers. The battery was silenced during the initial assault but at 05:25 hours guns from two of the batteries fired on Allied minesweepers. The battery was only finally silenced when overrun by the Americans in the last week of June. When it was captured it was discovered that only one casemate had been damaged, probably by naval gunfire. [49] At Houlgate 102 Halifaxes of 6 Group dropped mostly 500lb bombs on the battery but the gun crews were not silenced permanently and it remained a thorn in the

---

47   *Mosquito Thunder: No 105 Squadron RAF At War 1942-45* by Stuart R. Scott (Sutton Publishing 1999).
48   The 1st Battalion, 22nd Infantry attempted to capture the Crisbecq battery on 7 June at the same time as the 2nd Battalion was attacking Azeville. It was beaten back by a strong counter-attack and fire called in from the Azeville battery by the Ste-Marcouf battery commander Oberleutnant zur See Walter Ohmsen. Next day, the battalion tried again, this time after a 20-minute preliminary bombardment from artillery, mortars and ships. The infantry followed a creeping barrage towards the bunkers. By now the garrison had been reinforced by elements of the 919th Infanterie Regiment and the fighting became hand to hand in the trenches. There was another counterattack and again they were shelled by Azeville. They were also hit by Nebelwerfers. After Azeville was captured, the Americans decided to go round Ste-Marcouf and merely contain it for the time being with infantry and tank destroyers while they pressed on up the coast. By 12 June, the 2nd Battalion, 39th Infantry discovered that the battery had been abandoned. The previous

side of the Allies until 19 June when the battery was temporarily put out of action, again by naval gunfire. The guns were still intact when it was captured in August. No aircraft were lost on the raid but a 426 'Thunderbird' Squadron Halifax at Linton-on-Ouse crashed and exploded near Bircham Newton killing all the crew.

During the next hour and a quarter the remaining four batteries were bombed. At Les Longues between 'Omaha' and 'Gold' beaches the battery survived intact after the raid by Lancasters and was still operational after another attack at dawn by American bombers and a bombardment by the naval forces off shore. The Lancaster piloted by Squadron Leader Arthur William Raybould DSO DFM on 582 Squadron was lost in the attack. A 578 Squadron Halifax, which crashed into the sea near the Cherbourg Peninsula and a 76 Squadron Halifax failed to return from the 4 Group raid by 101 aircraft on the battery at Mont Fleury, which was believed to contain several Russian 122mm guns.

At Pointe-du-Hoc, (Ste-Pierre-du-Mont), 3.7 miles west of Vierville, a cliff rising 100 feet high from a very rocky beach a six-gun battery (thought to be 155mm, with a range of 25,000 yards) could engage ships at sea and fire directly onto 'Utah' and 'Omaha'. The gun positions, which were considered to be the most dangerous battery of all, were bombed throughout May, with a heavier than average attack by both day and night three days before D-Day and it now received the heaviest and most concentrated attack of the night with 637 tons being dropped on it by 108 Lancasters of 5 Group.

During the next hour and a quarter the remaining four batteries were bombed. At Les Longues between 'Omaha' and 'Gold' beaches the battery survived intact after the raid by Lancasters and was still operational after another attack at dawn by American bombers and a bombardment by the naval forces off shore. The Lancaster piloted by Squadron Leader Arthur William Raybould DSO DFM on 582 Squadron was lost in the attack. A 578 Squadron Halifax, which crashed into the sea near the Cherbourg Peninsula and a 76 Squadron Halifax failed to return from the 4 Group raid by 101 aircraft on the battery at Mont Fleury, which was believed to contain several Russian 122mm guns.

At Pointe-du-Hoc, (Ste-Pierre-du-Mont), 3.7 miles west of Vierville, a cliff rising 100 feet high from a very rocky beach a six-gun battery (thought to be 155mm, with a range of 25,000 yards) could engage ships at sea and fire directly onto 'Utah' and 'Omaha'. The gun positions, which were considered to be the most dangerous battery of all, were bombed throughout May, with a heavier than average attack by both day and night three days before D-Day and it now received

night, Ohmsen had been ordered to withdraw. He was awarded the Iron Cross 1st Class on 13 June. *Hitler's Atlantic Wall* by Anthony Saunders (Sutton Publishing 2001).

49 At La Pernelle there were two batteries, the first one with four 105mm guns in casemates, the second with three 170mm guns in open emplacements. The guns of the first battery faced out to sea rather than across the Bay of the Seine. It was bombed several times before D-Day when it was shelled by the monitor HMS *Erebus*. The guns of the second battery, known to the Germans as 'Essen' had a greater range than those at the other battery and could fire on the landing beaches. However, Essen lacked the necessary rangefinder and fire-control equipment to fire accurately on moving ships. In a bombing raid on 9 May, one of the guns was damaged and removed to Cherbourg for repair but it was never returned. Following this and other raids, the remaining guns were moved about half a mile inland and hidden. Before the Germans retreated from the area, the guns were spiked without being fired in anger. *Hitler's Atlantic Wall* by Anthony Saunders (Sutton Publishing 2001).

the heaviest and most concentrated attack of the night with 637 tons being dropped on it by 108 Lancasters of 5 Group.

'You did famously last night in the face of no mean difficulties. Fire from the coastal batteries, which were your targets, has been reported as virtually negligible. All four radar targets were put right out. The next few days will necessarily be the critical period of this operation. Calls upon you may be heavy and the weather may not be easy. I know that you will do your damnedest to meet all assignments with that efficiency and determination which has characterised the whole of your share of Overlord to date.'
    Air Marshal 'Bomber' Harris in a signal to the Mosquito PFF marker squadrons.

'The meeting of 6 June was organised on a squadron basis, with all available aircrew in the Squadron Briefing Room. It was mainly to clear the air on what was happening. For the past 2-3 months the media had expected D-Day at almost any time. Our target patterns in that period often suggested 'today could be the day'.' In fact, I was not informed that it had happened until we returned after the operations of 5/6 June. At our flying height and with much broken cloud lower down, we mostly saw little of remark on the 6th.'
    Wing Commander H. J. Cundall DFC AFC, 105 Squadron CO.

The squadron ORB recalls Cundall's address:[50]
'At 14.00 hours he told them that their work of the preceding night had put nearly all the coastal batteries in the invasion area out of action. As far as the squadron was concerned the invasion would mean a tremendous amount of extra work. All leave would have to be suspended and 6 crews would be required to stand by at 30 minutes readiness, 24 hours to the day. The normal working day for aircrew not at 30 minutes readiness would start at 16.00 hours. No aircrew would be allowed away from the flights for more than 3 hours and then only on condition that they remained at the end of a telephone. All officers and airmen were ordered to carry [side-] arms at all times.'

One Lancaster on 50 Squadron at Skellingthorpe was lost. The only crewmember who survived managed to evade capture. One of two Lancasters on 97 Squadron that were lost was flown by the CO, Wing Commander Edward James 'Jimmy' Carter DFC who was shot down by a Ju 88. Carter's crew, which included Squadron Leader Martin Bryan-Smith DFC* MiD the squadron gunnery leader and Flight Lieutenant Albert Chambers DFC, the signals leader, was lost without trace. The other Lancaster was flown by Lieutenant Finn Yarde Jespersen DFC. The Norwegian pilot and his crew also perished. At 06:30 three companies (225 men) of the US 2nd Ranger Battalion, using rocket propelled grapple hooks attached to climbing ropes and portable extension ladders scaled the cliffs within ten minutes after landing and captured the position. To everyone's surprise the six guns had long since been relocated to a well camouflaged emplacement but unguarded in an orchard 2½ miles further inland with ammunition piled up neatly and they were pointed at 'Utah' Beach. Ranger Alban Meccia recalled. 'There wasn't one bomb crater near them.'

50 *Mosquito Thunder: No 105 Squadron RAF At War 1942-45* by Stuart R. Scott (Sutton Publishing 1999).

AIR FORCES AVAILABLE FOR OPERATION OVERLORD
AIRCRAFT ON OPERATIONAL STATIONS 6 JUNE 1944
A. Summary by Types:

	Operational & Non-operational	Operational	Effective Strength
Heavy bombers	3,958	3,455	3,130
Medium and light bombers	1,234	989	933
Fighters and lighter bombers	4,709	3,824	3,711
TOTAL	9,901	8,268	7,774

B. Summary by Command:

	Operational & Non-operational	Operational	Effective Strength
8th Air Force			
Heavy bombers	2,578	2,243	1,947
Fighters	1,147	961	961
Ninth Air Force			
Medium bombers	624	513	467
Light bombers	228	165	156
Fighters	1,487	1,132	1,123

	Operational & Non-operational	Operational	Effective Strength
RAF Bomber Command			
Heavy bombers	1,380	1,212	1,183
Light bombers	134	98	97
2nd TAF			
Medium bombers	88	67	67
Light bombers	160	146	146
Fighters	1,006	856	831
ADGB			
Fighters	1,072	875	796
TOTAL	9,901	8,268	7,774

Operational aircraft with crews available
Luftflotte 3 commanded by Generalfeldmarschal Hugo Sperrle could only field 890 aircraft of all types, of which 497 (or 56 per cent) were operational on 6 June.

Ouistreham was the last target to be attacked, between 05:02 and 05:15 hours. All but one of 106 Lancasters of 3 Group dropped their 1,000lb bombs onto the 8 Group markers. Although they destroyed service buildings, the casemates remained intact and the guns appeared intact when captured late on D-Day. In all RAF Bomber Command flew 1,211 sorties; a new record.

The 'Sky Scorpions' target for 6 June was St. Lô. The Liberators were to hit the rail yards, prevent the enemy from moving in troops and supplies that could be used against the invasion force. Lieutenant Duane Hall's crew was told that take off was

15:55. Bob Sherwood translated that to 3.55. He never could get used to military time.

The gunnery instructor met him at the plane, as he had promised. He moved along with Bob, joining him in the inspection of all the turrets, the gun-sights, the bomb fuses and bomb rack release boxes. Occasionally, he would offer a suggestion. 'Straighten the cotter pins safeties in the nose and the tail fuses before you take off. That way you won't have any trouble getting them out while you're climbing to altitude. You won't have enough light in the bomb bays with the doors closed and the racks full. The dim bulkhead lights aren't enough. Always carry a flashlight. Check the bomb shackles for chewed-up ears on the release levers. If necessary, get the shackle changed before take-off. Wipe the oil off the guns. Otherwise the bolt will freeze. You'll get a big temperature drop after 10,000 feet. If the chamber is empty and the guns freeze, you'll have no guns for the whole mission. You won't be able to charge them. The gun heaters won't thaw them. Take off with a round in the chamber. When you test fire over the Channel, that first round will blow the bolt free and the ammo will feed. First three rounds will be slow and then the guns will take off at their regular rate of fire, 1,000 rounds per minute. And don't forget to go to the tail turret and reach your hand up into the discharge chute. Sometimes a spent cartridge case will fall crossways in there. More cases will pile up on top of the jam. It will eventually stop the guns from firing. You won't be able to clear the stoppage in the air.'

The take-off and climb to altitude went smoothly. They found their proper position in the formation. An hour and a half later they were leaving the coast and flying above the overcast Channel. As they neared the French coast they could see the intense activity opposite the landing beaches. Even at this day's operational altitude of 17,000 feet and despite the drifting cloud cover, they could see the approaches to the beaches crammed with ships. There were ship convoys strung out all the way back to England. It looked like you could walk back.

Every Allied plane that could fly was up this day. They converged on the landing area from every point of the compass. Some singly, some in ragged 'vics' of three. Occasionally, Bob would see proud, tight formations of 30 to 50 Spitfires or P-47s, flashing their way in from the sea, going to unknown targets. Over 8500 Allied planes were aloft. No German aircraft were seen. The Sky Scorpions dropped their load on St. Lô and exultantly turned for home, shedding altitude rapidly. A short mission, they landed in just five and half-hours. They had slammed all twelve of the 500lb super demo bombs right into the rail junction. The RDX explosive was great stuff, more bang per ton than TNT. What a great mission. God bless that Canadian scientist for creating RDX. Bob Sherwood realized that he was now sweating. The plane was making its careful way along the perimeter track going to its hardstand. 'Damn, I forgot to turn off my heated suit,' he said. He found out later that no one had encountered much flak. No fighters were seen by the Group. The whole 8th Air Force had only lost very few planes. Hall's crew were not virgins anymore and they had done well. 'This whole thing is going to be a snap. Damn those lying Stateside instructors,' thought Sherwood.

At Hethel Lieutenant Marcus V. Courtney's crew in the 389th Bomb Group was scheduled to fly deputy lead. The young pilot had attended Duke University and was known throughout the southeast for his dance band, 'Vince Courtney and his Duke Ambassadors'. They played at summer resorts, filling in for big name

bands. In Tucson, Arizona in 1943 his bombardier, John B. Connor, a newly commissioned 2nd Lieutenant, soon struck up a strong friendship with his pilot:

'Our crew completed training December 1943 in Lincoln, Nebraska where we were assigned a brand new B-24J. I was also married there, with Vince being my best man. The remainder of the ten man crew and an Air Force nurse (maid of honour) were the only people that attended the wedding ceremony at the base chapel. We arrived in England in January 1944 for combat training and eventually became a lead crew in the 564th Squadron. On the night of 5 June, while waiting for the weather to clear, the bombardier of the lead aircraft in cleaning his hand gun accidentally shot a bullet through his foot. Since I was on the deputy lead crew and had the same briefings as the lead bombardier, the decision was made to substitute me on the lead crew rather than switch the entire crews. I moved my flying gear from our plane to the lead aircraft and prepared for the mission. My place on Vince's crew was taken by a lieutenant flying his 25th or last mission. The rest is history. We completed our mission. Cloud coverage prevented us from seeing the Channel or the invasion. We dropped our bombs on the beach head fortifications using radar techniques then returned to reload, since it was a short mission. Upon landing, the group chaplain met our crew to notify me that Vince Courtney's crew was missing. Since I was the only survivor of his crew I was relieved from the second mission that day.'

Lieutenant Courtney and the crew of *Shoot Fritz, You've Had It* crashed and exploded at Northrepps near Cromer on the North Norfolk coast during assembly, killing all ten men on board.

'Today is D-Day and everyone is alert to the highest pitch. Although we've been waiting for this day for a long time, now that it is here everyone is talking about the invasion and giving his own individual opinion of what is to come. For the past month bases have been restricted and then the restriction lifted only to be posted again. So when the restriction came yesterday, June 5, no one thought much about it. But when the reports came in that British Tommies were called out and told to report to base, when we had three different alerts scheduled for today, when the first take-off was at 03:00 (unusual in that it was so early), it started us all to thinking that this might at last be it. At 03:00 the new crew that is sleeping in the same Nissen hut with us, came in from guarding the planes.

After being over here for a while, one gets used to having the lights put on at all hours of the night and don't take notice to it or wake up from the lights being snapped on. Therefore it was odd how everyone snapped wide awake at the click of the light switch although they were all in the soundest of sleep. We all must have gone to sleep thinking of the impending invasion and the new crew verified our suspicions by telling us the news just came through that this was D-Day. Knowing we could learn no more, we all went back to sleep like veterans and a few of us got up for breakfast at 06:30. After making a fire, heating water and shaving, I hopped on my bike and was over to the line in time 'to sweat the boys out.'

Bill Francis of Chenango Bridge, New York, in the 93rd Bomb Group, 8th Air Force at Hardwick began writing these words on the morning of 6 June so that he could capture and retain his own thoughts and feelings on this eventful day.

'I knew when the orderly awakened me that morning that something unusual was afoot, as it was not our day to lead. At briefing I found the answer to my question. We were not going to fly the usual large squadron and group formation but rather small groups of six planes each. Every lead navigator that could be rounded up was required for this maximum effort. The rest of my crew were held in reserve for a later raid but for this early effort, I was assigned to another crew. I'm sure they were not pleased to have a strange navigator forced on them and I did not relish flying without my crew. A strong bond of trust developed among crewmembers, as it was a life or death situation on every mission. There was great excitement when the curtains concealing the route map were drawn back at briefing and we were informed that, 'This is it' - D-Day - and that the landing was to be made in Normandy. Surprise? No, but fear of the unexpected? Yes. I fully expected the Wehrmacht and the Luftwaffe to resist with every ounce of strength available to them. My concern was fighter opposition to our bomber force. I was really fearful that this might be my last mission. Little did I know how overwhelming our air strength was and that the German defenders had no chance whatsoever of inflicting any serious losses, much less of turning this aerial armada back. Take off was at 03:00 hours. We were told in no uncertain terms that we were to fly a fixed and preset course to and from the target area. Once we broke the coast of England and passed over the Channel, there could be no alteration in course for any reason whatsoever that would be tolerated. We were told that British fighters had instructions that any plane flying out side of the narrow prescribed corridor or any plane aborting and flying the wrong direction would be shot down without exception. The point was made so clear that I believed it 100 percent and so did everyone else. One thing that did please me was the fact that I was not going to miss out of the invasion. I really wanted to be a part of the show and would have been greatly disappointed had I not been selected to lead the flight.'

Second Lieutenant John W. McClane, navigator, 44th 'Flying Eightballs' Bomb Group, 8th Air Force at Shipdham, Norfolk.

Combat crews in the 446th at Bungay (Flixton) airfield were tumbled out of their bunks during the night of 5 June and the Tannoy system summoned them to a main briefing at 22:30. Top brass from both 2nd Bomb Division and Wing headquarters had descended on the base and senior officers had quickly disappeared behind locked doors for a hastily convened conference. Field Order No.328 came in over the teletape machines throughout the three Divisions. At Flixton, flying control was the first to receive the news. To almost everyone's surprise and delight, the 'Bungay Buckaroos' had been selected to lead the entire 8th Air Force over the invasion coast of France on D-Day. Four more briefings followed into the small hours of 6 June.

The briefings given by Captain Arthur P. Hurr were the longest and most detailed the group had ever received. Crews were advised that six Liberator elements would take off at ten-minute intervals. Major Milton R. Stahl concluded the briefing: 'You are to strike the beach defences at Pointe de la Percèe, dropping your bombs not later than two minutes before zero hour [06:30]. Landing craft and troops will be 400 yards to one mile offshore as we attack and naval ships may be shelling our targets onshore. Deadline on our primary target is zero hour minus two [06:38]. After that, bomb the secondary target, which is the road junction in the Forest of Cerissy, or the target of last resort, which is the choke point in the town of Vire.'

Squadron operations were notified that the mission was to be a maximum effort, so that ground crews would have to pull out all the stops. Orders for bomb loading and fuelling were issued earlier than usual and no one a permitted to leave the base. At Seething nearby the 448th crews were called to the briefing room at 2300 and Colonel Jerry Mason said: 'This is it.' Their target was 'Omaha' Beach.

'June 6, D DAY. This is it. This is what it is all about. COMBAT. I was assigned to another crew for my first flight. It was not a standard practice, but the crew that I flew with was short their regular navigator that day, DNIF (duty not involving flying), or something. The Army had set up a special fund to buy fresh eggs on the English black market. Only crew members, flying combat on that particular day, were served fresh eggs, two each. Everyone else ate those horrible powdered eggs. Have your two fresh eggs anyway you want them. I have seen near fights when Cookie didn't cook them just right. It was jokingly called 'The Last Breakfast.' I ate my first 'Last Breakfast' and went to briefing. A curtain covered the wall behind the podium. The Command Pilot for the mission mounted the rostrum and the curtain was dramatically removed showing a map of the Continent with our day's work laid out. The CP announced the target, the way we were to get there, also, the pit falls and dangers. Flak areas were shown in red. Aircraft and positions in the formation were assigned. The Weather Officer guessed at the weather and the Chaplain performed the Last Rights. Good luck!

'Scared? You better believe it. Pre-flight, engines started, taxi into position.

'Off we go into the wild blue yonder...' (The Air Corps Song)

'D-Day morning, the wild blue yonder was anything but blue. There was an overcast at about 200'. The 95th used Horham Buncher for our climbing pattern. Our pattern intertwined with the climbing pattern of a nearby B-24 base. Take off, IAS 155 mph and climb 500 feet/minute to altitude. In the soup, it was impossible warn the pilot of approaching aircraft, instead you said, 'There went a B-24 at 11 o'clock.'

'Just getting to altitude under such conditions was a hairy task, at best. We broke out on top at 19,000 feet, rendezvoused and headed across the English Channel for our target, Falaise, a French town just inside the Normandy coast. Through rare breaks in the clouds, we glimpsed the armada in the Channel below us. It looked as though you could have walked across, stepping from boat to boat. Our orders were visual bombing only. Nobody knew what was going to happen on the ground. We were there to support, not jeopardize our ground forces.

'Every available plane was in the air that morning and traffic was ONE WAY. At navigation school, we had been told that fighters in the air resembled a swarm of bees. Sitting in the nose of the B-17, I kept pointing out swarms to the bombardier.

'Enemy fighters?'

'No, ours.'

'With each new appearance, same question, same answer. I was not nervous. My course in aircraft identification at Selman Field was a complete bust. I know that the bombardier would be glad to get his regular navigator back. Our target was socked in, so we turned, flew down the Cherbourg peninsula, turned and started for home.

'DO NOT LAND WITH ARMED BOMBS. GET RID OF THEM OVER THE NORTH SEA.' We got rid of ours.

'We landed safely and now, I was a combat veteran. Bitch, if you must, about flying combat, but a nice warm bunk and hot meals were waiting for you if and when you returned. The Red Cross girls were serving hot coffee and doughnuts to men that had braved the skies, today. Think of those poor bastards on the ground, on the beach head. Warm bed, hot meals, hot coffee and doughnuts, girls. GIRLS!'

2nd Lieutenant William 'Bill' O. Gifford, 95th Bomb Group, 8th Air Force.

Index

ABC ('Airborne Cigar') 146-147, 171
Aber, Major Earle J. 138
Ajax, HMS 47, 49
Alexander, Ensign Joseph 93-94
Arbib, Robert S. Jr 20
Arnn, Sergeant Roy 101-103
Arnold, Captain William John 98-101
Augusta, USS 109

Bacon, Chief Yeoman William Garwood 96-98
Barclay, H. L. 88
Barker, Brigadier General R. 17
Barker, Harry 146
Bashford, Sergeant Anthony 37, 39
Bassingbourn 153
Baumgarten, Private Harold 111
Bayfield, USS 27, 101
Bearden, James Hollis 108
Bedell Smith, Lieutenant General Walter 30
Betz, Franklin L. 154-155
Bletchley Park Manor 77
Bodell, Lieutenant Stanley C. 95
Bodney 151
'Bodyguard', Operation 76-78
Bourgoing, M. de 139
Boxted 165
Branham, Felix 105-106
Braybrook, Lieutenant Roderick 95-96
Brixham 26
Brown, Ordinary Seaman Jack 'Buster' 24
Brown, Sergeant Major William 'Bill' 45
Bruce, Stan 81
Budzik, Flying Officer Kazik 156
'Bulbasket', Operation 36-37
Bungard, Ordinary Seaman Kenneth 19-20
Burn 151
Bury St Edmunds (Rougham) 143
Bush, Captain Eric 106

Caesar, Jan 63
Campbell, Doon 74
Canham, Colonel Charles D. 111
Capa, Robert 108
Cassidy, Ordinary Seaman Geoffrey 24-25
Century Network 34
Chapman, Robert R. 115-116
Charlesworth, Mrs. J. 65

Chelveston 138
Cheshire, Wing Commander Leonard VC 168
Chilbolton 164
Chodzko, Lieutenant Michael 89
Churchill, Winston 17, 22, 28, 75-76, 133, 141, 145
Collins, Brigadier Tom 18
Collins, Major General Lawton L. 'Lightning Joe' 29
Cook, Sergeant Johnny 151
Cormeau, Yvonne 32-33
Corry, USS 174
Costello, John 89
Cotterell, Major Anthony J. 50-57
Courage, Captain Richard 31
Courtney, Lieutenant Marcus V. 178-179
Creasy, Rear Admiral George 30
Cruise, Pfc Palmer Jr 117-121
Cundall, Wing Commander H. J. 176

Danae, HMS 106
de Guingand, Major General Sir Francis 'Freddie' 30, 61
Debden 163
Degnan, I. J. 114
Dengate, Flight Lieutenant Frank Hercules 'Herks' 150-151
Dickie, Wing Commander E. 141
Dieppe 28
Dolim, Lieutenant Abe 138
'Double Cross' 76-77
Duff, Robin 95
Dunnet, Robert 88
Duxford 157-159

East Kirkby 147-148
Eckstam, Lieutenant Eugene E. 25-26
Eisenhower, General Dwight D. 17, 20-22, 28-31, 41-42, 70-71, 74, 76, 98, 111, 125, 141
El Alamein 52, 77, 83
'Enigma' 77
Esclavon, Joseph Henry 91-93

Feinberg, Captain Bernard S. 106
Fenwick-Wilson, Wing Commander 146
Flagg, Maro P. 110-111
'Flashlamp', Operation 171
Flixton 180
Folkingham 32

Forrester, Lieutenant Colonel Michael 82
Francis, Bill 179-180
Full Sutton 174
Fussell, Private Peter   71

Gabreski, Lieutenant Colonel Francis S. 'Gabby' 156, 160
Gallacher, Squadron Leader J. F. C. 172
Gallant, Ralph E. 114
Gallipoli 106
Gellhorn, Martha 136-137
General George O'Squire 108
Gerow, General Leonard T. 'Gee' 29
Gifford, 2nd Lieutenant William 'Bill' 181-182
Gilbert, Flight Lieutenant Geoffrey H 'Taffy' 172
Giles, Staff Sergeant Henry 90
Glasgow, HMS 47
'Glimmer', Operation 145-148
Goathland, HMS 106
Goodman, Flight Lieutenant J. R. 'Benny' 173
Goodson, James 163
Goodwin, Bill 63
Great Ashfield   155
Great Dunmow 74
Green, Wing Commander F A . 174
Grundfast, Sam   109
Grune, Philip 163-164

Halesworth   63
Halm, Panzer Leutnant Gunther   83-84
Hammersley, Flight Sergeant, Roland 'Ginger' 147-149
Hammersley, Walter Alfred 148-149
Hammerton, Lieutenant Ian 43-44
Hardwick 179
Harrington 35
Harris, Air Marshal Sir Arthur Travers   133-134, 176
Hassell's Hall 35
Hausdorfer, Obergefreiter T. W.   140
Hayball, Doris   65
Heintz, André   139-140
Hemingway, Ernest   137
Hennessey, Lance Corporal Patrick L. M. 44
Hibbard, John   155
Hicks, Technical Sergeant Howard   116-117
Hilary, HMS 95
Hill, Brigadier James 46-47
Hitler, Adolf 79, 84
Hobart's 'Funnies' 41-43
Hodges, General 155
Holfineier, Herbert 164
Holt, Lieutenant Colonel H. Norman 161-163
Honour, Lieutenant George 72-73
Hooper, John 123-126
Hoskins, Mary   75
Hottelet, Richard C.   74

Houlgate 38, 149, 174
'Houndsworth', Operation 36
Howard, Lieutenant Ron 72
Howes, Ena 73
Hudspeth, Lieutenant Ken   72
Hughes, Captain J. H. B. 106
Hughes, Terry 89
Humphrey, Flight Lieutenant W. E. G. 172

Ingersoll, Ralph 69-70
Irvine, Jean   70-71

Jackson, George 65

Kellerman, Steve 17-108
Kent, HMS 79
Kimbolton 155
Kingsford-Smith, Wing Commander Rollo 149-150
Kingston-McGloughry, Air Commodore E. J. 134
Knettishall 145
Knilans, Flight Lieutenant Hubert C. 'Nick' 168

La Pernelle 147, 174
Lancaster-Rennie, Jean 138
Lane, George 38-39
Lanyi (Lane), Gergi   38-39
Largs, HMS   62
Lecheminant, Roger   39-40
Leigh-Mallory, AVM Sir Trafford 29-31, 133
Leighton-Porter, Christabel 84-86
Les Longues 175
Levitt, Sergeant Saul 143-145
Linton-on-Ouse 172, 175
Littlar, Bob   67-68, 89
Longues-sur-Mer 47
Lovat, Lord 74
Lynn, Vera 65
Lyons, Daniel, Frank 68-69

Macksey, Lieutenant Kenneth 40
Mailey, Ron 80
Maisy 174
'Mandrel' 171
Marcks, General der Artillerie Erich 141
Martin, Joseph 96
Martin, Major Peter 39
Mason, Colonel Jerry 181
McClane, 2nd Lieutenant John W.   135, 180
McElhinney, P. 66
McFarlane, Private Ken 63-64
McKee, Sergeant Jim 126
McLaughlin, Larry 96
Merrill, Flight Lieutenant 151
Michie, Ian A. 95
Molesworth 141
Mont Fleury 175

Montgomery, Field Marshal Sir Bernard 28, 30-31, 41-42, 61, 70-71, 108, 131
Moon, Admiral Don 27
Moorehead, Alan 74, 88
Morgan, General Frederick E. 17
Morrow, Lieutenant Albert 25
Mountbatten, Lord Louis 17
'Mulberry' 19
Murrow, Ed 74

Nelson, Thomas A. 139
Netley 99
Newton, 1st Lieutenant Samuel 'Sam' 153
Norfolk House 19, 133
Normanton, Major Tom 71
Northrepps 179
Nowlan, Mrs. Nellie 88

O'Neill, William Thomas 111-113
Oatman, Bill 121
'Oboe' 169, 172, 174
Old Buckenham 155
Oliver, Corporal Walter William 40
Orion, HMS 95
Orr, Larry 101
Orsdel, Jim Van 116
Ouistreham 149, 168, 171, 177
Owen, Flight Lieutenant Charles 171

Patience, Rifleman Eric 86-87
Patton, Lieutenant General, George S. 75, 77
Pavlovsky, Helen 66
Pelorus, HMS 106
Phillips, Flight Lieutenant Eric 'Phil' 112, 147
Pointe-du-Hoc 34, 175-176, 181
Porcella, Private Thomas W. 32
Portal, Marshal of the RAF, Sir Charles 133
Powell, Robert 'Punchy' 151
Pyle, Ernie 107

Quincy, USS 174

Ramillies, HMS 62
Ramsay, Admiral Sir Bertram 29-30, 70-71, 133
Rankin, Robert J.165
Rees, Major Goronwy 129-133
Rehr, Carleton R.129-132
Rehr, Louis S. 129-132
Richardson, Wilbur142-143
Riou, HMS 25
Robb, AVM James M. 30
Roberson, Staff Sergeant Perry 155
Rogers, David 'Buck' 137
Rommel, Feldmarschall Erwin 29, 31, 36, 38-39, 75, 82-83, 89, 155
Rommel, Manfred 82-83

Rougham 143
Rubin, Manny 26-27
Ryan, Cornelius 74

Safford, Ralph 156
'Samwest', Operation 37
Scott, Lance Bombardier Frank 64
Seething 135, 138, 181
Self, Sergeant George 45-46
Skellingthorpe 176
Skidmore, Flight Officer Charles E. 'Chuck' Jr 122-123
Slapton Sands 24-27, 29
Smith, Ben Jr 141
Snoltz 68-69
SOE 33-34
Southwick House 70-71
Speidel, Generalmajor Hans 82- 83
Stagg, Group Captain John 22, 30
Standing, Michael 94-95
Ste Martin-de-Varreville 173
Steer, Lance Corporal Geoff 67
Stewart, Mrs. E. 65
Stiles, 1st Lieutenant Bert 153
Stonehouse, Phil 171
Studland Bay 45
Summersby, Kay 70
Svenner 50, 62
Swindon 121

Talley, Colonel B. B. 114-115
'Tarbrush', Operation38
'Taxable', Operation 140-141, 168-170
Tedder, ACM 30-31
Telford, June 81
Tempsford 35
Terry, Colonel 153
Thompson, Commander Walter 75
Thornton, Jack 44
Thruxton 163
Tibenham 140
Tibor, Robert P. 160-161
'Tiger', Operation 29
'Titanic', Operation 142-143
Torquay 26
Townsley, William D.104
Trott, Pilot Officer Kenneth 126-128
Tuff, Colour Sergeant Jim 79-80
Tuscaloosa, USS 140
Tute, Warren 89

'Ultra' Secret 77
Upottery 137

Valachovic, 2nd Lieutenant Paul 62-63
Verlaine, Paul34

Voght, Grenadier Robert 104-105
Von Ribbentrob, SS-Obersturmfuhrer Rudolf 31
von Rundstedt, Feldmarschall Gerd22, 34, 79

Wall, Patrick 123
Walter, Brigadier Arthur 19, 45
Wanner, Lieutenant Ed   140
Ward, Lieutenant (JG) Simon V. 109-110
Warlimont, General Walter   84
Warner, Flight Lieutenant David 135-136
Warren, Lieutenant Colonel 71-72
Warspite, HMS 62
Watkins, Captain Ernest 57-61
Weinshank, Technical Sergeant Fritz 23-24, 27, 31, 32
Wentworth Golf Club 74
Weymouth 24-25, 61, 92-93, 102, 105, 107

White, Lieutenant John A. 135, 139
Whittlesea, Margaret   107
Wilby, A. F. 106
Wills, Colin 88
Wingfield, Lance Corporal 86
Wood, Arthur 'Chippy' 35-37
Woodhall Spa 168, 173
Wooldridge, Lieutenant Roy 38-39
Woolfox-Lodge 146

X-craft 72-73

Younger, Lieutenant Colonel Allan 37

Zemke, Colonel Hubert 'Hub' 165-166
Zuckerman, Professor Solly 134